Timothy Green Beckley's Big Book Of WEREWOLVES

IN REALITY! IN FOLKLORE! IN CINEMA! AND IN LUST!

Revised Edition

ISBN 1-60611-011-X
ISBN 978-1-60611-011-9

Published by Global Communications/Mr. Creepo Productions
Box 753 · New Brunswick, NJ 08903

Staff Members
Timothy G. Beckley, Publisher
Carol Ann Rodriguez, Assistant to the Publisher
Sean Casteel, General Associate Editor
Tim R. Swartz, Graphics and Editorial Consultant
William Kern, Editorial and Art Consultant

Sign Up On The Web For Our Free Weekly Newsletter
and Mail Order Version of Conspiracy Journal
and Bizarre Bazaar
www.ConspiracyJournal.com

Order Hot Line: 1-732-602-3407

Timothy Green Beckley's Big Book Of
WEREWOLVES

IN REALITY! IN FOLKLORE! IN CINEMA! AND IN LUST!

Covers, Titles, Layout and Composition by William Kern

CONTENTS

AN AMERICAN WEREWOLF IN MANHATTAN

By Timothy Green Beckley - aka "MR UFO" & "MR CREEPO"

I used to hang out on Times Square. Frankly, I found it very inspiring.

Ok! It was a bit sleazy, but where else could you get two franks for a quarter, drink an Orange Julius, go to see a double feature and still have money to get home?

True, you had to step over a few winos and the closest thing to Disney on Broadway at the time was a family of mice playing in the bags of garbage along the curb.

I remember one movie called ***"The Abominable Snowman Versus The Wolfman."*** I met the producer years later by "coincidence." Turns out he was a big believer in UFOs and so we had a lot in common to chat about. Some of the films with werewolves in them were made on a shoestring—or better yet—with a bunch of long, tangled wigs purchased in a store on Forty Second Street that catered to prostitutes who walked along what was then known as (we're talking the Sixties here) the infamous "Minnesota Strip". So called because most of the "working girls" came from—well, Minnesota.

I must have seen more horror movies than anyone else hanging around this grimy center of American culture. A lot more guys were squatting in the nearby porno theaters, but the admission cost was three bucks to get in and I only had a fin and a half to spend to hang out all day. And besides I never cultivated an appreciation for the smell of vomit and urine, and the moaning and groaning of the couples on the screen were nothing compared to people being ripped apart by a crazed hairy beast with claws ten times as sharp as Freddy Kruger's nails.

To go back a bit in time, I had gotten hooked on horror movies pretty early on. The house I resided in was haunted, so phantoms and creepy creatures were nothing too far out of the ordinary. And I blame a lot of my horrific fantasies on none other than Nancy Davis, who later became the First Lady of the land when she married actor Ronald Reagan. You see, even as a precocious preteen, I was more interested in the macabre than in math. ***"Donovan's Brain"*** (starring Nancy D.) was a flick made in 1953 in which the brain of a mobster was kept in a jar filled with a pumping apparatus that for all intents and purposes kept him "alive," or at least on the cusp of human survival.

Now this might have been a wild concept in the early Fifties, but don't forget that slugger Ted Williams and supposedly Uncle Walt's brains are frozen somewhere in a similar fashion.

My mother, realizing that this film might have a traumatic effect on my young psyche, made me go to bed before the picture aired on primetime television. Yet through the walls I could hear this incredible sound—this eerie hypnotic pumping—going on and on and ad infinitum, as the brain was gaining strength and energy and blood began to flow to it through the use of an artificial pump attached to the brain's arteries.

Well, believe me, mother knows best. From that moment on and for many years, I had to sleep with a night light on for fear of the dark, the sound of the pump seemingly matching the rapid beating of my heart.

As creepy as it sounds—for after all I am now Mr. Creepo, host of low budget, B-movies available in chain saws (I mean chain stores) everywhere—whenever I see a werewolf movie this unholy sensation starts to take over my body. There were films in the Sixties like Curse of the Werewolf and a little later on Shadow of the Werewolf that made my flesh crawl. And years later, when Michael Jackson paid homage to werewolves everywhere with the making of his video Thriller somehow I had to get involved.

Now having "grown up" (yah right, me grown up), I had turned my 42nd Street obsession into a career. I was hired as a movie review critic for a famous men's magazine and for five years edited a magazine called Adult Cinema Review. God should condemn me not so much for my being a heretic, but because I had to sit through hundreds of bad movies and take copious notes for articles only the most demented could possibly enjoy. But I did get to meet a lot of underground movie producers. Some were borderline "gangsters" involved in some pretty sleazy sidelines—or at least were accused of such—while others were just pleased to be able to make movies and realized it would be very difficult to break into Hollywood's main stream; so they produced adult movies that made it "big" on the drive-in circuit and in the double feature grind houses of the era that screened week after week such notable epics as I Spit On Your Grave and Three On A Meat Hook. It might be "ugly" to some, but it was entertaining to millions and it was an honest living.

Along came 1983 and Michael Jackson's **Thriller** was being aired around the clock on MTV. The beat was captivating and the video had all the elements that drew me to it...dancing zombies and the transformation of a human into a werewolf. Again, somehow I had to "involve" myself. At the time I was dating a very attractive, highly educated lady who was also involved in editing a rival magazine who knew just about everyone "who was anyone" in the adult entertainment business. After downing a bottle of Dewers and eating a couple of moldy cheese sandwiches, we hit upon the idea of doing a triple XXX parody of **Thriller**.

1984 Driller Premier Party poster

Cast and Dancers From the 1984 movie, "DRILLER!"

The result is an 80 minute "for adults only" motion picture called **Driller** that for two weeks in 1984 was the number one video release in the adult category (no you never could rent it at Blockbuster). It sold thousands of copies, played in drive-ins where the cities' community boards were liberal minded, and received a lot of press. The "mainstream" media accused us of ripping off Michael Jackson, yet they gleefully went along with the gag and printed photos of our look-alike cast of zombies and dancers on their front pages.

The men's magazines went wild, noting how "over the top" the entire project was. The main attraction that made this so off the wall was that it was the first film to combine horror and elements of erotica.

I mean our werewolf had "what it takes" and our zombies did more in the graveyard than would be allowed in any cemetery that I know of. I will leave the rest to your imagination, though for a rather measly $20 I will gleefully send you an autographed copy of **Driller** on DVD as long as you sign a waiver that you are over 18 and of "stable mind." The transfer isn't the best. It was shot on 35mm film for theatrical release, but our distributor screwed us in numerous ways, including making inferior prints and later putting out an unauthorized version of the film after their distribution contract with us had legally expired. But it's worth the few bucks just to see how much I love werewolves and how much werewolves can love (if you get my drift).

So now you can see the appeal that werewolves have had in my life. Most of you reading this book know of my ages-long fascination and involvement with UFOs and the paranormal, but probably do not realize there are many sides to this "whacko's" personality. I have been a publisher since the age of 14 and have been "hooked up" with other writers and researchers to bring to the public what I consider to be the most authentic material available in the conspiracy, UFO and alternative markets. This book is no exception as we delve into the phenomenon of shape- shifting, Lycanthropy and crypto-zoological beasts out of our wildest nightmares. We have compiled a virtually exhaustive history of the subject in legend, in lore, in lust, in the movies and, without a doubt, in reality.

Sean Casteel takes us on a present day hunt along with the help of field investigators Nick Redfern and Linda Godfrey, who have confronted "creatures of the full moon" as part of their self appointed task of proving the "unreal" is very real. My old buddy Brad Steiger has been walking the beaten—or should I say un-beaten?—path for many a moon (full or not). Emmy Award winning documentary producer Tim R. Swartz has co produced a few of my—or I should say Mr. Creepo's—B movie thrillers, including Blood Sucking Vampire Freaks, Sandy Hook Lingerie Party Massacre and Skin Eating Jungle Vampires. Tim S. has seen more werewolf films than a werewolf hunter has silver bullets. We are honored that he has dug into his private photo and poster collection to make this book a must for all motion picture buffs of horror films.

And let us not forget the unequaled examination of the subject by Sabine Baring-Gould. Described as "a British antiquarian and eclectic scholar," in addition to his unparalleled look at werewolves in an historical vein, he was also a writer of hymns such as "Onward Christian Soldiers," penned a collection of ghost stories titled Mehalan and must have just about turned into a turnip writing The Lives Of The Saints, which runs a hefty sixteen volumes. . . Anyone wanting to review it let me know will you?

Well, lately I've felt something strange hanging outside my window. So let me close for now and call my friends at Azure Green and see if they can overnight me some wolf's bane before it starts to get messy around these parts.

Timothy Green Beckley
aka Mr UFO – Mr Creepo
MRUFO8@hotmail.com

1. For those looking to dig deeper into my career as a pulp book and magazine editor/publisher trek on over to: www.BadMags.com
2. Driller can be ordered from
Global Communications , Box 753, New Brunswick, NJ 08903

Author, editor and motion picture producer, Timothy Green Beckley, poses with an Oriental Shapeshifter.

The beast from the motion picture, "Driller."

THE TERRIBLE HUNGERS OF REAL-LIFE VAMPIRES, WEREWOLVES AND GHOULS
by Brad Steiger

SOMETIMES one hears it said that hell and the devil are but projections of one side of the human psyche. Without attempting to determine the truth or error of such a conjecture, it would appear that the imagination is, indeed, as Shakesphere said, capable of "seeing more devils than hell can hold."

There are, however, some things which defy even the most lurid imagination. When oterwise representative specimens of humanity develop a thirst for human blood and/or flesh, and oters rob graves in order to satisfy their sexual hungers, it is enough to make even the most jaded cast about for an explanation.

Man has not always had modern psychiatry to explain such peculiar and incomprehensible behavior in terms of sadism and sexual perversion. In times past, evil spirits got the blame. This was only logical, for were not supernatural emissaries of evil responsible for such cataclysms as lightning and thunder, earthquakes, fires, sickness, and warts on the nose?

It was easy enough to lay blame for a bloodless, mutilated corpse on wild animals. But when, immediately after such a discovery, a man would be found wandering in a daze with fresh on his beard or fragments of human flesh sticking to his clothing, some other explanation was needed.

Clearly, early man reasoned, it must be the work of devils. Men simply did not do such things of their own volition. Those who did were most certainly possessed. Since those possessed behaved like wild animals, it followed that the deman-men must somehow take the form of wild animals. Belief in the transformation of men into carnivorous animals, or lycanthropy, led to the formation of the legends of the vampire, the werewolf, and the ghoul.

Vampirism is recognized today as a condition of deep psychosis in which one believes that his or her life can be sustained only by fresh blood obtained from human victims. There is also a form of sexual perversion in which the deviate is aroused by the thought of drinking or sucking human blood. In order to achieve sexual satisfaction, the deviate must somehow satisfy his terrible thirst. Those having a knowledge of sexual symbolism will readily discover a wealth of such conversions in the vampire legend.

According to legend, a vampire was the restless soul of a dead person, which needed regular draughts of human blood to sustain its existence. It was believed that the vampire did its hunting in the form of a huge bat, a form that it could assume at will. The vampire would leave its place of burial at night to suck the blood of living persons and had to return to its grave before daybreak.

It was further believed that a person who met death at the hands (or fangs, more properly) of such a creature also became a vampire. In some regions it was thought that a vampire was the soul of an excommunicate, kept by the devil for his own purposes. Vampires were reputed to favor their relatives and friends as victims, especially those who were young and healthy.

If young and healthy victims are considered choice fare for vampires, then Hungary's Countess Elizabeth Bathory must be deemed discriminating. Over six hundred girls and young women were drained of their lives in order to appease the beautiful but perverted noblewoman's strange lusts.

Except for her zest for the taste of blood, the ravishing vampire of Castle Czejthe bore little resemblance to the traditional image of her breed. The Countess' sensual body could hardly be likened to the withered cadavers that by night forsook their coffins to steal the lifeblood of others. Elizabeth's lusty blood blood was very much her own.

Kings and cardinals, bishops and judges were proud to call themselves Bathory, as were princes and warriors. Gyorgy Thurzo, prime minister of Hungary, was Elizabeth's cousin.

On New Year's Eve of the year 1610, Prime Minister Thurzo, the governor of the Nvitra Province, and the village priest, along with a detachment of soldiers and police, stealthily climbed the bleak hill to Castle Cezjthe. The night was cold, and the memebrs of the company shivered as the black sky showered cold rain on them. But not all of the chill could be attributed to the weather.

As Count Thurzo stood by the castle's huge, vault-like doors, waiting for the others to join him, he thought of the day, just a little over a week earlier, when King Mattias had summoned him.

"Thurzo," the king had begun in serious tones, "isn't the Countess Nadasdy of Csejthe a kinswoman of yours?"

The prime monister had paled. So, it's come at last, he thought, then answered, "Yes, your majesty. A cousin."

"I've been hearing strange and terrible things about the countess," said the King. "The village priest says that the villagers are afraid she is a vampire, and they want something done. Do you know anything about it?"

Count Thurzo knew. He had heard many stories of the mysterious disappearances of a number of children and young women from Czejthe, and of travelers who had never been heard of after they had reached the village. He had heard, too, of the midnight sorties of Castle Csejthe's emblemed coach into the village, "which had caused the terrified peasants to lock and bolt their doors. He had remembered one trembling peasant who had come to him with a report of screams of agony and the sweet stench of burning human flesh that sometimes drifted down from the castle into the village when the wind was right.

"I've heard a few wild tales, your majesty. But I'm sure there is an explana—"

King Mattias cut him off.

"I'm not so sure the stories are wild, Thurzo. Those people are frightened, and badly. I order you to take whatever men you need and personally see what's going on in that castle!"

"Yes, your majesty."

The wind walied through the battlements of Castle Csejthe, startling the prime minister back to the present. By this time the raiding party had assembled. Testing the castle's door and finding it ajar, Count Thurzo walked straight in, closely followed by his men. The sight that greeted them caused Thurzo's hand-picked professionals to shudder.

The village priest fell to his knees and crossed himself. In the center of the great hall lay the chalk-white corpse of a young girl with a jagged cut in its throat, obviously drained of every drop of blood. A short distance away sprawled another girl, whose nude form looked as if it had been used as a cushion for giant pins. Although she, too, had been drained of a large amount of blood, this one was still alive and gasping.

Two seasoned policemen turned away in horror from the next spectacle. Chained to a pillar at one end of the hall was the charred corpse of yet another of the vampire's victims. This one had been set afire before being bled dry. Her death had obviously been a mercy.

"Your Excellency, look here!" cried the prime monister's sergeant.

The raiders hastened down the dark stairway to the dungeon area. Horror gave way to rage when they discovered dozens of girls and young women penned up like cattle. Many were weak and thin from repeated bleedings, while others were fat and healthy. Count Thurzo's party had found a veritable human slaughterhouse. A clamor of oaths and threats rose among the band, as they went about freeing the captives.

"Silence!" ordered the prime monister in a harsh whisper. "We have not yet found everything we came for. Quickly now, upstairs!"

The raiders had not yet been discovered. Swiftly they ascended the steps leading from the dungeon, and with eyes averted, crossed the great hall once more. Count Thurzo thought for a moment, then decided to enter the banquet hall. The prime minister had chosen New Year's Eve for his expedition with the thought that the raiding party might have a better chance of gaining entrance undetected because of the probable festivities which would be taking place. But no one was prepared for the kind of celebration actually in progress.

Devils would have delighted in the vampires' orgy that the raiders interrupted.

The walls of the banquet hall fairly oozed blood. There was so much blood on the floor that the heels of the soldiers' jackboots were stained. Three nude female bodies in various stages of mutilation lay on the floor and another served as the *piece de resistance* in the center of a table, which had been spread with a gore-soaked tablecloth of the finest white linen. The Nadasdy's expensive silver lay scattered about the room. On the table stood goblets containing liquid too dense and too red to be wine.

A fifth victim hung from the ropes that bound her to a pillar near the revelers. Around the table sat Countess Elizabeth Bathory-Nadasdy; Lloona Joo, the Countess' advisor in devil worship; Barsovny and Orvos, Lesbian pplaymates and procurors to the countess; and other celebrants—completely in the nude.

The raiders, too stricken for action or words, watched as Barsovny tightened a cord around the victim's throat until the juglar vein, swollen with blood, stood out. Orvos was ready with a stiletto.

"Me!" cried out the Countess, as though in the arms of a lover. "Me!"

She sprang in front of the doomed girl. Orvos made a jab with the pointed dagger, and a stream of crimson spewed out under pressure, drenching the waiting Countess, who screamed in pleasure and rubbed her naked breasts with bloody hands.

"Hold!" choked out Count Thurzo. "In the name of God, hold!" The dagger clattered to the floor. Several of the revelers screamed.

"Hello, cousin," gurgled Elizabeth, drunk on blood or wine or both. "Welcome!"

The celebrants were placed under arrest. All were taken to a nearby jail, except Elizabeth, who was placed under heavy guard in her apartment.

When the trial convened with Theodosiue de Sluzo of the Royal Supreme Court presiding, the tale of an eleven-year reign of terror unfolded. It was revealed that the Countess Bathory had not only drunk the blood of her victims, but had bathed in it as well, in the belief that such a process would keep her skin soft and white and youthful. De Sluzo and twenty other judges heard accounts of murder, torture, human sacrifice, preverted sexual acts, orgies of blood drinking and blood baths such as seldom reach the ears of man. There could be no doubt as to the verdict.

Lloona Joo was sentenced to death by burning after having her fingers torn off one by one. The others met swift justice under the headsman's axe—all except Elizabeth.

The beautiful vampire of Csejthe was found guilty with the others, but because of her high station and noble birth, the court delayed passing sentence. She was, however, never to see the light of day again. Her castle apartment was sealed up except for narrow slits to provide ventilation and to allow her guards to pass food to her. The countess was then fifty, was said to be still beautiful and remarkably youthful for her age. Four years after the stonemasons sealed her in, the Countess Elizabeth Bathory-Nadasdy died—but not from a stake through her heart.

Perhaps in Elizabeth's case, the fury of a woman scorned was matched, even surpassed, by the wrath of one deserted while caught up in the hot whirlwind of first passion.

Would the ardent young countess have gone to such gruesome lengths if her smoldering desire had been granted satisfaction through normal sexual expression? What kind of man was Count Nadasdy, who preferred the masculine society of army camps to the bedroom of his young and beautiful bride? Was the vampire instinct already rampant in the mind of Countess Bathory?

"Vampire" conjures up for most an image quite different from that embodied by the beautiful, perverse Countess Bathory. Movie-goers of twenty years ago and late show devotees will remember Bela Lugosi's portrayal of Count Dracula, the central character of Bram Stoker's classic vampire novel of the same name. In the movie version of the book and in the subsequent films based upon it, the presentation was always the same.

The story would open with a view of the vampire's coffin hidden away in a remote burial vault or the secret chamber of a deserted mansion. And then—"screee-e-ch!" The lid would slowly raise, revealing the cadaverous figure of Dracula, dressed somberly in black, with the Dracula family crest worn at his collar. With eyes gleaming malevolently, he would step gracefully from the casket, black cloak swirling, and transform himself into a bat.

A short time later, the bat could be seen flying through the window of a bedroom, where slept his always beautiful victim with her bare throat white in the moonlight. The sexual symbolism is obvious, and it is just as apparent today in the popular figure of television's matinee idol vampire, Barnabas Collins, of *Dark Shadows.* But real life vampires seldom operate with such dignity and poetry.

An example is the case of Italy's Vincent Verzini, whose vampiric crimes were comitted durinf the years 1867-1871. The sexual nature of the twenty-two year old Verzini's acts is unmistakable. He achieved orgasm, it is reported, by grasping his female victim by the throat, first chocking her, and then tearing her flesh with his teeth. He then proceeded to suck the blood through the wound.

One day pretty Maria Previtali, nineteen-year-old cousin of Verzini, went out into the fields to work. Suddenly she became aware of fottsteps other than her own. Frightened, she looked over her shoulder. Vincent was following.

Maria's footsteps picked up speed, as she fought back a wave of fear and panic. She thought of fourteen-year-old Johanna Motta, who had been viciously murdered the preceeding December as she traveled on foot to a nearby village.

She remembered how she had lain awake that night, too frightened to sleep, and listened to Papa as he told his wife of the incident.

"Si, Mama," Papa had said, his voice filled with emotion, "her throat was black and blue, and her mouth was full of dirt. All of her clothes were ripped off and her thighs were bruised with teeth marks.

"Her belly was wide open, and her insides pulled out. And, Mama, *per Dio,* the parts that make her a woman had been torn right off!"

Maria shuddered and started to run. She remembered Mrs. Frigeni, who had gone out to work in the fields one morning, and by nightfall, had still not returned. When her husband had gone out to look for her, he found her naked and mutilated body. She had been strangled with a leather thong and flesh had been torn from her abdomen.

Maria was almost breathless now. Vincent had recently been in trouble for chocking women. Mario could run no more. Her footsteps faltered, and two powerful hands grabbed her.

She felt herself thrown to the ground. Fingers like bands of steel closed around her throat. She could not even scream. Only a miracle could save her. She started to faint, and the hasty vampire loosened his grip. Drawing in her breath, the courageous girl brought up her knee and kicked her insane cousin in the stomach.

As he staggered, Maria sprang to her feet, rubbing her burning throat.

"Vincent," she gasped, "are you crazy? You trying to kill me?"

Maria's blow had drained the erstwhile vampire of his thirst. He got to his feet, muttering obscenities and threats, then staggered off across the field. Maria ran home and told her horrified mother, who took her at once to the village prefect.

Verzini was immediately arrested, and after being questioned at length, made a full and detailed confession. He was tried, convicted, and sentenced to life imprisonment.

Although Vincent Verzini's examiners found "no evidence of psychosis," there can be little doubt that his vampirism was the expression of deep derangement and sexual perversion. That this is the case is shown lucidly by Verzini's own words:

"I had an unspeakable delight in strangling women, experiencing during the act erections and real sexual pleasure. The feeling of pleasure while strangling them was much greater than that which I experienced while masturbating. I took great delight in drinking Motta's blood. It also gave me the greatest pleasure to pull the hair-pins out of the hair of my victims.

"It never occurred to me to touch or look at the genitals...*It satified me to seize the woman by the neck and suck their blood.*"

Not manifestly sexual were the vampirish acts of John Haigh, British killer of nine. Haigh's thirst for human blood is believed by some authorities to have been somehow linked to his religious fanaticism.

Haigh was obsessed with the Old Testament admonitions to "drink water out of thine own cistern and running waters out of thine own well." It would be fascinating to know the processes by which Haigh's twisted mind shaped this thought to cause him to start drinking his own urine and blood.

Yes, the religious vampire's first taste of human blood was that of his own. He became involved in an automobile crash in which he suffered a scalp wound which bled profusely. The blood flowed down his face and into his mouth, creating a thirst which would lead him to the gallows.

Perhaps the wound's accompanying blow deepened Haigh's psychosis. Shortly after the incident, he had a dream which he interpreted to mean that his religious fervor had sapped his strength and he could only restore his energies by the regular consumption of fresh human blood.

In keeping with the religious trend of his sickness, Haigh evolved a ritual. First he would sever the jugular vein of his victim, then he would carefully draw off the blood a glassful at a time. The actual drinking of the vital fluid was observed with great ceremony. Haigh later became convinced that his faith, too, could be sustained only by the sacrifice of others and the drinking of their blood.

It is accepted today that the drinking of both blood and urine are perverted sexual acts, affording gratification and pleasure to the psychotic or deeply neurotic who indulge.

It is believed that Haigh participated in homosexual acts as a youth. It is interesting to note that he claimed to have been seduced by a homosexual member of a religious sect prior to his own deviation.

Is it possible that feelings of guilt arising from these events drove the impressionable Haigh to offer such terrible propitiation? Or did he mistake the intoxication which reportedly comes from blood-drinking for religious ecstasy? As fascinating as these questions are, they will never be answered in the case of John Haigh, the vampire, who in August, 1949, was delivered to the hangman.

The vampire, the restless soul of a dead person which must drink the blood of others to sustain its "life," is highly suggestive of the pathologically immature, dependent personality, who cannot fend for himself in the business of living, but must attach himself to a more productive personality, just as the vampire attaches itself to the creatures on whose blood is feeds. Such individuals almost always subconsciously desire to return to the stae of complete dependence characteristic of the pre-natal state. Psychoanalysts usually disclose that, in extreme cases, the grave comes to symbolize the womb. This is often the true motive behind some individuals' incestuous desire for intercourse with their mother. The vampire's nightly return to its grave greatly resembles such a state of mind. The vampire's fangs are clearly phallic symbols, both in form and function. The vampire's predilection for its relatives resembles the incestuous cravings of the deviate, a form of infantile sexuality, as further symbolized by the vampire's relish for the young.

Blood sucking itself is significant. Psychologists say thsat any neirotic act involving this act is a sign of mother-fixation.

A stake through the heart to kill a vampire is strongly suggestive of fear (connected hatred) of the father figure.

It appears, therefore, that the true lair of the vampire must be sought in the hidden and forgotten areas of the human mind, rather than in secluded burial vaults and the cobweb-laced ruins of deserted mansions; and that the terrible thirst of real-life vampires must be understood in the light of the frustration and misdirection of the most basic of human needs: the need to love and reproduce one's own kind.

*****

During the Middle Ages and the period known as that of the Great Witch Mania, it was natural to explain the deviations of men in terms of demonaology. Prevalent at the same time was a belief in the transformation of men into wolves (perhaps the source of the modern designation for a certain lascivious breed of male creature) and other carnivorous animals.

The belief that a creature half-human and half-animal was unholy reaches back into dim antiquity. Thus, the ancient Israelites are instructed through the *Book of Leviticus*: "And you shold not lie with any beast and defile yourself with it, neither shall any woman give herself to a beast to lie with it... ." (18:23) Such practices were associated with worship of the pagan diety Moloch, and any offspring of such a union was classed as an evil apirit.

The most common manifestation of lycanthropy was the werewolf. A less-fastidious cousin of the vampire, this half-man half-wolf was said to go about committing murder, rape and cannibalism.

One day in the town of Dole, France, in the year 1573, a wooden stake was set up in the public square and straw and faggots piled at its base. A figure with long, matted hair and tattered remnants of clothing was dragged in chains and under heavy guard to the stake and tied securely to it.

This being accomplished, the sheriff unrolled an official looking document and read in a loud voice:

"In the name of His Majesty, by the grace of God King of France: It is proven that on a certain day, shortly after the Feast of St. Michael last, Gilles Garnier, being in the form of a wolf, seized upon in a vineyard a young girl, aged about ten or twelve years, she being in the place commonly called as Gorges, the vineyard de Chasteonoy, hard by the Bois de Serre, about a mile from Dole, and there he slew and killed her both with his hands seemingly paws, as with his teeth, and having dragged her body with his hands and teeth into the aforesaid Bois de Serre, he stripped her naked and not content with eating heartily of the flesh of her thighs and arms, he carried some of the flesh to Apolline his wife at the hermitage of Saint-Bonnot, near Amanges, where he and his wife had their dwelling"

The official's voice cracked, and he paused to clear his throat. The crowd let out its breath as one. A priest made the sign of the cross and chanted in Latin as the sheriff began to read again.

In trite, unemotional language, a story of murder and cannibalism unfolded that caused the sale of fresh meat in Dole to fall off for a week afterwards. In revulsion the people listened as the damnation of Gilles Garnier, convicted werewolf, proceeded.

"...Unto customary place of execution, and that there by aforesaid Master Executioner he shall be burned and his body reduced to ashes."

The hooded executioner approached and with a flourish placed his torch on the dry straw. Flames shot up, and the "werewolf" screamed his way into oblivion with a cry of pain that may very well have come from either man or beast.

About a month before Christmas, 1598, Antoinette Duprey, eleven years old, paused on a Paris street to absorb the full joy of a snowflake kiss on her cheek. From the door of a tailor shop a soft voice spoke.

"Salut, Cherie."

"Bon jour, M'sieur."

"What a beautiful child you are. Do you live near?"

"No, M'sieur. It is a distance from here. It was such a nice day for a walk I lost count of the blocks."

"Tiens! You must be cold. Will you not come into my shop where it is warm? And I have some chocolate ready."

The child shook her long, blond hair. It was growing late, and Maman would be worried. But yet... .

"Merci, M'sieur. But only for a minute."

"But of course. Pretty girls should not be out after dark."

The little girl's minute turned into eternity. She never came out of the tailor shop alive. But a friend of her family had seen her enter the shop, and when he discovered that Antoinette was missing, he informed the police. At the sadistic tailor's trial it was testified that once the child entered the shop the tailor changed himself into a wolf and sprang upon her, ripping off her clothing and biting and clawing at her frail child's body.

It was further avowed that this fiend prowled the woods by night, snarling and drooling at the mouth, and tearing out the throats and entrails of helpless passersby.

Barrels of bleaching bones were found in the accused tailor's cellar, along with other things too hideous to describe.

Quickly the werewolf was condemned to the stake. His executioners, who had seen all manner of villains burned, stopped their ears, so great was this fiend's blasphemy, even as the flames burned the flesh from his bones. The magistrate ordered that the court records pertaining to the case be burned in the same fire.

If there seems to be a dearth of werewolf cases today, it is only because the beast has had his name changed by modern psychiatry. Nowadays he is called by such names as "sadist," "pervert," or "psychotic sex offender." From time to time, nevertheless, one sees the "werewolf" label attached to sex crimes by sensationalists publications. Such was the case of William Johnston.

William Johnston, alias H. Meyers, alias Harry Gordon, sadistic killer of three women, did not claw or bite his victims to death. He did his namesake justice, however, with a straight razor. Like London's infamous "Jack the Ripper," Johnston chose prostitutes for his victims.

On the night of April 6, 1935, Betty Coffin turned a corner and started to walk down San Francisco's Market Street. As she passed the streetlamp, she glanced at her wristwatch. It was 2:30 A.M., and Betty's feet hurt. She had covered a lot of concrete during the last three hours and was about to call it a night. Then she saw him.

It was too late to play games. She walked right up to the heavy-set, slightly drunk man, who was dressed as a seaman, and propositioned him.

"Sailor, do you know a nice place where a girl can get some rest?"

"Huh? Oh, yeah, sure," replied the man, his eyes snapping awake.

Half an hour later, Betty Coffin stood sleepily by as her "client" scribbled on a registration card in a cheap waterfront hotel. A minute "Mr. and Mrs. Harry Meyers" started up the stairs to their room. The night clerk noted later that the couple's only luggage was a bottle of whiskey and a little box that protruded from Meyers' pocket.

Two hours late Meyers came down alone.

He approached the night clerk. "Where can I get a beer and a sandwich," he yawned.

"There's a place on the corner," answered the drowsy clerk. "Just turn left after you go out the door."

"Thanks. Can I get you anything?"

"Nope."

But the big man was already on his way.

At eight o'clock a chambermaid entered the Meyers' room using a passkey. She placed her broom against the wall and started to open the window. Then she looked at the sprawled figure on the bed. Her scream brought the manager from downstairs. The nude body of Betty Coffin lay on the blood-soaked sheets. Her face had been beaten savagely, and her mouth taped shut. The corpse was stiped with gaping wounds in regular patterns, as if she had been raked again and again by the claws of a wild beast. Blood-stained fragments of clothing were strewn about the room.

The dead girl had not been sexually assaulted—at least not in the normal way.

Said Inspector Allan McGinn of the San Francisco Police: "The man who does a job like this is the type that strikes again and again. He doesn't stop at one murder. *It just whets his appetite for more."*

The inspector was right. The most arduous of police work failed to turn up the killer, and five years later he struck again. On June 25, 1940, the body of Mrs. Irene Chandler was found in another waterfront hotel in the same circumstance as that of Betty Coffin. Causes of death were listed as strangulation and loss of blood. Mrs. Chandler was known to the police as a "seagull," a streetwalker who catered to sea-faring men. This time the "werewolf" left his claws behind: a rusty, blood-stained razor.

Time was running out for the werewolf-killer. The Sailor's Union of the Pacific supplied to the police a picture of a man who fit the killer's description. On July 8, 1940, a San Francisco detective confronted Harry W. Gordon at a sailor's union meeting.

"We want to talk to you at headquarters," said the officer quietly.

The blond werewolf's shoulders slumped. He offered no resistance as he was taken to jail.

After intense questioning, Gordon broke down.

"I'll talk!" he cried. "I'll tell you everything. I'm glad to get it over with. I killed Betty Coffin and Irene Chandler."

The officers were not prepared for Gordon's next words: "And I killed my first wife in New York, too!"

On September 5, 1941, Harry W. Gordon took his last breath in San Quentin's lethal gas chamber. The werewolf's savage hunger was quieted at last.

*****

Stranger even than the thirst of the vampire and the hunger of the werewolf is the grisly appetite of the ghoul. A ghoul has been defined as a demon which robs graves to devour the corpse. This act is termed "necrophagia," literally "eating of the dead." But the concept of ghoulishness has been extended by custom to include a number of other practices, including sexual intercourse with and mutilation of the dead, both termed "necrophilia."

A classic case of necrophilia is that of Sergeant Bertrand, a soldier in the French army in the mid-1800s. Bertrand was only twenty-five at the time of his arrest; by then the history of his ghoulish career read like a book of the damned. His behavior eventually came to the attention of his superiors, and he was placed under the care of Dr. Marchal de Calvis.

At his first meeting with the doctorBertrand described himself as a successful Don Juan, a claim frequently the boast of impotents and deviates.

"I have had many women," he told de Calvis, "and I have always satisfied them completely."

"But of course," cajoled the physician, "and I suppose you started at quite a young age."

Bertrand's composure was a bit ruffled.

"Very yong. And even before that I was extremely active. Such was my maleness at the age of nine that I was forced to relieve myself by hand seven or eight times a day."

Dr. de Calvis made notes on a pad, then studied his pen.

"remarkable! But at what age did you turn to women?"

"Thirteen, maybe fourteen."

"Tell me about it."

Bertrand's eyes glowed. There was no mistaking the pleasure in his voice as he spoke:

"The sight of female clothing was sufficient to arouse me. In my mind I could see a room full of women, all at my disposal. In my mind I would torture them in every possible way, according to my desire. I would imagine them as dead before me, and I would defile their corpses."

"I see," mused de Calvis. He was beginning to sense the true nature of his patient's deviation. "Was this when you first made love to a corpse?"

"No," replied the sergeant. "At first it was with the bodies of animals I found dead along the roadside. Sometimes, when I could not find one, I was forced to kill."

"Most regretable," said the doctor, feigning sympathy. "But what about your first experience with the corpse of a human?"

"It was in 1847 at a cemetary near Bere," said Bertrand slowly. "A comrade and I happened to wlak by a newly-made grave. Suddenly, I was struck with a terrific headache , and my heart began to pound. I trembled all over. As soon as I could get away, I returned to the spot and dug up the body. Then I chopped it up with a pick and spade. I kept it up until my desire was releived. Only then did my headache leave me."

In subsequent interviews Bertrand related numerous graveside orgies similar to the foregoing. He told of the time he had swum a ditch of icy water to reach a fresh grave. So great had been his passion that night that he had not even noticed the chill.

This was Bertrand's first actual sexual contact with a corpse, that of a seventeen-year-old girl.

"I cannot describe my sensations," Bertrand told Dr. de Calvis, "but all the joy procured by possessing a living woman was as nothing with the pleasure I felt."

The sergeant went on to describe his mutilation of the body, as before, and its return to the grave. Bertrand told the doctor that he thought the motivating force behind his deeds was the urge to destroy.

"The urge to dismember the bodies was incomparably more violent in me than the urge to violate them."

Small wonder, in the light of happenings like this, that superstitious folk of earlier times whispered of drooling demons that came down from the hills to desecrate graves, assault and cannibalize even bodies in advanced stages of decay.

Another real-life ghoul by the name of Ardisoon is reported to have exhumed the bodies of females aged three to eighty, and indulged in oral sex acts with them. He was arrested after he had taken home the corpse of a three-year-old girl on whom he practiced certain abominations until the stench betrayed him.

Even more remarkable is the case of the female necrophagiac who opened the caskets in her family vault and devoured the genitals of her dead husband, her brother and her son.

In 1957, Ed Gein, a middle-aged bachelor farmer from Plainsfield, Wisconsin, confessed to stealing a dozen female bodies from freash graves in the community cemetary. Although he replaced most of the pieces after he had dismembered the bodies, he kept a collection of sex parts and noses in a box. He also saved ten of the skulls and upholstered some of his furniture with human skin. Gein progressed from grave-robbing to murdering two women, and when the sheriff entered his farmhouse, he was horrified to find one of the victims strung up by her heels, decapitated and eviscerated. The necrophagiac's neighbors later recalled with great unpleasantness that Gein was forever bringing them portions of "venison." While under psychiatric examination, Gein told the analyst that he had never shot a deer in his life.

A mitigating case can be made for those suffering from the ghoul psychosis in that they disturb only corpses, which, of course, cannot suffer further. But this in not likely to assuage the feelings of thier victims' survivors. And would ghoul suddenly turn werewolf if no cadavers were available to him? Would he turn upon the living to satisfy his strange and terrible hunger?

What is the true nature of the real-life vampires, werewolves and ghouls? Perhaps a clue is to be found in the self-evaluation of Sergeant Bertrand:

"The urge to dismember . . . was incomparably more violent in me than the urge to violate. . ."

Whatever the answer, another question remains: Can there be a vein of truth in the old beliefs, that such atrocities are the work of evil spirits who have taken possession, body and soul, of the perpetrators?

It might be argued that, as in the case of the poltergeist, a person in the appropriate frame of mind might serve as a medium thhrough which these entities can satisfy their unholy cravings.

Older stories carry accounts of men and women changing themsleves into blood-sucking bats, voracious wolves, or red-eyed, fang-toothed demons. More recent accounts report nothing of the sort. But actually, the discrepancy is of small significance. If the *mind* of the "ghoul" has undergone change to the point where he believes himself to be such a creature, it is of slight consequence if his form changes.

The Countess Bathory made a formidable vampire with the scissors from her maid's sewing kit. Harry W. Gordon's razor served ost adequately as werewolf's claws and fangs. Sergeant Bertrand was not hampered in his ghoulish pleasures by the fact that he worked with a pick and shovel or sword rather than a monster's paws.

Our age of scientific reason leads us to explain the acts of these and others like them in clinical terms of psychosis and sexual perversion, and to view perversion itself as a sign of negative psychic forces at work on the mind of man. Where mosr logically could such forces be focused than on the instinct to propagate life? As sex produces life, so it is that perversion produces death.

"It (necrophilia) is a true perversion," writes Dr. Erich Fromm. "While being alive not life, but death is loved, not growth but destruction."

Instead of in the supernatural, then, it appears that the origin of history's recorded vampires, werewolves, and ghouls must be sought in the wastelands of man's subconscious.

❏

Brad Steiger is the author of 200 books on the paranormal; his most relevant being *The Werewolf Book: An Encyclopedia of Shape Shifting Beings.*

Go to www.BradandSherry.com <http://www.bradandsherry.com/> for full details of his career.

Real Life Werewolves
They're Not The Stuff Of Hollywood!

By Sean Casteel

Sean Casteel is a journalist who has interviewed numerous luminaries in the field of UFO and paranormal research. He is a Contributing Editor to "UFO Magazine," and contributes regularly to "Mysteries Magazine" and "The Conspiracy Journal." He has written several books for Inner Light/Global Communications, including "UFOs, Prophecy and the End of Time" and "The Excluded Books of the Bible." Casteel has also appeared on the popular radio programs "Coast To Coast" and "The Kevin Smith Show." He has a website at www.seancasteel.com

LINDA GODFREY

People come to the study of werewolves in many different ways. For Linda Godfrey, it all started when she was working as a reporter for a county newspaper called "The Week" based in Delavan, Wisconsin.

"It just came to my attention," Godfrey said, "that people around the town of Elkhorn, which is my hometown, were seeing some kind of wolf-like creature that just walked around on two legs around a stretch of county road called Bray Road, just outside of town. They were even phoning in reports to the County Animal Control Officer. When I checked with him, I found out this was true, and that in fact he had a manila file folder marked 'werewolf,' because nobody knew what else to call this thing, and he didn't either."

So Godfrey had an interesting story virtually dumped in her lap. She would eventually come to write three books dealing with these strange sightings and become a well known crypto-zoologist in her own right. But back again to the beginning.

"When I interviewed the witnesses," she said, "I became very impressed that they didn't seem like they were making it up or trying to pull a hoax or anything

like that. They were a fairly diverse group. So we ran the first story and I dubbed it 'the Beast of Bray Road' because that was where the first reported sightings came up. It's certainly by far not the only place where it's been seen. But I liked the term 'beast' better than 'werewolf' because we really didn't know what it was, and I still don't know what it is. But 'beast' can refer to any kind of animal. That story ran December 1, 1991, and it's never stopped since."

EYE WITNESS ACCOUNTS

The initial stories were fascinating, to say the least.

"There was a witness," Godfrey said, "who was a young, single mother named Lori Endrizzi, and she happened to see this creature at night. She noticed it because it was kneeling by the side of the road in a way that an animal really can't normally manage. It was using its paws to hold up what looked like a chunk of road kill that it was eating from. It scared her a lot. She went to the library to look up and see what it could be, and the only thing she found that looked like it were pictures of werewolves. She was one of the ones who reported it to the Animal Control Officer."

Another young woman, named Dorothy Gipson, thought that she had hit something with her car.

"She felt a bump," Godfrey explained, "stopped and got out of the car to see if she'd hit somebody's pet dog or something like that. Then, as she described it, she said this 'thing' came running at her and she could hear its feet very heavily pounding the pavement—but only its hind feet. It was running upright at the car. At that point, she hopped back in and sped off, but it did lunge at her car and left some scratch marks, which I did see. There wasn't any way to prove, really, what they were from, but she had a set of evenly spaced scratch marks on the rear end of her car."

Equally strange is the story of a group of schoolchildren who had been out sledding on Bowers Road, which runs parallel to Bray Road, not very far away.

"They saw what they thought was a dog kneeling by a little bit of open water," Godfrey said. "They thought it was kneeling and trying to drink. When they went over to pet it, the so-called 'dog' stood up. That's when they realized it was no dog and they took off running. It actually chased them, and this is what usually happens when people are chased: it broke off the chase and they were able to continue safely home. But they were really frightened out of their wits."

One of the children who was part of the incident was a classmate of one of Godfrey's sons.

"My son told me that he really didn't think this kid was making it up," Godfrey said, "or that any of them were."

continued >

20

THE WEREWOLF GOES NATIONWIDE

The sightings on Bray Road continued apace for a little while after the period discussed above, and then dropped off for about the next ten years. But the sightings continued elsewhere, and Godfrey's first reports for the county newspaper soon became a national news story.

"I was on 'Inside Edition,'" she said, "and from then on, just about any time someone wanted to talk about werewolves, they would call me. Because there really aren't any other large bodies of contemporary accounts of something that sounds and looks like a werewolf."

After having a kind of crypto-zoological greatness thrust upon her, Godfrey quickly became one of the few experts on the subject of werewolves, a term she disdains, by the way.

"I like to call it a 'man-wolf' instead," she said, "because it has less Hollywood baggage. 'Werewolf' implies it's a human changing into a wolf. So much of what we think of as the werewolf legend began in Hollywood. The full moon, the silver bullets, all that sort of thing. So it's true that every indigenous people and culture around the world has its own traditions of men that can change into some other type of animal. But a lot of that is more related to shamanistic traditional tribal rites than it is to an actual physical being turning into a Lon Chaney style werewolf. There's a difference.

"The shamans are thought," she continued, "to perhaps be able to create a psychic impression or a thought form that they can throw off from themselves. I don't entirely discount that idea."

Godfrey also considers the possibility—which she calls the "Indigenous Dog-Man Theory"—that perhaps some strain of canine has managed to adapt a more upright stance because it gave them advantages in running around in swamps, for instance, which might be easier on two legs than four.

"And it's more efficient to carry prey," she said, "in your upper arms than to drag it away in your mouth. They may have adapted to this and become a little more intelligent as a result, too, and so have been able to remain very elusive. Also, it would not have changed their outward appearance very much. Many witnesses have reported seeing it running both on hind feet and four legs, and it can go back and forth between the two. We've even had track evidence of this in some other states. But if you found a dead one, you probably would just think here's a really large wolf or wolf-hybrid. So those are I think more likely explanations than the traditional Hollywood werewolf."

Godfrey said that the sightings reports pour in at the rate of one to two a week, and come to her from all over the country, including New Jersey, Georgia, Kentucky, Tennessee, Texas and Oklahoma, with more recent sightings coming from Iowa.

"They seem more confined to the Midwest and the East Coast," she said. "So I don't know if they're stopped by the Great Plains there because there's no cover for them to move around. They do seem to prefer to have some kind of cover, whether it's a forest or a cornfield or something like that. They also seem to follow water and water sources. There's almost always some source of water nearby a reported sighting."

PARANORMAL POSSIBILITIES

Again, the idea of a paranormal origin for the werewolves is a thorny one to grapple with. In medieval times, for instance, people who were accused of being a werewolf were generally believed to have achieved the transformation through magical means.

"They would apply a special salve," Godfrey said, "or they would have a belt made out of wolf hide that they could put on them. Then there were chants and rites to be performed that would transform them. But it didn't necessarily mean that their body physically transformed. Often it was understood that their spirit or their astral body would take on the form of a wolf and go out from them while their actual physical body lay sleeping. And if the wolf form was wounded somehow, say somebody shot it in the leg, then a corresponding wound would be found on the person's own leg, without the actual human body ever having changed or moved from the spot. That was the way that they would identify a werewolf. They'd say, 'Well, I shot it in the leg and then they found somebody sleeping with a bullet hole in their leg in the same spot.'

"So that's actually really very close to the idea of the shaman tradition that you have with Native Americans and other indigenous people where, through some sort of magical rite, either a thought form or a spirit double goes out from the body, or in some cases forms around the body, kind of like a supernatural costume, if you will, that the person can move around in. And underneath is his physical body, but around him is this illusion of the form of an animal. In Tibet, they call these thought forms a tulpa, but it has parallels in many other cultures as well.

"There are other people who believe that entities may be conjured up by means of other magical rites, and that these entities wouldn't be based on human beings. They would be some other type of spirit that could take on the shape of a werewolf, and hopefully go out and do things for whoever had conjured it up. Some people believe that's possible, and other people don't."

DOWNRIGHT MEAN LOOKING

Wherever the creatures come from, they consistently project an aura of evil and meanness, according to the many witnesses Godfrey has spoken to.

"Something I really get very often from people," she said, "way more often than not, is a sense of fear emanating from it. They just get really unnerved. They feel that it's glaring at them, that it's sort of sneering. That it's somehow getting across to them that it has the upper hand and that it could follow them or do bad things to them if it wanted to. But in most cases, once they're good and scared, what it does is makes its escape. Whether it's been chasing them or just watching from the roadside, there's almost always some kind of cover, and as soon as it can get to that cover, it just tries to get away."

Godfrey stopped counting after a hundred sightings and now estimates the total to be around two hundred. But in all those sightings, only one person has ever reported being injured by the werewolf. A man in Quebec told her he had had his hip grazed by the tooth of a werewolf, which left a jagged cut behind. The man sent Godfrey a photo of the wound, which of course remains inconclusive.

"In all these other cases," she said, "you would think that somebody would have been hurt by now, or reported that it ripped their arm or bit them on the leg or something like that. It just doesn't happen. It has such a consistently clear behavior that I think that that really is another indication that people aren't making this up. There's something strange that's really going on."

The werewolves, along with the aura of fear they project, also seem to make a kind of telepathic contact with some witnesses.

"People will say to me," Godfrey said, "and usually it's at the end of the report, they'll say, 'There's one other thing. I hope you don't think I'm crazy but I felt that I was getting a mental message from it.' And not in the King's English, you know. It's not like they're hearing words in their head, but they feel that they're getting a definite impression that they can understand. They usually translate it as something like, 'You shouldn't be looking at me. If you tell anyone I'll come and get you. I'm here, you're there. You can't get me,' that kind of thing. Very challenging, and it kind of shakes them up."

DON'T LAY YOUR BIGFOOT ON MY WEREWOLF

Godfrey allowed as how the Bigfoot is sometimes said to send a similar kind of telepathic message, but in the case of the Bigfoot, witnesses usually "hear" something much more benign than what is projected by the more aggressive man-wolf. Meanwhile Godfrey bristles at those who say the man-wolf is just another version of the Bigfoot only with a longer snout.

"You've really got definite primate characteristics on the one hand," she said, "and really definite canine characteristics on the other hand. Not only does the werewolf have a long pointed snout—whereas even baboons can have snouts, but they're not long and pointed—they also have ears on top of their heads, sharp pointed ears that look like a German shepherd or wolf ears, from most accounts. The bodies taper towards the hips and they're much more slender than you would find on any kind of a primate. There are tails often seen, and most important, anyone who gets a clear look at it will report that the legs looked like they were bent backwards. That's because a canine walks on its toe pads and its heel is up above the ground. Where we're expecting to see a knee bending forward, we're seeing what's actually the heel, bending what looks to us like backwards but it's actually just the normal heel joint, it's just off the ground.

"So it looks very different," Godfrey continued. "We have had photos of the footprints of this thing, and they look like very large, somewhat elongated wolf or dog prints. When the track medium is the right kind, you can see claw marks, little points where the claws extend, and this would not be the case with a primate. They're not Bigfoot tracks, let's put it that way."

IS LUST IN THE PICTURE?

Godfrey was asked the inevitable question, is the werewolf or man-wolf perhaps a metaphor for human lust?

"I think that's a legitimate question," Godfrey responded. "But I believe, from everything I've read and studied, there would be more of a metaphor for human violence, the desire to shed blood that's connected with eating flesh. I think that if you're looking for the metaphor for lust, that kind of goes more with a vampire. Now, in Eastern Europe, the werewolf and the vampire are almost one and the same being. They're very close to one another, like they've morphed into the same creature.

"But I think there isn't a real big sexual connotation with these things. It's more all about power and violence and people being scared that they're going to be eaten. Whereas the vampires are seductive, they come into people's bedrooms. I can really see the lust argument much more readily with a vampire than a werewolf. I do think there is some merit to the argument that we do have these archetypes in our mind and that with all the violence that's going on in the world—it's a way of externalizing the violence that we fear.

"And there is another theory," she went on, "if you want to combine the two, that posits that perhaps they are a type of psychic vampire, feeding not on lust or blood but on fear, on the strong emotions caused by fear, and that that explains why they're interested in coming across as fearsome, making this big attack, eliciting strong emotions from people. Then they would have what they want and make their exit. This would argue for them being other-dimensional beings, if that were true."

BRAY ROAD REVISITED

After a long absence, the sightings have started up again in the Bray Road area around Elkhorn, which leads Godfrey to wonder if the man-wolf has some kind of cyclical migration route that has brought it around full-circle to the place where Godfrey first became aware of its existence. One more recent incident occurred in March, 2008.

"A man was leaving a mobile home park," Godfrey recounted, "that is maybe half a mile from one end of Bray Road, when he spotted a creature running away from that same park area. He was visiting someone there. He had heard that a lot of cats had been going missing from around the mobile home park. He saw this creature. Didn't know what it was. It was large, running on two feet. Kind of suspecting where it was going, he trailed it and caught up with it again near Bray Road, just in time to see it disappearing into some brush. But he did report that it had the same characteristics that people usually describe, which is six to seven feet tall, covered with dark gray or brown fur, and walking just as easily on two feet as four. And looking either like a very overgrown canine or a wolf."

After nearly twenty years of collecting werewolf sightings and conducting thorough research, the obvious question becomes "Just what does Godfrey herself think is really going on?

"I don't know," she said. "I still really don't know, because I haven't been able to observe it in motion. I think perhaps if I did, that might help me make up my mind. I generally go between two theories—the indigenous dog-man that I described before or some sort of inter-dimensional being that is similar to what my Native American friends think it is, a creature that can be corporeal but perhaps can pop back into another dimension when it needs to. With modern physics now saying that there probably are at least eleven dimensions if not more, you know, it opens up that possibility. I think that science is leading us to a place where we can accept that fact, that there may be worlds beyond our own five senses, beyond what we can see.

"So I kind of go back and forth between those two. I can see a good case for either one of them. And until I can lay eyes on one myself, I'm probably not going to be able to say with any conclusiveness that I feel it's one thing or the other. I just hope to keep researching."

WHAT ABOUT UFOs? DEMONS? BLACK MAGIC?

There are even more alternate theories that also tantalize. Is there any direct connection to UFOs, for instance?

"I've never run across a direct link between werewolves and UFOs," Godfrey said. "It's true that odd phenomena tend to occur within the same geographical area. I know in *Hunting the American Werewolf*, I talk about the Jefferson County Square of Weirdness. I've identified a 13-square mile area that includes all kinds of strangeness, from UFO sightings to weird large birds being seen, to Bigfoot sightings and man-wolf sightings. And all of this stuff is going on within the same confined area.

"It's very similar to what Fortean researcher John Keel referred to as a 'window area,'" she continued. "His belief was that there are certain places where dimensions perhaps intersect and that things can go back and forth, if they know where to look. It's like something crawling out the window from another dimension. So perhaps there is a relationship in that way. But I don't have any kind of report of someone saying they saw the werewolf come out of a UFO or that a UFO was hovering directly overhead when they saw it or anything like that to directly link the two."

And what about the idea that a werewolf is some kind of demon?

"Demon is another one of those very loaded words," Godfrey answered. "I think maybe a better way to describe that would be the idea of some sort of pre-existing entity or an entity that is somehow conjured up from somewhere else. Christians might call that a demon; people of other religions might call it an evil spirit. There are different terms for it. I think that's another possibility. I can't say for sure, but there are many people who believe that's what it is."

As to the idea that some kind of "conjuring" is involved, wouldn't that imply an awful lot of black magicians skulking around out there in the Wisconsin woods?

"I don't know if there are that many black magicians," Godfrey replied, "who have done this over the ages, too. Because you're talking about not only two thirds of the United States, and other countries—I mean, I get reports from France and Australia and other places—so if that were true, there would have to be a widespread cadre of people with this amount of esoteric knowledge and skill, adept at pulling this kind of thing off. And they would have to be doing it rather regularly and for their own reasons. I would suspect that a much smaller number of people, if this were possible, would be interested in pursuing such a thing."

Whether we're dealing here with a recent form of more highly evolved Dog-Man type creature, or thought forms created by certain shamanistic adepts and then turned loose on an unsuspecting world, or Man-Wolves crossing over from other dimensions than our own, or even wolf-like demons conjured by black magicians with a darkly malevolent intent, the mystery of the werewolf persists in haunting the imagination, but is keeping its secrets nonetheless.

[More information can be found on Linda Godfrey's website at beastofbrayroad.com You can also email Linda from the site and tell her about your own sightings of werewolf-type creatures. Her books include The Beast of Bray Road, Hunting the American Werewolf and most recently Werewolf.]

Werewolf and Monster Hunter Nick Redfern Goes Wild in the Jungle

NICK REDFERN

When he was five years old, British researcher and author Nick Redfern went on a family vacation to Scotland and visited Loch Ness. He was told the story of the alleged monster that dwelt there by his father. That initial brush with the paranormal made a lasting impression on Redfern, and he has devoted his adult life to the pursuit of strange animals, UFOs, and other "out there" entities, including collecting sightings reports of werewolves on both sides of the Atlantic.

Redfern has authored three books on crypto-zoology: Three Men Seeking Monsters, Memoirs of a Monster Hunter and Man Monkey, and he comes with admirable credentials for an interview about werewolves.

continued >

27

THE HEXHAM HEADS

Redfern started off with an interesting werewolf story from the early 1970s that took place in England.

"There was a very, very strange werewolf case," Redfern said, "in a town in the north of England called Hexham, and this involved something that came to be known as the Hexham Heads. Two young boys were playing in their backyard one day and dug up these two small stone heads from the garden. They were shown to various archeological experts who concluded that the heads were probably ancient Celtic in origin, so going back a very long time. Well, the heads were brought into the house and examined. One looked like an obviously male-type head; the other one looked female and almost witchlike, with a beaked nose as well, like a classic witch from folklore.

"And after the heads were brought into the house," he continued, "a lot of weird paranormal activity began to happen. Not just in that house but in the neighboring house as well. The family that found it experienced strange noises and doors slamming, things like that. But the people who lived next door actually were awakened in the middle of the night by—for want of a better term—this manifestation of a werewolf in the bedroom. Literally a manlike figure, hairy, but with a large, imposing, wolf-like head. This went on on several occasions, and again it was accompanied by poltergeist-type activity, with the creature just appearing and vanishing in the blink of an eye. So it had kind of an air of the paranormal or the occult to it rather than just a straightforward flesh and blood animal that science hasn't identified."

Redfern said that the heads were next turned over to an expert in Celtic history and archeology named Dr. Anne Ross. She began to experience the same poltergeist manifestations in her own home, as well as the appearance of the identical hairy, manlike figure with the wolf's head. The Hexham Heads went through several subsequent owners before they were lost completely to the pages of history.

But not before they piqued the boundless curiosity of the young Redfern, who heard the story when it was first reported by the BBC, implanting a deep desire to know more about werewolves. He began to collect stories on the subject whenever and wherever he could.

REPORTS FROM THE UNDERGROUND

"Over time," he said, "digging into the issue of mystery animals in general, people would say to me, 'Oh, I saw a lake monster in this particular lake, or I saw a Bigfoot-type creature.' But for every 20 or 30 cases like that, you get one where somebody said, 'Well, I was driving home late one night and I saw this weird, wolf-like creature at the side of the road. As I got close to it, it seemed to rear up on its hind legs from a four-legged position, as if it could walk on four legs and two. It backed off into the trees and it looked like the closest thing you could imagine to a werewolf.'

"And these stories were all coming in from people," he continued, "none of whom knew each other, just up and down the country. And then over time, I began to realize there was like a whole underground collection of reports, but nobody had made the connection that these things were being seen all over the place."

Having collected werewolf reports for many years, Redfern has come to prize most the stories that have paranormal overtones, as if the sheer strangeness makes them more believable.

"One that I investigated," he said, "involved a guy who said he'd seen this werewolf-type creature chasing and attacking a herd of sheep. This was in Dartmoor, a very windswept, spooky, foggy moorland. He'd seen this creature pursuing the sheep, but the weirdest thing of all—it was as if the bottom part of the creature's legs, from the knees down, was missing or transparent, as if it was almost spectral rather than like a three-dimensional animal. But he said that it was as if the creature was obviously in our realm of existence because it was chasing the sheep. But it was as if it was blinking out as well and just flickering on and off almost like a faulty light bulb or something like that."

Another similar incident took place in the same county as the previous one, Devon. The rather frightening creature seen there has come to be called the Abbottsham Werewolf and was sighted in the early 1970s.

"People reported seeing this large wolf-like creature," Redfern said, "but in some of the cases there were stories of this creature again kind of striding purposefully on four legs and then, when it needed to get out of the area quickly, you know, if somebody had seen it with their car headlights late at night, it would rear up on to its hind legs and just fly off at high speed."

Rendlesham Forest is a location famous for the UFO sightings that took place there over the holidays in 1980-81, and which continue to be controversial in the present day, with various military witnesses still at odds with debunkers over what really happened there.

"But Rendlesham Forest has been a hotbed of weirdness for years," Redfern said. "Black cat reports, ghostly black dogs, and a weird creature that's come to be known as the 'Shug Monkey.' And 'shug' is a mutation on an old English word that means 'demon' and goes back centuries. Most people describe the Shug Monkey as looking like a cross between a large ape and a huge dog, the body being like a dog but the head being like a silver-backed gorilla or something like that.

"I interviewed one guy about seven years ago," he continued, "who told me that he'd been walking through Rendlesham Forest in the mid-1970s and he'd seen this creature. The body was like a very, very shiny silky black cat, but huge, ten to twelve feet long, a massive animal, but he said the head was clearly canine. It looked very much like a German shepherd, pointed ears, elongated jaw line, etc. He was just literally petrified, rooted to the spot, and didn't know what to do.

"He realized of course that it wasn't a normal animal of the sort that probably anyone had seen before, certainly in the physical world, shall we say. He just watched it. He said it was about 20 or 30 feet in front of him and just came looming out of the bushes and kind of turned towards him and glared in his direction. He said the glare was kind of strange. It almost gave off a feeling of intelligence as if it was saying, 'Well, come on then, if you think you can take me on.' Almost like goading him and confronting him. Eventually it just went on its way, ignored him, and vanished into the trees."

The person who told the story to Redfern also said that he didn't feel he had seen the Shug Monkey because the creature he did see definitely had a canine-type head as opposed to a primate one. Like Linda Godfrey said earlier in this chapter, we are dealing with something much different than a Bigfoot or any type of apelike creature.

INVOKING THE WEREWOLF

Many of the cases reported to Redfern occur in areas where there has been a whole range of other weird activity, as with Rendlesham Forest, which is also home to a certain amount of occult activity, like witchcraft and people holding ancient black rites and rituals in the woods, including the sacrifice of animals.

"We're not entirely sure," he said, "what the nature of all these incidents are, but certainly there appears to be a high degree of invoking involved in some respects. That even applies to the Hexham Heads case, with these heads having been found buried in the backyard. Where you have invoking and you have black arts groups, doing rites and rituals in the woods, invariably, these are the same locations where these wolf-like entities appear.

"And I think it would be stupid," he added, "to ignore that fact and just try to follow the flesh and blood angle, or the mysterious animal that science hasn't identified yet. I think it's far stranger. Now, we could address all sorts of areas: are they literally demonic? Are they something from another realm of existence? It could be explained by quantum physics, for example, which is looking into the feasibility of things like parallel universes, parallel realms. Is it possible that ancient man knew something about this and was able to tap into these realms of existence?

"Another theory that I find interesting is the Tulpa theory," he said, "the idea that we're literally able to conjure these things up, creating, in simplistic terms, mind monsters. There's a long history of that. It's particularly prevalent in Tibetan cultures, the idea that deep meditation and thoughts, where you focus on one particular image, and over weeks of preparation and ritual you can externalize something you've been heavily concentrating on and give it some sort of quasi-existence in the real world."

The problem then becomes that these mind monsters cling very tenaciously to life and can actually free themselves from their creator, like giving birth to an insane child.

"So that's another theory," Redfern said, "the idea that we ourselves are creating them and then they're getting out of hand."

REDFERN MEETS A WEREWOLF

Redfern has a story of his own personal encounter with a werewolf-type creature.

"Now people have said," he began, "and maybe they're right, that because I investigate these things and write about them—I was actually ironically writing about werewolves when this experience happened—people say, well, it was on your mind and it could have been your mind playing tricks, which it could have been. I always admit that before I tell people this story."

It was late 2002, and Redfern had been doing some investigations and was deeply into writing and researching. He had even been trying to conjure a werewolf himself, what he called "controversial attempts to raise these things."

"Me and my wife had gone to bed," he recounted, "and it was about three in the morning. I had what I can only term a classic example of sleep paralysis. You're in bed, you're semi-awake, but you're literally unable to move. And more often than not, these experiences are accompanied by a feeling of dread, a feeling that there's an evil, menacing force in the room."

Redfern, in his semi-comatose state, began to see the image of a wolf-like creature walking on two legs down the corridor towards his bedroom.

"The best way I can describe it," he said, "was as if it was wearing a black cloak from the neck to the feet, buttoned up or pulled tight, with the collar turned up, with a hood, and poking out of the hood was this large, wolf-like face. The closer it got to the bedroom, the more I struggled to move, the more the feeling of dread built up and built up. I had this feeling of it getting closer to the door and coming in the room and making like a very weird and ominous—like a fast guttural growl. But if you can imagine, instead of just an animal growling, the growl would sound like language almost. I know that sounds strange, but if you imagine that a dog could talk when it growls and it actually had inflection in its voice. It was a growl but you could understand it was a fast-spoken language as well. That's when the intensity got to fever pitch point, at which point I managed to wake up and got this fleeting glimpse of this thing just vanishing backwards into the hallway."

There was a very oppressive atmosphere in the Redferns' apartment for the next two days, and the couple performed a cleansing ceremony using sage to sort of clear the air, which apparently worked for them.

"That was a very weird situation to be in," he said, "and that made me appreciate the enormity of what potentially you could do if you are able to manifest these things. If they're not necessarily good and again tenacious of life and then they start stalking you or whatever. A lot of people roll their eyes when I tell them that story, but that's honestly from the heart how it happened."

Redfern plans to continue trying to conjure these creatures himself, however.

"Particularly with werewolves," he said, "I think that because of the nature of the reports, I don't think we can say we're dealing with normal flesh and blood animals. So my next hope would be, by continuing to do these investigations, that if I can for the most part rule out the flesh and blood angle, the next step is to really try and invoke one myself. I actually do stuff like this quite a lot, and it disturbs some people when I tell them."

For instance, Redfern will go into the woods and get his mind focused, by chanting or just trying to achieve an altered state of thought, after which he envisions what he seeks to manifest in the hope that he can conjure something up.

"My hope would be that I would be able to get past the point of just doing that," he explained, "and then try to understand where they're actually coming from. Is it that the human mind has the ability to externalize something and give birth to a mind monster? Or is it that we're opening a doorway to somewhere else? Even if we don't understand how we're doing it or why we're doing it. I would hope that in time I might be able to understand what that is, where it is, and how it works. It's a long shot, but I think unless we take the time to do it, we'll never get the answers. All we'll end up with is reports, and yes, reports are great. You can fill book after book with reports, but at the end of the day, all you've got is testimony. I would like to get past that point to where we can say that now we've got an idea of where they're coming from."

THE LUST QUESTION

When asked the obligatory question about werewolves as a metaphor for human lust, Redfern responded by saying, "The human mind is a complex thing. I think that culturally, at a kind of sociological level, there are certain archetypes that everybody's brain locks onto. I don't doubt the possibility that in some cases some of the reports could fall into that category. But I would have to say honestly that the ones I've looked into, I don't think so. No one's ever said to me that there's been like a sexual aspect to it. It's just been outright menace, more than anything else. To put it bluntly, I've never come across anyone who's had like a psychic experience and said, 'I got f***ed by a werewolf.' That's not happened yet.

"Now I will tell you," he continued, "that I did interview someone who was a member of a Goth group of people who lived in Glasgow, in Scotland. They were into werewolves and would hold werewolf parties, and they'd make drinks that looked like blood out of tomato juice, that sort of thing. Basically that was an excuse to have a good old time, orgies, swinging or whatever. They kind of did it on the full moon, and they would have these parties and watch old Hollywood movies and howl and everything else.

"But that is an example of where werewolves have been used in relation to sexuality. But I think the important thing is that these were just a bunch of twenty-something Goths wanting to have a good time on a Saturday night. These weren't the werewolves themselves."

DON'T TRY THIS AT HOME, FOLKS!

Redfern unequivocally says that, of all the many strange things he has investigated, werewolves are the strangest of all.

"Purely and simply," he said, "because they seem to possess attributes of physical animals—people see them walking, getting up on two legs or getting on four legs—yet they also seem to possess paranormal aspects or attributes as well. And I think the fact that they seem to exude this air of menace is a pretty significant one, a unique one, and for that reason I tread carefully when I'm investigating these things, because, no pun intended, they come back and bite you on the ass. In the same way that you screw around with some of these weirder things and then it can start affecting you.

"And so I treat these cases and reports carefully and I would urge anyone who's had experiences with these things or is thinking about investigating them to tread equally carefully. Don't go into it thinking, 'Oh, all I need is a gun and a silver bullet and it's all going to be like some jolly Hollywood film.' It's not like that. It gets very, very weird and deep and dark the more you get into it. So I'd just say tread carefully."

[Doing a Google search for Nick Redern will turn up a plethora of information on a great many paranormal subjects, but for starters, his home page is at www.nickredfern.com/index.htm]

Werewolves in the Cinema by Tim Swartz

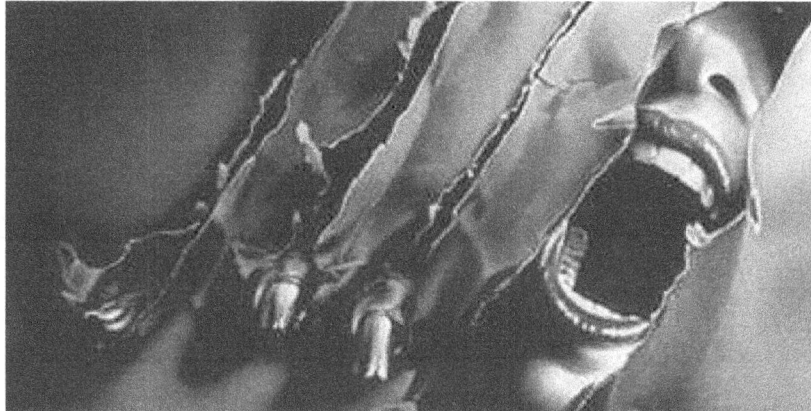

One of the most popular recurring screen monsters after the vampire is the werewolf. The werewolf in films has little to do with the "traditional" werewolf in history, which was more akin to a witch or satanic worshiper. In the movies, a werewolf is usually the unfortunate victim of fate and has little control of his transformations and subsequent actions.

The process of transmogrification from man to wolf is portrayed in films to be painful and the resulting wolf is typically cunning, merciless, and prone to killing and eating people without compunction regardless of the moral character of the person when human. The form a werewolf takes is not always an ordinary wolf, but is often more humanoid, powerful and larger than an ordinary wolf.

The first major Hollywood film to feature a werewolf was The Werewolf of London, starring Henry Hull. This film was also the first to use camera special effects, the multiple dissolve, to show the transformation from man to wolf. The werewolf, as portrayed by Hull, is less hairy and more akin to a "Dr. Jekyll and Mr. Hyde" character as he dons a cap for a night of hunting.

It wasn't until the 1941 Universal film The Wolf Man starring Lon Chaney Jr. The Wolf Man became firmly established as a horror classic. The Wolf Man was important for the mythos it added to the genre courtesy of the movie's writer, Curt Siodmak. The full moon and physical transformation was already vaguely in place, but Siodmak added the pentagram as the sign of the werewolf, the wolf's bane plant and the potential for silver to kill the werewolf. It is interesting that these points are now firmly routed in the mythology and taken almost as "fact" even though they were invented by a screenwriter.

Since that time the werewolf in film has enjoyed international popularity and rarely does a year go by without at least one film that features a lycanthrope. Each new decade brings a fresh reinterpretation on the werewolf film, the most recent influential film is 2003's Underworld that contains a rich mythology involving werewolves and their mortal enemies the vampire.

It has been fascinating watching the werewolf in film evolve. It will be even more interesting to see what new innovations will take place that will further carry the wolfman genre onto future movie screens.

The Werewolf: 1913
Bison Films (Canada)
A Navajo Witch Woman transforms her daughter into a wolf in order to attack the invading white men. An actual wolf was used in the transformation sequence.

Le Loup Garou: 1923
(France)
aka The Werewolf
Cast: Jean Marau, Madeleine Guitty
A murderer is cursed to be a werewolf by a priest.

Wolf Blood: 1925
Ryan Brothers Productions
Directors: George Chesebro, George Mitchell
Cast: George Chesebro, Marguerite Clayton
A transfusion of wolf's blood turns a man into a beast.

The Werewolf: 1932
(Germany)
Director: Friedrich Frier
Cast: Magda Sonja, Vladimir Sokolov
This is the first talkie to feature a werewolf. From the novel "Der Schwarze Mann" by Alfred Machard.

The Werewolf of London: 1935
Universal Pictures
Director: Stuart Walker
Cast: Henry Hull, Warner Oland
Wilfred Glendon (Hull) is an English botanist who journeys to Tibet in 1935 to find the elusive mariphasa plant. While there, he is attacked and bitten by a creature later revealed to be a werewolf. After he returns to London, Glendon is overcome by lycanthropy and tries to use the mariphasa flower to cure him before he kills the one he loves most.

The Wolf Man: 1941
Universal Pictures
Director: George Waggner
Cast: Lon Chaney Jr., Claude Rains, Ralph Bellamy, Maria Ouspenskaya, Bela Lugosi
Larry Talbot (Chaney) is bitten by a werewolf (Lugosi) while visiting a gypsy camp. He turns into a werewolf and is killed by his father (Rains) using a silver wolf's head cane. This movie brought silver, wolf's Bane, and the pentagram into the werewolf film genre.

The Mad Monster: 1942
Producers Releasing Corporation
Director: Sam Newfield
Cast: George Zucco, Glen Strange
An insane, but patriotic, scientist (Zucco) injects wolf's blood into a farmer (Strange) in order to create a superhuman soldier. The experiment goes awry and the farmer becomes a werewolf.

The Undying Monster: 1942
Fox Films
Director: John Brahm
Cast: James Ellison, Heather Angel, John Howard
The Hammonds are cursed with Lycanthropy, something that is found out after Howard goes on a rampage through the town, and is eventually shot by the police.

Frankenstein Meets the Wolf Man: 1943
Universal Pictures
Director: Roy Niel
Cast: Lon Chaney Jr., Bela Lugosi, Patric Knowles
Larry Talbot returns from his original role in The Wolf Man (1941), when his grave is broken into during a full moon. He locates the gypsy woman who goes with him to find Dr. Frankenstein. When they arrive Frankenstein is dead and his monster is trapped. Talbot accidentally releases him and the two monsters fight to the death.

Le Loup des Malveneur: 1943
(France)
aka The Wolf of the Malveneurs
Director: Guillaume Radot
Cast: Madeleine Sologne, Pierre Renoir, Gabrielle Dorziat
Reginald de Malveneur is a scientist attempting to discover the secret of total cellular rejuvenation. When a young governess, Monique Valory, arrives at the castle of the Malveneurs, she learns that Reginald has disappeared along with the gamekeeper. With the help of a young painter, Philippe, she begins to suspect that there is something strange at work in the household.

Cry of the Werewolf: 1944
Columbia Pictures
Director: Henry Levin
Cast: Nina Foch, Stephen Crane
Celeste La Tour (Foch) is a gypsy werewolf who tries to silence anyone that comes close to uncovering her secret.

House of Frankenstein: 1944
Universal Pictures
Director: Earle Kenton
Cast: Lon Chaney Jr., Boris Karloff
A mad doctor (Karloff) murders the proprietor of a carnival of horrors and captures Dracula, along with directions to Frankenstein's castle. There, he find the bodies of the Frankenstein Monster and Lawrence Talbot, the Wolf Man preserved in the frozen waters. After unthawing the two monsters things quickly get out of hand.

Idle Roomers: 1944
Columbia Pictures Corporation
Director: Del Lord
Cast: Moe Howard, Curly Howard, Larry Fine
The stooges are working as bellboys in a large hotel when a side show promoter shows up with "Lupe," a wild wolfman who promptly escapes. The stooges try to capture the wolfman by playing music to calm him, but music makes the wolfman go berserk and soon the stooges are the ones trying to run away. The boys end up caught in an elevator with the wolfman who shoots them into the sky.

Return of the Vampire: 1944
Columbia
Black and White
Director: Lew Landers
Cast: Bela Lugosi, Nina Foch, Matt Willis
Vampire Armand Tesla (Lugosi) is unearthed by a stray bomb. Workers, having no knowledge of vampire lore, remove the stake from his heart bringing him back to life. He becomes a part of the London elite and eventually enslaves a werewolf (Willis). The werewolf gets tired of being a slave and drags Tesla into the sun where he dissolves into a skeleton.

House of Dracula: 1945
Universal Pictures
Director: Erle Kenton
Cast: Lon Chaney, John Carradine, Lionel Atwill
Universal Pictures once again pairs a Mad Doctor (Onslow Stevens), Dracula (Carradine), the Wolfman (Chaney) and the rest of the gang for one final get together. Talbot (Chaney) is finally cured by the doctor whose attempts to also cure Dracula backfire, turning himself into a vampire as well. Much like both Frankenstein Meets the Wolfman (1943) and House of Frankenstein (1944), Frankenstein's monster is revived and there's a lot of action at the end. Talbot finally walks away cured, that is until he makes a reappearance in Abbot and Costello Meet Frankenstein.

She Wolf of London: 1946
Universal Pictures
Director: Jean Yarbrough
Cast: June Lockhart, Don Porter, Sara Haden
The Allenbys are haunted by the curse of lycanthropy, which Lockhart suspects she has inherited after several murders. However, in a plot twist, the killings were actually committed by a demented murderer.

Abbott and Costello Meet Frankenstein: 1948
Universal Pictures
Director: Charles Barton
Cast: Bud Abbot, Lou Costello, Lon Chaney Jr.
A parody of the Universal monster movies featuring Abbot and Costello as delivery men who stumble into the weird world of Count Dracula, Frankenstein's monster and Larry Talbot (Chaney) once again as the Wolfman.

The Werewolf: 1956
Clover Films
Director: Fred Sears
Cast: George Lynn, Steven Rich
Steven Rich plays a man with radiation poisoning who, when looking for an experimental treatment, instead is turned into a werewolf.

The Daughter of Dr. Jekyll: 1957
Scope
Director: Edgar Ulmer
Cast: John Anger, Gloria Talbott
Gloria Talbott goes to England in order to claim an inheritance from her deceased father who it turns out is the infamous Dr. Jekyll. A series of murders occur after she is arrived, thus leaving her the suspect. However the criminal is her father's former aid who is a werewolf. He's found, and strangely, is killed by a stake driven through his heart by villagers.

I Was a Teenage Werewolf: 1957
Sunset Productions
Director: Gene Fowler Jr.
Cast: Michael Landon, Whit Bissell, Tony Marshall
Michael Landon is a teenager who is sent to a psychiatrist in order to control his outbreaks. Instead, the psychiatrist uses hypnosis and a special serum to turn into a werewolf. His transformations occur whenever he is aroused and hears a loud noise, such as a doorbell or a telephone.

El Castillo de los Monstruos: 1957
Producciones Sotomayor
aka Castle of the Monsters
Director: Julian Soler
Cast: Antonio Espino, Evangelina Elizondo
The Mexican equivalent to the string of Universal Films in the mid-forties such as House of Dracula (1945) in which for some reason or another every imaginable movie monster converges on one castle to cause terror. In this case, the reason is to disrupt the honeymoon of a couple (Espino and Elizondo). Featured in the castle are: The Creature from the Black Lagoon, Frankenstein's Monster, the Mummy, and the Wolfman.

How to Make a Monster: 1958
AIP
Director: Herbert Strock
Cast: Robert Harris, Paul Brinegar, Gary Conway
In one of the more interesting monster movie plots, a studio costumer is dejected after production is changed from horror to movie musicals. In order to fight the men at the top he uses special makeup and hypnosis in order to turn two of his actors into Frankenstein's Monster and the Wolfman.

El Hombre y El Monstruo: 1958
Cinematographa Absa
aka The Man and the Monster
Director: Rafeal Baledon
Cast: Enrique Rabal, Abel Salazar
A concert pianist turns into a werewolf whenever he plays and only his mother's touch can change him back to human form.

La Casa del Terror: 1959
Diana Films
aka Face of the Screaming Werewolf
Director: Gilberto Martines Solares
Cast: Lon Chaney Jr., German Valdes
Lon Chaney Jr. plays not only a werewolf, but a mummified werewolf, who is resurrected by a thunderstorm and then terrifies the town.

The Curse of the Werewolf: 1960
Hammer Films
Director: Terence Fisher
Cast: Oliver Reed, Yvonne Romain
This is one of the few werewolf movies that use actual folklore and mythology in its plot. An adaptation of Guy Ender's novel The Werewolf of Paris, Leon (Reed) is born on Christmas Eve by a mute servant girl who was raped by a beggar. He is born with a patch of hair on his arm, which along with the Christmas Eve birth signifies lycanthropy. When he reaches adulthood the curse takes affect.

La Loba: 1964
Producciones Sotomayor
aka The She Wolf
Director: Rafael Baledon
Cast: Kitty de Hoyos, Joaquin Cordero
A young doctor (Cordero) who specializes in lycanthropy cases, but is a lycanthrope himself, meets the family of doctor Fernandes, who's daughter de Hoyas is also a werewolf. The werewolves fall in love, but the specially trained werewolf hunting dog and the doctor's assistant (Canedo) kill both werewolves, who die in each others arms.

Frankenstein's Bloody Terror: 1967
Maxper Producciones Cinematogrficas
Director: Enrique Eguiliz
Cast: Paul Naschy, Diane Konopka, Julian Ugarte, Rossana Yanni, Michael Manz
This movie marks the introduction of Count Waldemar Daninsky (Naschy), who happens to be a werewolf. In this, the first of many many to come, he meets a strange Hungarian couple (Ugarte and Yanni) who turn out to be vampires. Another couple (Konopka and Manz) befriend the werewolf who then kills the vampires and is then killed by Konopka.

Las Noches del Hombre Lobo: 1968
Kin Films (Spain/France)
aka Nights of the Werewolf
Director: Rene Govar
Cast: Paul Naschy, Monique Brainvill
In this film, Daninsky (Naschy) is a werewolf who is used by a mad scientist to kill his colleagues, but instead everyone ends up dying, including Daninsky.

Blood of Dracula's Castle: 1969
Paragon International Pictures
Directors: Al Adamson, Jean Hewitt
Cast: John Carradine, Paula Raymond, Alex D'Arcy
Count and Countess Dracula (D'Arcy and Raymond) live in a castle in the Mojave Desert. Their butler George (Carradine) keeps the basement stocked full of fresh victims. Things get interesting when a werewolf shows up along with a couple who claim to have inherited the estate.

El Hombre que Vino de Ummo: 1969
Producciones Jaime Prades/Eichberg Film/International Jaguar Cinematografica
Director: Tulio Demichelli
Cast: Michael Rennie, Paul Naschy, Karen Dor
An alien lands from the planet Ummo, and revives monsters in order to conquer the world. This includes Paul Naschy reprising his role as wolfman Count Waldemar Daninsky.

The Maltese Bippy: 1969
Metro-Goldwyn-Mayer
Director: Norman Panama
Cast: Dick Martin, Dan Rowan
A Rowan and Martin parody of monster movies where Dick Martin becomes convinced he is a werewolf.

The Werewolf vs. the Vampire Woman: 1970
Plata Films S.A.
Director: Leon Klimovsky
Cast: Paul Naschy, Paty Shepard, Gaby Fuchs
Paul Naschy returns after being resurrected when doctors remove a silver bullet from his corpse. He travels with two women to his castle in search of the vampire woman, who is revived by a drop of blood falling on her face. One girl is killed, the other is held until Walpurgis Night for a ritual. She is saved by Daninsky who dies in her place.

Dr. Jekyll and the Werewolf: 1971
Arturo Gonz·lez Producciones Cinematogrficas S.A
Director: Leon Klimovsky
Cast: Paul Naschy, Shirley Corrigan, Jack Taylor
Count Waldemar Daninsky (Paul Naschy) seeks the help of Dr. Jekyll to cure his lycanthropy.

The Fury of the Wolfman: 1971
Maxper Producciones Cinematogrficas
Director: Jose Maria Zabalza
Cast: Paul Naschy, Perla Cristal, Veronica Lujan
Following right on the heels of Dr. Jekyll y el Hombre Lobo (1971) Count Waldemar Daninsky (Naschy) returns from Tibet as a werewolf. He seeks the help of a female doctor (Cristal) but ends up turning her into a werewolf as well.

Werewolves on Wheels: 1971
Southstreet Productions
Director: Michel Levesque
Cast: Stephen Oliver, Severen Darden, Duece Berry
In this biker movie the leather-clad motorcyclists turn into werewolves thanks to a spell cast by a Satanist high priest (Severn Darden). Adam (Stephen Oliver) is the leader of a gang called The Devil's Advocates. His girl (D.J. Anderson) receives a request from a cult to offer herself to the Devil. She dances naked with a snake and before long is chomping on lover-boy Adam, which turns him into a werewolf too. The only one who can put an end to the mayhem is Tarot (Duece Barry), a biker with a background in the supernatural.

Frankenstein's Bloody Terror: 1972
Fenix/Comptoir Francais Du Film
Director: Jesus Franco
Cast: Dennis Price, Howard Vernon, Alberto Dalbes
Dracula is initially killed by Jonathan (Dalbes) only to be later brought back to life by a Baron, thus giving the Baron control of a horde of vampires. In order to once again stop the vampires Jonathan sets out with a werewolf to kill the Baron. He fails, however the Baron ends up killing the vampire horde and Count Dracula anyway. Jonathan rewards him by burning down his castle and killing him with the help from some gypsies.

Moon of the Wolf: 1972
Filmways Pictures
Director: Daniel Petrie
Cast: David Janssen, Barbara Rush, Bradford Dillman
A sheriff (Janssen) suspects that a werewolf is brutally killing off locals in his Louisiana town.

The Rats are Coming, The Werewolves are Here: 1972
Constitution Films Inc.
Director: Andy Milligan
Cast: Hope Stansbury, Jacqueline Skarvellis, Berwick Kaler
The Mooneys are struggling with genetic lycanthropy. One daughter, Diana, is sent to a Scottish medical school in order to help save the family, and returns with a new husband. The full moon causes the entire family to turn into werewolves, attacking Diana and her husband. The two manage to survive, but Diana later tells her husband that his only purpose had been to get her pregnant, she then changes into a werewolf and kills him.

The Return of Walpurgis: 1973
Lotus Films/Atlas International
Director: Carlos Aured
Cast: Paul Naschy, Faye Falcon, Vinc Molina, May Oliver
Paul Naschy as Daninsky is bitten by a beautiful woman (Oliver) and becomes a werewolf. His lover (Falcon) kills him with a knife fashioned from a melted silver cross, thus ending the curse.

The Boy Who Cried Werewolf: 1973
RKF/Universal
Director: Nathan Juran
Cast: Kerwin Mathews, Elain Devry, Scott Sealy
A boy witnesses his father being attacked by a werewolf, and then tries to convince both his mother and his therapist that his father is now a werewolf.

The Werewolf of Washington: 1973
Millco
Director: Milton Ginsberg
Cast: Dean Stockwell, Biff McGuire, Clifton James
A presidential aide turns into a werewolf after a trip to Hungary, and the U.S government then tries to cover it up.

Blood: 1974
Damiano Film Productions Inc./Bryanston Films Ltd
Director: Andy Milligan
Cast: Allen Berendt, Paula Adams, Eve Crosby
Dr. Orlovski (Allan Berendt), who is afflicted with lycanthropy, lives with the daughter of Dracula. There are also hordes of rabid bats flying around, turning the locals into blood-drooling cannibals.

The Beast Must Die: 1974
Amicus Productions
Director: Paul Annett
Cast: Calvin Lockhart, Peter Cushing, Charles Gray
An eccentric millionaire with a taste for the extravagant invites a group of people, who are all connected to a strange death, to his mansion. One of the invitees is supposedly a werewolf and the prey for the host's hunting party.

Legend of the Werewolf: 1974
Tyburn Film Productions Limited
Director: Freddie Francis
Cast: Peter Cushing, Ron Moody, Hugh Griffith
A traveling circus in 19th century France adopts and showcases a feral "wolf boy." He runs off to Paris, where he develops a jealous, overprotective crush on a prostitute, leading him to attack her client, incurring a pursuit by a determined police surgeon.

Scream of the Wolf: 1974
Metromedia Productions
Director: Dan Curtis
Cast: Philip Carey, Peter Graves, Don McGowan
An author is being stalked by a terrifying, mysterious beast. The creature is also being tracked by a big game hunter, who has come out of retirement to make one final big kill.

The Werewolf and the Yeti: 1975
Profilmes/Profilms
Director: Miguel Iglesias Bonns
Cast: Paul Naschy, Grace Mills, Castillo Escalona
Naschy reprises his role as Count Waldemar Daninsky who is bitten by a woman and turned into a werewolf. This time, however, he is eventually cured, but not before he gets into a fight with the Yeti.

Nazareno Cruz y el lobo (1975)
Choila Producciones Cinematogrficas
aka The Nazarene Cross and the Wolf
Director: Leonardo Favio
Cast: Juan JosÈ Camero, Marina Magali, Alfredo AlcÛn, Lautaro Mur˙a
Nazareno Cruz is the seventh son of a couple living in a high mountain village. According to a myth, a seventh son will become a wolf on nights of the full moon. Everyone in the village is relieved when this doesn't happen. The boy grows up and falls in love with a beautiful girl, Griselda. When he's 20 years old, he is visited by the Devil, who offers him the wealth of the world if he will turn his back on his love for Griselda, and if he fails to do this, he will become a wolf.

Werewolf of Woodstock: 1975
American Broadcasting Company
Cast: Tige Andrews, Belinda Balaski, Ann Doran, Meredith McRae, Andrew Stevens
After Woodstock has ended, a hippie-hating farmer (Tige Andrews) gets turned into a werewolf when he gets a massive jolt of electricity from a leftover piece of equipment one of the bands left behind. The farmer keeps transforming during electrical storms and killing everyone who gets in his way. After being chased to the top of a power station, he is shot with a silver bullet and falls to his death.

Wolfman: 1979
EO Productions
Director: Worth Keeter
Cast: Earl Owensby, Kristina Reynolds, Ed Grady
Colin Glasgow (Owensby) inherits the "Devil's curse," when his father dies. He soon discovers that his father was a werewolf and that he is to follow in his footsteps.

The Return of the Wolfman: 1980
Dalmata Films
Director: Jacinto Molina (Paul Naschy)
Cast: Paul Naschy, Silvia Aguilar, Azucena Hernandez
In this film, Paul Naschy makes his directorial debut. Once again Count Waldemar Daninsky is resurrected as a werewolf and uses his limited time to kill Countess Bathory.

The Howling: 1980
AVCO Embassy Pictures
Director: Joe Dante
Cast: Dee Wallace, Patrick Macnee, Dennis Dugan
Possibly one of the most influential werewolf movies ever made. News anchor Karen (Wallace) is used as a decoy to catch a psychopath. It is later found that the psychopath is a werewolf. Karen follows up on the story which leads her to the Colony, a remote spa that's sole population is a coven of werewolves. She escapes after burning the werewolves in a barn. As she reports her story, she transforms into a wolf on air, only to be shot to death by her lover.

An American Werewolf in London: 1981
Lycanthrope Films
Director: John Landis
Cast: David Naughton, Jenny Agutter, Griffin Dunne
A movie that really broke new ground using special effects to transform a man into a wolf. Two American students (Naughton and Dunne) come across the Slaughtered Lamb Pub while traveling through England. They are warned to stay on the roads and off the moors but stray from the road. They are attacked by a werewolf who kills Dunne and mauls Naughton. He wakes up in a hospital and has reoccurring nightmares through which he learns that he has become a werewolf. Naughton has a relationship with his nurse and eventually dies when he is in wolf form.

Wolfen: 1981
Orion Pictures
Director: Michael Wadleigh
Cast: Albert Finney, Diane Verona, Gregory Hines
Wilson (Finney) is a police detective who investigates a series murders in the Bronx. Along with his partner (Verona) and Hines, they soon discover that the killers are 'wolfen,' descendants of Indians who prey on the white man.

Full Moon High: 1982
Filmways Pictures/ Larco Productions
Director: Larry Cohen
Cast: Adam Arkin, Alan Arkin, Ed McMahon
Tony, a high school quarterback is taken on a trip to Romania where, as a direct quote from the video box states: "Tony (Arkin) is bitten by a werewolf - and that's when things really start to get hairy!"

The Beast and the Magic Sword: 1983
Aconito Films
Director: Jacinto Molina (Paul Naschy)
Cast: Shigeru Amachi, Beatriz Escudero, Junko Asahina
Naschy returns as director and once again plays wolfman Count Waldemar Daninsky. This time he is in sixteenth century Japan seeking a cure for his curse.

Children of the Full Moon: 1984
ITC Entertainment
Director: Tom Clegg
Cast: Christopher Cazenove, Diana Dors
A couple discovers a remote mansion whose occupants are a kindly old woman and very mysterious children, all who turn out to be werewolves.

Leviatan: 1984
Continental Motion Pictures
Director: Claudio Fragasso
Cast: Alice Cooper, Victoria Vera
Rock superstar Vincent Raven (Alice Cooper) returns to his boyhood home for a video shoot. The sheriff warns him that there have been several grisly murders lately. The authorities think it is wild dogs, but Raven (the werewolf) knows the truth.

The Company of Wolves: 1984
Palace Pictures
Director: Neil Jordan
Cast: Angela Lansbury, Sarah Patterson, David Warner
This movie is dreamlike and full of symbolic folklore about werewolves. Grandmother (Lansbury) tells her granddaughter (Patterson) strange tales about maidens falling in love with handsome strangers with a smoldering look in their eyes. All the stories are somehow reducible to loss of innocence, and fear of/hunger for a newly acquired sense of sexuality.

Silver Bullet: 1985
Paramount
Director: Daniel Attias
Cast: Gary Busey, Everett McGill, Corey Haim, Megan Follows
Based on Stephen King's book "Cycle of the Werewolf." A new Minister (McGill) moves into town and at the same time a series of grizzly murders occur. A paraplegic boy (Haim) believes that a werewolf is responsible for the murders, and tries to convince his family likewise. Only his sister (Follows) believes him, and together they seek out the identity of the werewolf.

The Howling II - Your Sister is a Werewolf: 1985
Hemdale
Director: Philippe Mora
Cast: Christopher Lee, Annie McEnroe, Reb Brown
Plot: Christopher Lee and Reb Brown are werewolf hunters who travel to Transylvania and run across an entire village of werewolves. This coven is led by Striba (Danning) the queen witch of Transylvania. A really bad sequel to a great movie.

Teen Wolf: 1985
Atlantic
Director: Rod Daniel
Cast: Michael J. Fox, James Hampton, Susan Ursitti
Michael J Fox plays a high school student who finds out that because of a family curse, he is a werewolf. However, instead of seeing it as a curse he uses it to become the most popular kid in school.

She Wolf: 1987
K-Beech Video Inc.
Cast: Anne Borel, Frank Stafford
Daniella (Borel) has inherited the werewolf curse from an ancestor. When the moon turns full, the she-wolf stalks the night.

Howling III the Marsupials: 1987
Bacannia
Director: Phillipe Mora
Cast: William Yang, Deby Wrightman, Christopher Pate
In one of the weirdest werewolf movies ever conceived, a mutant strain of werewolves survives as an Australian species. Full of strange concepts that include marsupial werewolves with pouches to carry their young!

Werewolf: 1987
Fox TV
Director: David Hemmings
Cast: John York, Lance LeGault, Chuck Connors
One of the first series carried by the newly formed Fox TV. A graduate student is bitten by his best friend who is a werewolf. Consequently, he turns into a werewolf himself, and to break the curse he must find and kill the original werewolf.

Teen Wolf 2: 1987
Atlantic
Director: Christopher Leitch
Cast: Jason Bateman, Kim Darby, John Astin, Paul Sand
Todd (Bateman) is accepted to a university on a boxing scholarship, although his boxing abilities are questionable. What he doesn't know is that he was accepted in hopes that he would have the same curse (lycanthropy) as his cousin Scott.

The Howling 4 - The Original Nightmare: 1988
Allied Entertainment
Director: John Hough
Cast: Romy Windsor, Michael Weiss, Anthony Hamilton
Marie (Windsor) is an author plagued by dreams of werewolves. Thinking the dreams are caused by stress, she and her husband (Weiss) take a holiday to the town of Drago. She soon discovers that her dreams were premonitions of the future, as everyone in Drago is a werewolf.

Lone Wolf: 1988
Prisim Entertainment (Uk)
Director: John Callas
Cast: Shelly Beatie, Dyan Brown, Ann Douglas, Kevin Hart
A computer genius puts his talents to work to expose the werewolf that's been preying on local high-school students.

My Mom's a Werewolf: 1989
Crown International
Director: Michael Fischa
Cast: Diana Barrows, Ruth Buzzi, Tina Caspary
When a lonely housewife decides to lunch with a pet shop owner, she is unaware that he is a werewolf. Things go too far and she soon becomes one as well.

The Howling V- The Rebirth: 1989
Allied Vision/Lane Pringle
Director: Neal Sundstrom
Cast: Ben Cole, William Shockley, Mark Sivertsen, Clive Turner, Phillip Davis
In the Middle ages, residents of a castle in Budapest committed suicide to severe the bloodline of a werewolf. However, a baby survives. In 1989 the Count summons a variety of people to the castle to discover the werewolf's descendant. Shortly after they arrive, the suspects are eliminated one by one by the real werewolf.

Mom: 1990
Trans World Entertainment
Director: Patrick Rand
Cast: Jeanne Bates, Art Evans, Stella Stevens
During a time when the city of Los Angeles is terrorized by animal attack style murders, a kindly elderly lady provides a nomad with room and board. It turns out that he is a werewolf and is responsible for the recent killings. He bites the elderly woman, turning her into a hungry werewolf. Now her son must try to prevent the both of them from doing any more harm.

The Howling 6 - The Freaks: 1991
Allied Vision/Lane Pringle
Director: Hope Perello
Cast: Bruce Martin Payne, Brendaan Hughes
A drifter Ian (Hughes) ventures into the town of Canton Bluff seeking work. He soon finds work restoring the town's church. He seems distant to the townsfolk and when a traveling freak show ventures into town, the reason becomes clear, Ian is a werewolf. He is kidnapped by the show's proprietor Harker (Payne who is a vampire himself) and put on display. After the carnival is stormed by the townspeople Ian kills Harker and once again takes to the road.

Huntress - Spirit of the Night: 1991
Torchlight Entertainment / New City Releasing
Director: Mark Manos
Cast: Jenna Bodnar, Charles Copper, Ion Siminie
Tara returns to her ancestral estate only to have her clothes explode off her body and a white light enter her chest. Afterwards she's tormented by strange desires and dreams of running through the woods. Her cave-dwelling boyfriend is no help to her. Meanwhile, false friends plot to steal her inheritance and a determined hunter seeks to slay the new werewolf in town.

Full Eclipse: 1993
HBO/Tapestry Films/Citadel Entertainment
Director: Anthony Hickox
Cast: Mario Van Peebles, Patsy Kensit, Bruce Payne
Peebles is recruited to be a part of an elite Los Angeles police team comprised of werewolves.

Wolf: 1994
Columbia
Director: Mike Nichols
Cast: Shirin Devrim, Jack Nicholson, Allison Janney
Will Randal (Nicholson) is bitten by a wolf that he encounters while driving late at night. From that point on, his life begins to change. Using his newly acquired wolf instincts, he gains an advantage over colleagues and foes alike.

The Howling - New Moon Rising: 1995
Allied Vision
Director: Clive Turner
Cast: Clive Turner, John Huff, John Ramsden, Cheryl Allen
Ted (Turner) arrives in Pioneer Town and discovers that there has been a mysterious murder. A priest (Huff) explains to the detective (Ramsden) the history of the werewolf curse, and that Ted was once present at the slaughter at a Budapest castle. More deaths occur, and Ted is arrested. A young woman (Allen) helps Ted escape, and then reveals to him that she is in-fact the werewolf.

Project Metalbeast: 1995
Blue Ridge Entertainment/Prison Pictures
Director: Alessandro de Gaetano
Cast: Barry Bostwick, Kim Delaney, John Marzilli
In Hungary, CIA agent Donald Butler (Marzilli) heads an operation in search of werewolf blood, in hopes of using it to create a superior soldier. After killing the werewolf, and injecting himself with the blood, Butler is turned into a werewolf and is killed by his partner (Bostwick). Twenty years later, scientist Anna De Carlo experiments with a new metallic flesh called BioFerron. Butler's corpse is grafted with the BioFerron, and the Metal Beast is created.

Bad Moon: 1996
Badwolf Productions/Morgan Creek
Director: Eric Red
Cast: Michael Pare, Mariel Hemmingway, Mason Gamble
An adventurous photojournalist, Ted (Pare), encounters a horrific, half-human beast that savagely murders his girlfriend. In a violent battle, Ted manages to kill the creature - but not before he receives a vicious bite that leaves him scarred forever. Ted returns to the home of his sister, Janet (Hemmingway), his beloved 10-year-old nephew, Brett (Gamble) and their dog Thor. Things soon begin to go bad, especially when the family dog, a big German Shepherd named Thor, just can't accept the werewolf among them.

American Werewolf in Paris: 1997
Hollywood Pictures
Director: Anthony Walker
Cast: Tom Everett Scott, Julie Delpy
Three friends are on a thrill seeking tour across Europe where they meet the daughter conceived in "An American Werewolf In London" (1981) and save her from jumping off the Eifel Tower. They get involved in a plot for an underground group of werewolves who want to use a serum to transform whenever they want.

Werewolf Reborn: 1998
Full Moon/Tempe Video
Director: Jeff Burr
Cast: Bogdan Cambera , Len Lesser, Robin Downes
Fourteen-year-old Eleanor Crane goes to visit her older cousin Peter in a remote Eastern European village, and receives an unexpectedly cold welcome from the villagers, who are plagued by a deadly curse - and from her cousin, who hides a deadly secret of his own.

Eyes of the Werewolf: 1999
Sterling Entertainment/SNJ Productions
Director: Jeff Leroy
Cast: Stephanie Beaton, Mark Sawyer, Deborah Hurber
An industrial accident leaves Rich (Sawyer) blind and at the mercy of an unscrupulous surgeon who performs an experimental eye transplant. Unknown to everyone, including the doctor's band of organ snatching murderers, the eyes were pulled from the sockets of a werewolf. All hell breaks loose, for Rich and everyone he comes in contact with, during the next full moon.

Rage of the Werewolf: 1999
Brimestone Productions
Director: Kevin Lindenmuth
Cast: Tom Nondorf, Joe Zaso, Santo Marotta
New York, sometime in the future; an asteroid collides into the moon which causes it to orbit closer to the Earth - causing a proliferation of werewolves.

Ginger Snaps: 2001
TVA International
Director: John Fawcett
Cast: Katharine Isabelle, Emily Perkins, Mimi Rogers
On the night of Ginger's first period, she is savagely attacked by a wild creature. Ginger's wounds miraculously heal but something is not quite right. Now Brigitte must save her sister and save herself.

Dog Soldiers: 2002
Kismet Entertainment Group
Director: Neil Marshall
Cast: Sean Pertwee, Kevin McKidd, Emma Cleasby, Liam Cunningham, Thomas Lockyer
A squad of British soldiers on training in the lonesome Scottish wilderness discovers a wounded Special Forces captain and the savaged remains of his team. As they encounter ranger Megan it turns out that werewolves are active in the region. They have to prepare for some action as the there will be a full moon tonight.

Wolves of Wall Street: 2002
A.C.H. GmbH
Director: David DeCoteau
Cast: Eric Roberts, Elisa Donovan, Michael Bergin, William Gregory Lee, Jason-Shane Scott
On the advice of a bartender familiar with the Wall Street crowd, Jeff applies to the Wolfe Brothers brokerage firm for his dream job as a stock broker. He is forced to abandon his love and values for cunning and instinct. After a change of heart, he finds that leaving the brotherhood is harder than joining.

Dark Wolf: 2003
20th Century Fox
Director: Richard Friedman
Cast: Samaire Armstrong, Ryan Alosio, Andrea Bogart, Kane Hodder
Josie, a waitress who discovers that the blood in her veins is of noble werewolf descent and that a werewolf is after her because it needs to mate.

Underworld: 2003
Lakeshore Entertainment
Director: Len Wiseman
Cast: Kate Beckinsale, Scott Speedman, Michael Sheen
A war has been going on for centuries between vampires and werewolves, never seen by human eyes, until one of the werewolves by the name of Lucian (Michael Sheen) finds out about one human that can bond with vampire blood and Lycans blood, Michael (Scott Speedman). Selene (Kate Beckinsale) is the vampire Death dealer that finds out why the Lycans are following Micheal and falls in love with him. Kraven (Shane Brolly) is the leader of the vampire house after Viktor (Bill Nighy) dies and wants Selene by his side.

Ginger Snaps 2: Unleashed: 2004
49th Parallel Productions
Director: Brett Sullivan
Cast: Emily Perkins, Katharine Isabelle, Tatiana Maslany
The second part of the "Ginger Snaps" trilogy picks up after the first one. Ginger has turned into a werewolf and her sister Bridgitte has infected herself with Ginger's blood. In order to keep herself from becoming like her sister, she must inject herself daily with monkshood. After barely escaping a werewolf that has found her, she awakes in a clinic that treats drug addiction. With her monkshood taken away, Bridgitte can't escape what she is becoming.

Ginger Snaps Back: The Beginning: 2004
Combustion Inc.
Director: Grant Harvey
Cast: Katharine Isabelle, Emily Perkins, Nathaniel Arcand, JR Bourne, Hugh Dillon
Set in 19th Century Canada, Brigette and her sister Ginger take refuge in a Traders' Fort which later becomes under siege by some savage werewolves. And an enigmatic Indian hunter decides to help the girls, but one of the girls has been bitten by a werewolf. Brigitte and Ginger may have no one to turn to but themselves.

Romasanta: 2004
Lions Gate Films Home Entertainment
Director: Paco Plaza
Cast: Julian Sands, Elsa Pataky, John Sharian
In 1850 wolves plague the forests and people are disappearing. The mutilated cadavers present precise surgical cuts along with savage gashes. It's a contradiction that terrorizes the local villagers, who are too frightened to enter the forests. Rumors about the legend of the "Werewolf of Allariz" spread. Barbara and her sister Josephine live in an isolated house in the forest. They only feel safe when a traveling vendor by the name of Manuel Romasanta comes to visit. But why is Manuel not afraid to enter the forest and what secrets are hidden under the roof of his wagon?

Van Helsing
Universal Pictures: 2004
Director: Stephen Sommers
Cast: Hugh Jackman, Kate Beckinsale, David Wenham, Will Kemp
Based on a version of the character of Abraham Van Helsing from Bram Stoker's novel Dracula, the film also incorporates characters from other works such as the film The Wolfman into the narrative, and draws particularly on literary classics of the gothic horror canon such as Mary Shelley's novel Frankenstein.

The Beast of Bray Road: 2005
The Asylum
Director: Leigh Slawner
Cast: Jeff Denton, Thomas Downey, Sarah Lieving, Joel Hebner
Based on actual accounts of werewolf sightings in Walworth County, Wisconsin, the film follows a local sheriff who is finally forced to accept that a string of horrifying deaths is linked to a predator which possesses DNA of both man and wolf.

Cursed: 2005
Dimension Films
Director: Wes Craven
Cast: Christina Ricci, Jessie Eisenberg, Joshua Jackson, Shannon Elizabeth
Ellie has been taking care of her younger brother Jimmy since their parent's death. One night after picking him up from a party they are involved in a car accident on Mullholland Drive. While trying to rescue a woman from the other car a creature attacks and kills her, also injuring both Ellie and Jimmy. After some research Jimmy realizes the creature could only have been a werewolf.

Wolfsbayne: 2005
Bloody Moon Films
Director: Ben Dixon
Cast: Jim O'Rear, Gunnar Hansen, Linnea Quigley
In 1590, the Diet of Augsburg ruled that gypsies were the spawn of Satan and, therefore, had no rights whatsoever. The ruling allowed Christians to kill gypsies without penalty, which sparked the church to organize a small group of religious assassins to carry out the dirty work. Unfortunately, the band of killer priests were not informed that the gypsies had made a pact of protection with a powerful werewolf clan, so all hell broke loose. Four hundred years later, the bloody war between the church, gypsies and werewolves rages on and it's up to a small-town police chief to end it or die trying.

Underworld: Evolution: 2006
Lakeshore Entertainment
Director: Len Wiseman
Cast: Kate Beckinsale, Scott Speedman, Bill Nighy, Shane Brolly
The movie continues the saga of war between the Death Dealers (vampires) and the Lycans (werewolves). The film traces the beginnings of the ancient feud between the two tribes as Selene (Kate Beckinsale) and Michael (Scott Speedman), the lycan hybrid, try to discover the secrets of their bloodlines. All of this takes them into the battle to end all wars as the immortals must finally face their retribution.

Skinwalkers: 2007
Lions Gate Films
Color 110 min
Director: James Issac
Cast: Jason Behr, Elias Koteas, Rhona Mitra, Kim Coates, Natassia Malthe

Creatures, bound by the blood of the wolf, that can kill with curses and move at lightening speed, watching the night sky for the rise of the blood-rd crescent moon. They are Skinwalkers. They feed on our flesh and thirst for the taste of human blood. The red moon signals each pack, divided by principles, hell bent to survive an ancient prophecy.

Werewolf: The Devil's Hound: 2007)
Lionsgate Films
Director: Gregory C. Parker & Christian Pindar
Cast: Kirsten Babich, Christy O. Cianci, Michael Dionne, Phil Gauvin

Kevin has a late night encounter with the blood thirsty Christine that prompts him to slowly turn against his family and co-workers. Now, with the help of the quirky werewolf hunter Kwan, two families will unite for one common cause.

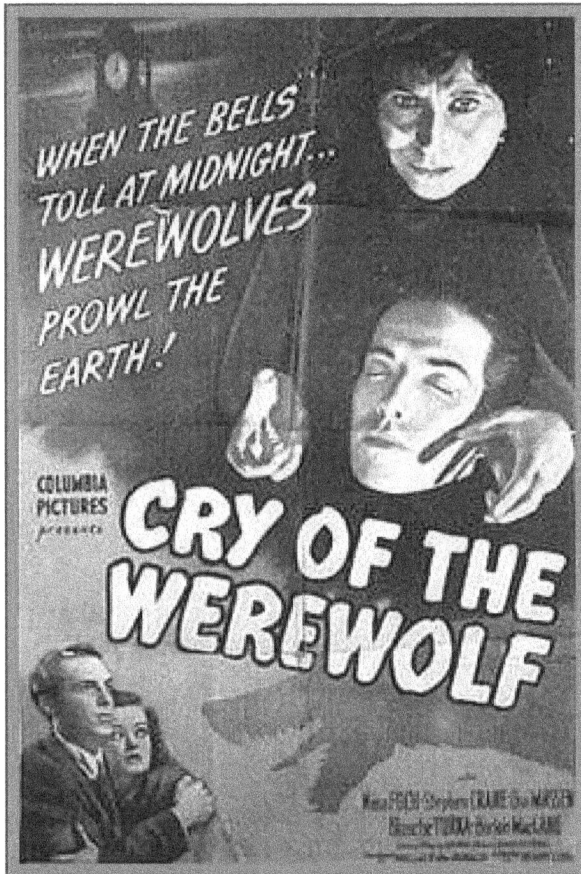

LEGEND OF THE WEREWOLF

LE LOUP DES MALVENEUR

THE MAD MONSTER

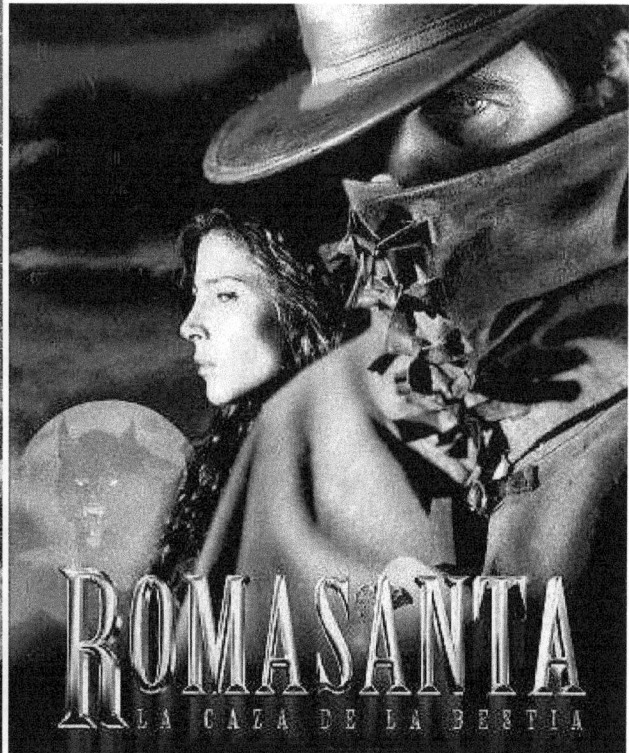

ROMASANTA
LA CAZA DE LA BESTIA

Skinwalkers

THE MONSTER

THE WOLFMAN

THE UNDYING MONSTER

WEREWOLF OF LONDON

THE WEREWOLF VS. VAMPIRE WOMAN

WEREWOLVES ON WHEELS

The WOLF MAN

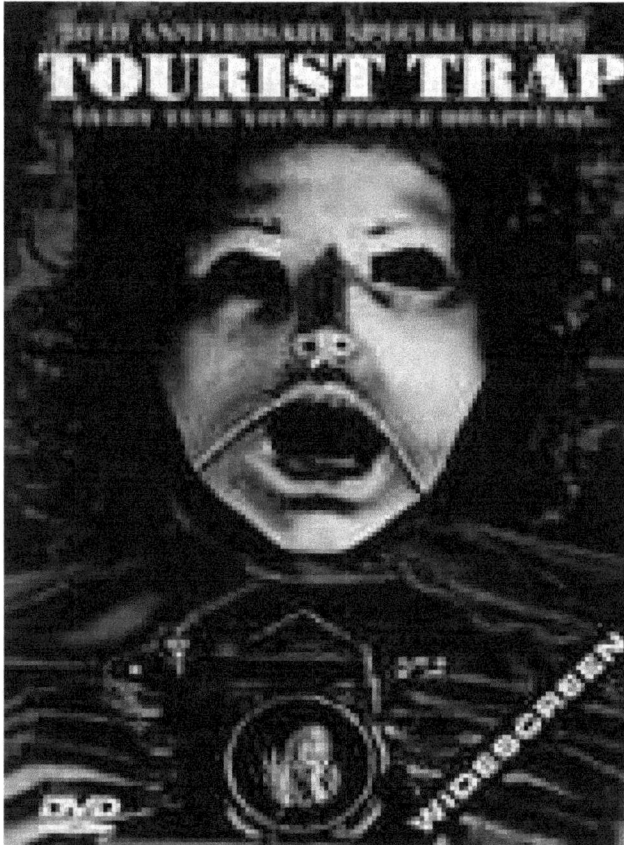

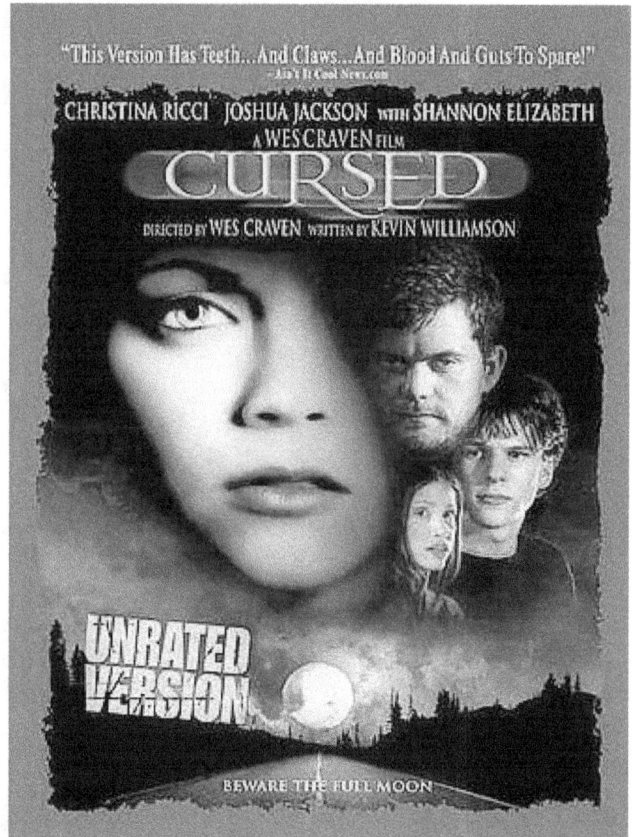

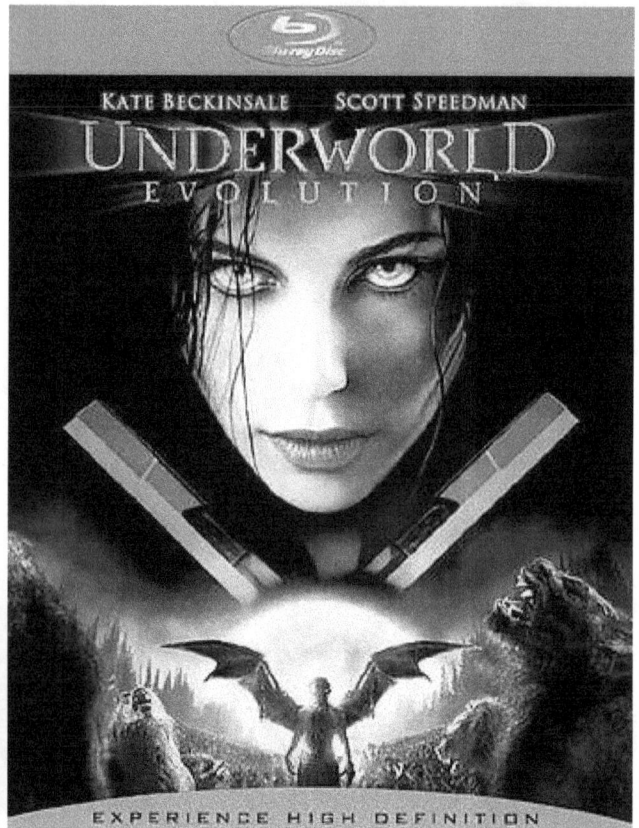

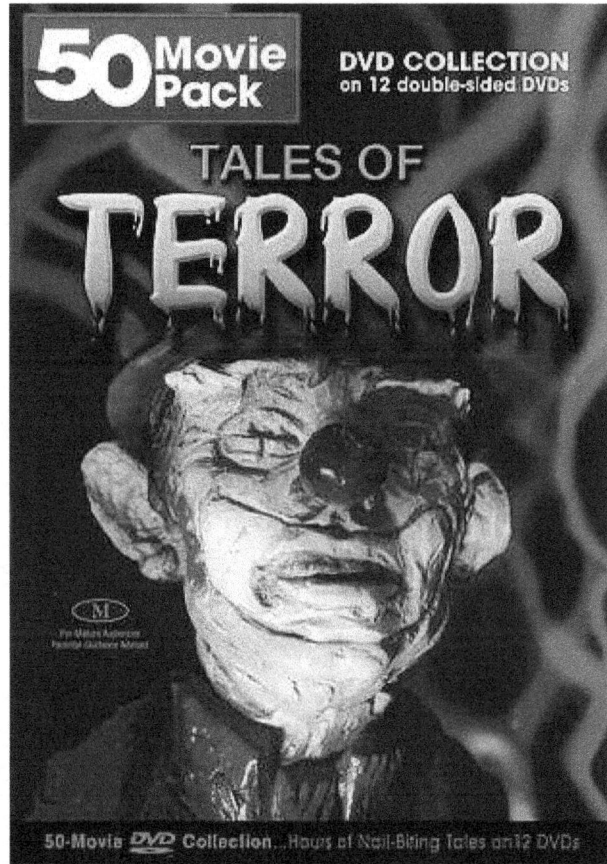

Werewolf of Ansbach Execution

Werewolfs (300 Women) in Julich (Germany)
woodcut, Augsburg 1591

18th Century Engraving

Fredrick Madden
Cambridge, 1832

Beast of LeGevaudan

Beast of LeGervaudan

Hartmann Schedel
Liber Cronicarum
Numberg Germany, 1493

Marco Polo: Lykanthrope, Island auf Andaman;
Painting in manuscript, France, 15th Century

Werewolf in Battle
woodcut, colortet, 15th Century

Hans Weiditz
Straburg, 1516

Maurice Sand
Les Lupins
from Légendes Rustiques

Werewolf (magician) and Cat (witch)
woodcut Mailand, Italy
from E-M. Guazzo: Compendium...1628

"He soon emerged in the form of a wolf"
THE WERE-WOLVES.

Scene from a Russian Tale

Ch. Le Brun
France, 17th Century

Beast of LeGevaudan

THE BOOK OF WERE-WOLVES
by
SABINE BARING-GOULD

The Reverend Sabine Baring-Gould (28 January 1834 – 2 January 1924) was an English hagiographer, antiquarian, novelist and eclectic scholar. His bibliography lists more than 1240 separate publications, though this list continues to grow. His family home, Lewtrenchard Manor near Okehampton, Devon, has been preserved as he rebuilt it and is now a hotel. He is remembered particularly as a writer of hymns, the best-known being *"Onward, Christian Soldiers"* and *"Now the Day Is Over"*. He also translated the carol *"Gabriel's Message"* from Basque to English. He habitually wrote standing up, and his desk can be seen in the manor.

Because the family spent much of his childhood travelling round Europe his education was mostly conducted by private tutors. He spent a period of about two years in formal schooling, first at King's College School London (then located in Somerset House) and then, for a few months, at Warwick Grammar School. Here his time was cut short when a bronchial attack of the kind that was to plague him throughout his long life gave his father the excuse for another trip to the South of France for the sake of the boy's health. In 1853 he went up to Cambridge, earning the degrees of B.A. in 1857, then M.A. in 1860 from Clare College.

CONTENTS

TIMOTHY GREEN BECKLEY'S BIG BOOK OF WEREWOLVES

THE BOOK OF WERE-WOLVES
CHAPTER I
INTRODUCTORY

I shall never forget the walk I took one night in Vienne, after having accomplished the examination of an unknown Druidical relic, the Pierre labie, at La Rondelle, near Champigni. I had learned of the existence of this cromlech only on my arrival at Champigni in the afternoon, and I had started to visit the curiosity without calculating the time it would take me to reach it and to return. Suffice it to say that I discovered the venerable pile of grey stones as the sun set, and that I expended the last lights of evening in planning and sketching. I then turned my face homeward. My walk of about ten miles had wearied me, coming at the end of a long day's posting, and I had lamed myself in scrambling over some stones to the Gaulish relic.

A small hamlet was at no great distance, and I betook myself thither, in the hopes of hiring a trap to convey me to the posthouse, but I was disappointed. Few in the place could speak French, and the priest, when I applied to him, assured me that he believed there was no better conveyance in the place than a common charrue with its solid wooden wheels; nor was a riding horse to be procured. The good man offered to house me for the night; but I was obliged to decline, as my family intended starting early on the following morning.

Out spake then the mayor—"Monsieur can never go back to-night across the flats, because of the—the—" and his voice dropped; "the *loups-garoux*."

"He says that he must return!" replied the priest in patois. "But who will go with him?"

"Ah, ha,! M. le Curé. It is all very well for one of us to accompany him, but think of the coming back alone!"

"Then two must go with him," said the priest, and you can take care of each other as you return."

"Picou tells me that he saw the were-wolf only this day se'nnight," said a peasant; "he was down by the hedge of his buckwheat field, and the sun had set, and he was thinking of coming home, when he heard a rustle on the far side of the hedge. He looked over, and there stood the wolf as big as a calf against the horizon, its tongue out, and its eyes glaring like marsh-fires. Mon Dieu! catch me going over the marais to-night. Why, what could two men do if they were attacked by that wolf-fiend?"

"It is tempting Providence," said one of the elders of the village;" no man must expect the help of God if he throws himself wilfully in the way of danger. Is it not so, M. le Curé? I heard you say as much from the pulpit on the first Sunday in Lent, preaching from the Gospel."

"That is true," observed several, shaking their heads.

"His tongue hanging out, and his eyes glaring like marsh-fires!" said the confidant of Picou.

"Mon Dieu! if I met the monster, I should run," quoth another.

"I quite believe you, Cortrez; I can answer for it that you would," said the mayor.

"As big as a calf," threw in Picou's friend.

"If the loup-garou were *only* a natural wolf, why then, you see"—the mayor cleared his throat—"you see we should think nothing of it; but, M. le Curé, it is a fiend, a worse than fiend, a man-fiend,—a worse than man-fiend, a man-wolf-fiend."

"But what is the young monsieur to do?" asked the priest, looking from one to another.

"Never mind," said I, who had been quietly listening to their patois, which I understood. "Never mind; I will walk back by myself, and if I meet the loup-garou I will crop his ears and tail, and send them to M. le Maire with my compliments."

A sigh of relief from the assembly, as they found themselves clear of the difficulty.

"Il est Anglais," said the mayor, shaking his head, as though he meant that an Englishman might face the devil with impunity.

A melancholy flat was the marais, looking desolate enough by day, but now, in the gloaming, tenfold as desolate. The sky was perfectly clear, and of a soft, blue-grey tinge; illumined by the new moon, a curve of light approaching its western bed. To the horizon reached a fen, blacked with pools of stagnant water, from which the frogs kept up an incessant trill through the summer night. Heath and fern covered the ground, but near the water grew dense masses of flag and bulrush, amongst which the light wind sighed wearily. Here and there stood a sandy knoll, capped with firs, looking like black splashes against the grey sky; not a sign of habitation anywhere; the only trace of men being the white, straight road extending for miles across the fen.

That this district harboured wolves is not improbable, and I confess that I armed myself with a strong stick at the first clump of trees through which the road dived.

This was my first introduction to were-wolves, and the circumstance of finding the superstition still so prevalent, first gave me the idea of investigating the history and the habits of these mythical creatures.

I must acknowledge that I have been quite unsuccessful in obtaining a specimen of the animal, but I have found its traces in all directions. And just as the paléontologist has constructed the labyrinthodon out of its foot-prints in marl, and one splinter of bone, so may this monograph be complete and accurate, although I have no chained were-wolf before me which I may sketch and describe from the life.

The traces left are indeed numerous enough, and though perhaps like the dodo or the dinormis, the werewolf may have become extinct in our age, yet he has left his stamp on classic antiquity, he has trodden deep in Northern snows. has ridden rough-shod over the mediévals, and has howled amongst Oriental sepulchres. He belonged to a bad breed, and we are quite content to be freed from him and his kindred, the vampire and the ghoul. Yet who knows! We may be a little too hasty in concluding that he is extinct. He may still prowl in Abyssinian forests, range still over Asiatic steppes, and be found howling dismally in some padded room of a Hanwell or a Bedlam.

In the following pages I design to investigate the notices of were-wolves to be found in the ancient writers of classic antiquity, those contained in the Northern Sagas, and, lastly, the numerous details afforded by the mediéval authors. In connection with this I shall give a sketch of modern folklore relating to Lycanthropy.

It will then be seen that under the veil of mythology lies a solid reality, that a floating superstition holds in solution a positive truth.

This I shall show to be an innate craving for blood implanted in certain natures, restrained under ordinary circumstances, but breaking forth occasionally, accompanied with hallucination, leading in most cases to cannibalism. I shall then give instances of persons thus afflicted, who were believed by others, and who believed themselves, to be transformed into beasts, and who, in the paroxysms of their madness, committed numerous murders, and devoured their victims.

I shall next give instances of persons suffering from the same passion for blood, who murdered for the mere gratification of their natural cruelty, but who were not subject to hallucinations, nor were addicted to cannibalism.

I shall also give instances of persons filled with the same propensities who murdered and ate their victims, but who were perfectly free from hallucination.

CHAPTER II
LYCANTHROPY AMONG THE ANCIENTS

What is Lycanthropy? The change of manor woman into the form of a wolf, either through magical means, so as to enable him or her to gratify the taste for human flesh, or through judgment of the gods in punishment for some great offence.

This is the popular definition. Truly it consists in a form of madness, such as may be found in most asylums.

Among the ancients this kind of insanity went by the names of Lycanthropy, Kuanthropy, or Boanthropy, because those afflicted with it believed themselves to be turned into wolves, dogs, or cows. But in the North of Europe, as we shall see, the shape of a bear, and in Africa that of a hyéna, were often selected in preference. A mere matter of taste! According to Marcellus Sidetes, of whose poem {Greek *perï lukanærw'pou*} a fragment exists, men are attacked with this madness chiefly in the beginning of the year, and become most furious in February; retiring for the night to lone cemeteries, and living precisely in the manner of dogs and wolves.

Virgil writes in his eighth Eclogue:—

Has herbas, atque héc Ponto mihi lecta venena Ipse dedit Mris; nascuntur plurima Ponto. His ego sépe lupum fieri et se conducere sylvis Mrim, sépe animas imis excire sepulchris, Atque satas alio, vidi traducere messes.

And Herodotus:—"It seems that the Neuri are sorcerers, if one is to believe the Scythians and the Greeks established in Scythia; for each Neurian changes himself, once in the year, into the form of a wolf, and he continues in that form for several days, after which he resumes his former shape."—(Lib. iv. c. 105.)

See also Pomponius Mela (lib. ii. c. 1) "There is a fixed time for each Neurian, at which they change, if they like, into wolves, and back again into their former condition."

But the most remarkable story among the ancients is that related by Ovid in his "Metamorphoses," of Lycaon, king of Arcadia, who, entertaining Jupiter one day, set before him a hash of human flesh, to prove his omniscience, whereupon the god transferred him into a wolf:— [1]

[1. OVID. Met. i. 237; PAUSANIAS, viii. 2, ß 1; TZETZE *ad Lycoph.* 481; ERATOSTH. *Catas.* i. 8.]

In vain he attempted to speak; from that very instant His jaws were bespluttered with foam, and only he thirsted For blood, as he raged amongst flocks and panted for slaughter. His vesture was changed into hair, his limbs became crooked; A wolf,—he retains yet large trace of his ancient expression, Hoary he is as afore, his countenance rabid, His eyes glitter savagely still, the picture of fury.

Pliny relates from Evanthes, that on the festival of Jupiter Lycéus, one of the family of Antéus was selected by lot, and conducted to the brink of the Arcadian lake. He then hung his clothes on a tree and plunged into the water, whereupon he was transformed into a wolf. Nine years after, if he had not tasted human flesh, he was at liberty to swim back and resume his former shape, which had in the meantime become aged, as though he had worn it for nine years.

Agriopas relates, that Deménetus, having assisted at an Arcadian human sacrifice to Jupiter Lycéus, ate of the flesh, and was at once transformed into a wolf, in which shape he prowled about for ten years, after which he recovered his human form, and took part in the Olympic games.

The following story is from Petronius:—

"My master had gone to Capua to sell some old clothes. I seized the opportunity, and persuaded our guest to bear me company about five miles out of town; for he was a soldier, and as bold as death. We set out about cockcrow, and the moon shone bright as day, when, coming among some monuments. my man began to converse with the stars, whilst I jogged along singing and counting them. Presently I looked back after him, and saw him strip and lay his clothes by the side of the road. My heart was in my mouth in an instant, I stood like a corpse; when, in a crack, he was turned into a wolf. Don't think I'm joking: I would not tell you a lie for the finest fortune in the world.

"But to continue: after he was turned into a wolf, he set up a howl and made straight for the woods. At first I did not know whether I was on my head or my heels; but at last going to take up his clothes, I found them turned into stone. The sweat streamed from me, and I never expected to get over it. Melissa began to wonder why I walked so late. 'Had you come a little sooner,' she said, 'you might at least have lent us a hand; for a wolf broke into the farm and has butchered all our cattle; but though be got off, it was no laughing matter for him, for a servant of ours ran him through with a pike. Hearing this I could not close an eye; but as soon as it was daylight, I ran home like a pedlar that has been eased of his pack. Coming to the place where the clothes had been turned into stone, I saw nothing but a pool of blood; and when I got home, I found my soldier lying in bed, like an ox in a stall, and a surgeon dressing his neck. I saw at once that he was a fellow who could change his skin (*versipellis*), and never after could I eat bread with him, no, not if you would have killed me. Those who would have taken a different view of the case are welcome to their opinion; if I tell you a lie, may your genii confound me!"

As every one knows, Jupiter changed himself into a bull; Hecuba became a bitch; Actéon a stag; the comrades of Ulysses were transformed into swine; and the daughters of Prtus fled through the fields believing themselves to be cows, and would not allow any one to come near them, lest they should be caught and yoked.

St. Augustine declared, in his *De Civitate Dei*, that he knew an old woman who was said to turn men into asses by her enchantments.

Apuleius has left us his charming romance of the *Golden Ass*, in which the hero, through injudicious use of a magical salve, is transformed into that long-eared animal.

It is to be observed that the chief seat of Lycanthropy was Arcadia, and it has been very plausibly suggested that the cause might he traced to the following circumstance:—The natives were a pastoral people, and would consequently suffer very severely from the attacks and depredations of wolves. They would naturally institute a sacrifice to obtain deliverance from this pest, and security for their flocks. This sacrifice consisted in the offering of a child, and it was instituted by Lycaon. From the circumstance of the sacrifice being human, and from the peculiarity of the name of its originator, rose the myth.

But, on the other hand, the story is far too widely spread for us to attribute it to an accidental origin, or to trace it to a local source.

Half the world believes, or believed in, were-wolves, and they were supposed to haunt the Norwegian forests by those who had never remotely been connected with Arcadia: and the superstition had probably struck deep its roots into the Scandinavian and Teutonic minds, ages before Lycaon existed; and we have only to glance at Oriental literature, to see it as firmly engrafted in the imagination of the Easterns.

CHAPTER III
THE WERE-WOLF IN THE NORTH

In Norway and Iceland certain men were said to be *eigi einhamir*, not of one skin, an idea which had its roots in paganism. The full form of this strange superstition was, that men could take upon them other bodies, and the natures of those beings whose bodies they assumed. The second adopted shape was called by the same name as the original shape, *hamr*, and the expression made use of to designate the transition from one body to another, was at *skipta hømum*, or *at hamaz*; whilst the expedition made in the second form, was the hamfør. By this transfiguration extraordinary powers were acquired; the natural strength of the individual was doubled, or quadrupled; he acquired the strength of the beast in whose body he travelled, in addition to his own, and a man thus invigorated was called *hamrammr*.

The manner in which the change was effected, varied. At times, a dress of skin was cast over the body, and at once the transformation was complete; at others, the human body was deserted, and the soul entered the second form, leaving the first body in a cataleptic state, to all appearance dead. The second hamr was either borrowed or created for the purpose. There was yet a third manner of producing this effect-it was by incantation; but then the form of the individual remained unaltered, though the eyes of all beholders were charmed so that they could only perceive him under the selected form.

Having assumed some bestial shape, the man who is *eigi einhammr* is only to be recognized by his eyes, which by no power can be changed. He then pursues his course, follows the instincts of the beast whose body he has taken, yet without quenching his own intelligence. He is able to do what the body of the animal can do, and do what he, as man, can do as well. He may fly or swim, if be is in the shape of bird or fish; if he has taken the form of a wolf, or if he goes on a *gandreiæ*, or wolf's-ride, he is fall of the rage and malignity of the creatures whose powers and passions he has assumed.

I will give a few instances of each of the three methods of changing bodies mentioned above. Freyja and Frigg had their falcon dresses in which they visited different regions of the earth, and Loki is said to have borrowed these, and to have then appeared so precisely like a falcon, that he would have escaped detection, but for the malicious twinkle of his eyes. In the Vélundar kviæa is the following passage:—

I.

Meyjar flugu sunnan
From the south flew the maidens
Myrkviæ igøgnum
Athwart the gloom,
Alvitr unga
Alvit the young,
Orløg dr"gja;
To fix destinies;
ér · savarstrønd
They on the sea-strand
Settusk at hvilask,
Sat them to rest,
Drü sir suærnar
These damsels of the south
D"rt lÌn spunnu.
Fair linen spun.

II.

Ein nam eirra
One of them took
Egil at verja
Egil to press,
Føgr mér fÌra
Fair maid, in her
Faæmi ljüsum;
Dazzling arms.
÷nnur var SvanhvÌt,
Another was Svanhwit,
Svanfjaærar drü;
Who wore swan feathers;
En in riæja
And the third,
eirra systir

Their sister,
Var i hvìtan
Pressed the white
H·ls Vølundar.
Neck of Vlund.

The introduction of Smund tells us that these charming young ladies were caught when they had laid their swan-skins beside them on the shore, and were consequently not in a condition to fly.

In like manner were wolves' dresses used. The following curious passage is from the wild Saga of the Vølsungs:—

"It is now to be told that Sigmund thought Sinfjøtli too young to help him in his revenge, and he wished first to test his powers; so during the summer they plunged deep into the wood and slew men for their goods, and Sigmund saw that he was quite of the Vølsung stock. . . . Now it fell out that as they went through the forest, collecting monies, that they lighted on a house in which were two men sleeping, with great gold rings an them; they had dealings with witchcraft, for wolf-skins hung up in the house above them; it was the tenth day on which they might come out of their second state. They were kings' sons. Sigmund and Sinfjøtli got into the habits, and could not get out of them again, and the nature of the original beasts came over them, and they howled as wolves—they learned "both of them to howl. Now they went into the forest, and each took his own course; they made the agreement together that they should try their strength against as many as seven men, but not more, and. that he who was ware of strife should utter his wolf's howl.

"'Do not fail in this,' said Sigmund, 'for you are young and daring, and men would be glad to chase you.' Now each went his own course; and after that they had parted Sigmund found men, so he howled; and when Sinfjøtli heard that, he ran up and slew them all-then they separated. And Sinfjøtli had not been long in the wood before he met with. eleven men; he fell upon them and slew them every one. Then he was tired, so he flung himself under an oak to rest. Up came Sigmund and said, 'Why did you not call out?' Sinfjøtli replied, 'What was the need of asking your help to kill eleven men?'

"Sigmund flew at him and rent him so that he fell, for he had bitten through his throat. That day they could not leave their wolf-forms. Sigmund laid him on his back and bare him home to the hall, and sat beside him, and said, 'Deuce take the wolf-forms!'"—Vølsung Saga, c. 8.

There is another curious story of a were-wolf in the same Saga, which I must relate.

"Now he did as she requested, and hewed down a great piece of timber, and cast it across the feet of those ten brothers seated in a row, in the forest; and there they sat all that day and on till night. And at midnight there came an old she-wolf out of the forest to them, as they sat in the stocks, and she was both huge and grimly. Now she fell upon one of them, and bit him to death, and after she had eaten him all up, she went away. And next morning Signy sent a trusty man to her brothers, to know how it had fared with them. When he returned he told her of the death of one, and that grieved her much, for she feared it might fare thus with them all, and she would be unable to assist them.

"In short, nine nights following came the same she-wolf at midnight, and devoured them one after another till all were dead, except Sigmund, and he was left alone. So when the tenth night came, Signy sent her trusty man to Sigmund, her brother, with honey in his hand, and said that he was to smear it over the face of Sigmund, and to fill his mouth with it. Now he went to Sigmund, and did as he was bid, after which he returned home. And during the night came the same she-wolf, as was her wont, and reckoned to devour him, like his brothers.

"Now she snuffed at him, where the honey was smeared, and began to lick his face with her tongue, and presently thrust her tongue into his mouth. He bore it ill, and bit into the tongue of the she-wolf; she sprang up and tried to break loose, setting her feet against the stock, so as to snap it asunder: but he held firm, and ripped the tongue out by the roots, so that it was the death of the wolf. It is the opinion of some men that this beast was the mother of King Siggeir, and that she had taken this form upon her through devilry and witchcraft."—(c. 5.)

There is another story bearing on the subject in the Hrolfs Saga Kraka, which is pretty; it is as follows:—

"In the north of Norway, in upland-dales, reigned a king called Hring; and he had a son named Bjørn. Now it fell out that the queen died, much lamented by the king, and by all. The people advised him to marry again, and so be sent men south to get him a wife. A gale and fierce storm fell upon them, so that they had to turn the helm, and run before the wind, and so they came north to Finnmark, where they spent the winter. One day they went inland, and came to a house in which sat two beautiful women, who greeted them well, and inquired whence they had come. They replied by giving an account of their journey and their errand, and then asked the women who they were, and why they were alone, and far from the haunts of men, although they were so comely and engaging. The elder replied—that her name was Ingibjorg, and that her daughter was called Hvit, and that she was the Finn king's sweetheart. The messengers decided that they would return home, if Hvit would come with them and marry King Hring. She agreed, and they took her with them and met the king who was pleased with her, and had his wedding feast made, and said that he cared not though she was not rich. But the king was very old, and that the queen soon found out.

"There was a Carle who had a farm not far from the king's dwelling; he had a wife, and a daughter, who was but a child, and her name was Bera; she was very young and lovely. Bjørn the king's son, and Bera the Carle's daughter, were wont, as children, to play together, and they loved each other well. The Carle was well to do, he had been out harrying in his young days, and he was a doughty champion. Bjørn and Bera loved each other more and more, and they were often together.

Time passed, and nothing worth relating occurred; but Bjørn, the king's son, waxed strong and tall; and he was well skilled in all manly exercises.

"King Hring was often absent for long, harrying foreign shores, and Hvit remained at home and governed the land. She was not liked of the people. She was always very pleasant with Bjørn, but he cared little for her. It fell out once that the King Hring went abroad, and he spake with his queen that Bjørn should remain at home with her, to assist in the government, for he thought it advisable, the queen being haughty and inflated with pride.

"The king told his son Bjørn that he was to remain at home, and rule the land with the queen; Bjørn replied that he disliked the plan, and that he had no love for the queen; but the king was inflexible, and left the land with a great following. Bjørn walked home after his conversation with the king, and went up to his place, ill-pleased and red as blood. The queen came to speak with him, and to cheer him; and spake friendly with him, but he bade her be of. She obeyed him that time. She often came to talk with him, and said how much pleasanter it was for them to be together, than to have an old fellow like Hring in the house.

"Bjørn resented this speech, and struck her a box in the ear, and bade her depart, and he spurned her from him. She replied that this was ill-done to drive and thrust her away: and 'You think it better, Bjørn, to sweetheart a Carle's daughter, than to have my love and favour, a fine piece of condescension and a disgrace it is to you! But, before long, something will stand in the way of your fancy, and your folly.' Then she struck at him with a wolf-skin glove, and said, that he should become a rabid and grim wild bear; and 'You shall eat nothing but your father's sheep, which you shall slay for your food, and never shall you leave this state.'

After that, Bjørn disappeared, and none knew what had become of him; and men sought but found him not, as was to be expected. We must now relate how that the king's sheep were slaughtered, half a score at a time, and it was all the work of a grey bear, both huge and grimly.

"One evening it chanced that the Carle's daughter saw this savage bear coming towards her, looking tenderly at her, and she fancied that she recognized the eyes of Bjørn, the king's son, so she made a slight attempt to escape; then the beast retreated, but she followed it, till she came to a cave. Now when she entered the cave there stood before her a man, who greeted Bera, the Carle's daughter; and she recognized him, for he was Bjørn, Hring's son. Overjoyed were they to meet. So they were together in the cave awhile, for she would not part from him when she had the chance of being with him; but he said that this was not proper that she should be there by him, for by day he was a beast, and by night a man.

"Hring returned from his harrying, and he was told the news, of what had taken place during his absence; how that Bjørn, his son, had vanished, and also, how that a monstrous beast was up the country, and was destroying his flocks. The queen urged the king to have the beast slain, but he delayed awhile.

"One night, as Bera and Bjørn were together, he said to her:—'Methinks tomorrow will be the day of my death, for they will come out to hunt me down. But for myself I care not, for it is little pleasure to live with this charm upon me, and my only comfort is that we are together; but now our union must be broken. I will give you the ring which is under my left hand. You will see the troop of hunters tomorrow coming to seek me; and when I am dead go to the king, and ask him to give you what is under the beast's left front leg. He will consent.'

"He spoke to her of many other things, till the bear's form stole over him, and he went forth a bear. She followed him, and saw that a great body of hunters had come over the mountain ridges, and had a number of dogs with them. The bear rushed away from the cavern, but the dogs and the king's men came upon him, and there was a desperate struggle. He wearied many men before he was brought to bay, and had slain all the dogs. But now they made a ring about him, and he ranged around it., but could see no means of escape, so he turned to where the king stood, and he seized a man who stood next him, and rent him asunder; then was the bear so exhausted that he cast himself down flat, and, at once, the men rushed in upon him and slew him. The Carle's daughter saw this, and she went up to the king, and said,—'Sire! wilt thou grant me that which is under the bear's left fore-shoulder?' The king consented. By this time his men had nearly flayed the bear; Bera went up and plucked away the ring, and kept it, but none saw what she took, nor had they looked for anything. The king asked her who she was, and she gave a name, but not her true name.

"The king now went home, and Bera was in his company. The queen was very joyous, and treated her well, and asked who she was; but Bera answered as before.

"The queen now made a great feast, and had the bear's flesh cooked for the banquet. The Carle's daughter was in the bower of the queen, and could not escape, for the queen had a suspicion who she was. Then she came to Bera with a dish, quite unexpectedly, and on it was bear's flesh, and she bade Bera eat it. She would not do so. 'Here is a marvel!' said the queen; 'you reject the offer which a queen herself deigns to make to you. Take it at once, or something worse will befall you.' She bit before her, and she ate of that bite; the queen cut another piece, and looked into her mouth; she saw that one little grain of the bite had gone down, but Bera spat out all the rest from her mouth, and said she would take no more, though she were tortured or killed.

"'Maybe you have had sufficient,' said the queen, and she laughed."—(Hrolfs Saga Kraka, c. 24-27, condensed.)

In the Faroîse song of Finnur hin friæi, we have the following verse:

—Hegar Ìæ Finnur hetta sér.
When this peril Finn saw,
Mannspell var at meini,
That witchcraft did him harm,
Skapti hann seg Ì varglìki:
 Then he changed himself into a were-wolf:
Hann feldi allvél fleiri.
He slew many thus.

The following is from the second Kviæa of Helga Hundingsbana (stroph. 31):—
May the blade bite, Which thou brandishest Only on thyself, when it Chimes on thy head. Then avenged will be The death of Helgi, When thou, as a wolf, Wanderest in the woods, Knowing nor fortune Nor any pleasure, Haying no meat, Save rivings of corpses.

In all these cases the change is of the form: we shall now come to instances in which the person who is changed has a double shape, and the soul animates one after the other.

The Ynglinga Saga (c. 7) says of Odin, that "he changed form; the bodies lay as though sleeping or dead, but he was a bird or a beast, a fish, or a woman, and went in a twinkling to far distant lands, doing his own or other people's business." In like manner the Danish king Harold sent a warlock to Iceland in the form of a whale, whilst his body lay stiff and stark at home. The already quoted Saga of Hrolf Krake gives us another example, where Bødvar Bjarki, in the shape of a huge bear, fights desperately with the enemy, which has surrounded the hall of his king, whilst his human body lies drunkenly beside the embers within.

In the Vatnsdéla Saga, there is a curious account of three Finns, who were shut up in a hut for three nights, and ordered by Ingimund, a Norwegian chief, to visit Iceland and inform him of the lie of the country, where he was to settle. Their bodies became rigid, and they sent their souls the errand, and, on their awaking at the end of three days, gave an accurate description of the Vatnsdal, in which Ingimund was eventually to establish himself. But the Saga does not relate whether these Finns projected their souls into the bodies of birds or beasts.

The third manner of transformation mentioned, was that in which the individual was not changed himself, but the eyes of others were bewitched, so that they could not detect him, but saw him only under a certain form. Of this there are several examples in the Sagas; as, for instance, in the Hromundar Saga Greypsonar, and in the Fostbréðra Saga. But I will translate the most curious, which is that of Odd, Katla's son, in the Eyrbyggja Saga.—(c. 20.)

"Geirrid, housewife in Mafvahliæ, sent word into Bolstad, that she was ware of the fact that Odd, Katla's son, had hewn off Aud's hand.

"Now when Thorarinn and Arnkell heard that, they rode from home with twelve men. They spent the night in Mafvahliæ, and rode on next morning to Holt: and Odd was the only man in the house.

"Katla sat on the high seat spinning yarn, and she bade Odd sit beside her; also, she bade her women sit each in her place, and hold their tongues. 'For,' said she, 'I shall do all the talking.' Now when Arnkell and his company arrived, they walked straight in, and when they came into the chamber, Katla greeted Arnkell, and asked the news. He replied that there was none, and he inquired after Odd. Katla said that he had gone to Breidavik. 'We shall ransack the house though,' quoth Arnkell. 'Be it so,' replied Katla, and she ordered a girl to carry a light before them, and unlock the different parts of the house. All they saw was Katla spinning yarn off her distaff. Now they search the house, but find no Odd, so they depart. But when they had gone a little way from the garth, Arnkell stood still and said: 'How know we but that Katla has hoodwinked us, and that the distaff in her hand was nothing more than Odd.' 'Not impossible!' said Thorarinn; 'let us turn back.' They did so; and when those at Holt raw that they were returning, Katla said to her maids, 'Sit still in your places, Odd and I shall go out.'

"Now as they approached the door, she went into the porch, and began to comb and clip the hair of her son Odd. Arnkell came to the door and saw where Katla was, and she seemed to be stroking her goat, and disentangling its mane and beard and smoothing its wool. So he and his men went into the house, but found not Odd. Katla's distaff lay against the bench, so they thought that it could not have been Odd, and they went away. However, when they had come near the spot where they had turned before, Arnkell said, 'Think you not that Odd may have been in the goat's form?' 'There is no saying,' replied Thorarinn; 'but if we turn back we will lay hands on Katla.' 'We can try our luck again,' quoth Arnkell; 'and see what comes of it.' So they returned.

"Now when they were seen on their way back, Katla bade Odd follow her; and she lea him to the ash-heap, and told him to lie there and not to stir on any account. But when Arnkell, and his men came to the farm, they rushed into the chamber, and saw Katla seated in her place, spinning. She greeted them and said that their visits followed with rapidity. Arnkell replied that what she said was true. His comrades took the distaff and cut it in twain. 'Come now!' said Katla, 'you cannot say, when you get home, that you have done nothing, for you have chopped up my distaff.' Then Arnkell and the rest hunted high and low for Odd, but could not find him; indeed they saw nothing living about the place, beside a boar-pig which lay under the ash-heap, so they went away once more.

"Well, when they got half-way to Mafvahliæ, came Geirrid to meet them, with her workmen. 'They had not gone the right way to work in seeking Odd,' she said, 'but she would help them.' So they turned back again. Geirrid had a blue cloak on her. Now when the party was seen and reported to Katla, and it was said that they were thirteen in number, and one had on a coloured dress, Katla exclaimed, 'That troll Geirrid is come! I shall not be able to throw a glamour over their eyes any more.' She started up from her place and lifted the cushion of the seat, and there was a hole and a cavity beneath: into this she thrust Odd, clapped the cushion over him, and sat down, saying she felt sick at heart.

"Now when they came into the room, there were small greetings. Geirrid cast of her the cloak and went up to Katla, and took the seal-skin bag which she had in her hand, and drew it over the head of Katla. [1] Then Geirrid bade them break up the seat. They did so, and found Odd. Him they took and carried to Buland's head, where they hanged him. . . . But Katla they stoned to death under the headland."

[1. A precaution against the "evil eye." Compare *Gisla Saga Surssonnar*, p. 34. *Laxdéla Saga*, cc. 37, 38.]

CHAPTER IV
THE ORIGIN OF THE SCANDINAVIAN WERE-WOLF

One of the great advantages of the study of old Norse or Icelandic literature is the insight given by it into the origin of world-wide superstitions. Norse tradition is transparent as glacier ice, and its origin is as unmistakable.

Mediéval mythology, rich and gorgeous, is a compound like Corinthian brass, into which many pure ores have been fused, or it is a full turbid river drawn from numerous feeders, which had their sources in remote climes. It is a blending of priméval Keltic, Teutonic, Scandinavian, Italic, and Arab traditions, each adding a beauty, each yielding a charm, but each accretion rendering the analysis more difficult.

Pacciuchelli says:—"The Anio flows into the Tiber; pure as crystal it meets the tawny stream, and is lost in it, so that there is no more Anio, but the united stream is all Tiber." So is it with each tributary to the tide of mediéval mythology. The moment it has blended its waters with the great and onward rolling flood, it is impossible to detect it with certainty; it has swollen the stream, but has lost its own identity. If we would analyse a particular myth, we must not go at once to the body of mediéval superstition, but strike at one of the tributaries before its absorption. This we shall proceed to do, and in selecting Norse mythology, we come upon abundant material, pointing naturally to the spot whence it has been derived, as glacial moraines indicate the direction which they have taken, and point to the mountains whence they have fallen. It will not be difficult for us to arrive at the origin of the Northern belief in were-wolves, and the data thus obtained will be useful in assisting us to elucidate much that would otherwise prove obscure in mediéval tradition.

Among the old Norse, it was the custom for certain warriors to dress in the skins of the beasts they had slain, and thus to give themselves an air of ferocity, calculated to strike terror into the hearts of their foes.

Such dresses are mentioned in some Sagas, without there being any supernatural qualities attached to them. For instance, in the Nj·la there is mention of a man *i geitheæni*, in goatskin dress. Much in the same way do we hear of Harold Harfagr having in his company a band of berserkir, who were all dressed in wolf-skins, *ulfheænir*, and this expression, wolf-skin coated, is met with as a man's name. Thus in the Holmverja Saga, there is mention of a Bjørn, "son of *Ulfheæin*, wolfskin coat, son of *Ulfhamr*, wolf-shaped, son of *Ulf*, wolf, son of *Ulfhamr*, wolf-shaped, who could change forms."

But the most conclusive passage is in the Vatnsdéla Saga, and is as follows:— "Those berserkir who were called *ulfheænir*, had got wolf-skins over their mail coats" (c. xvi.) In like manner the word *berserkr*, used of a man possessed of superhuman powers, and subject. to accesses of diabolical fury, was originally applied to one of those doughty champions who went about in bear-sarks, or habits made of bear-skin over their armour. I am well aware that Bjørn Halldorson's derivation of berserkr, bare of sark, or destitute of clothing, has been hitherto generally received, but Sveibjørn Egilsson, an indisputable authority, rejects this derivation as untenable, and substitutes for it that which I have adopted.

It may be well imagined that a wolf or a bear-skin would make a warm and comfortable great-coat to a man, whose manner of living required him to defy all weathers, and that the dress would not only give him an appearance of grimness and ferocity, likely to produce an unpleasant emotion in the breast of a foe, but also that the thick fur might prove effectual in deadening the blows rained on him in conflict.

The berserkr was an object of aversion and terror to the peaceful inhabitants of the land, his avocation being to challenge quiet country farmers to single combat. As the law of the land stood in Norway, a man who declined to accept a challenge, forfeited all his possessions, even to the wife of his bosom, as a poltroon unworthy of the protection of the law, and every item of his property passed into the hands of his challenger. The berserkr accordingly had the unhappy man at his mercy. If he slew him, the farmer's possessions became his, and if the poor fellow declined to fight, he lost all legal right to his inheritance. A berserkr would invite himself to any feast, and contribute his quota to the hilarity of the entertainment, by snapping the backbone, or cleaving the skull, of some merrymaker who incurred his displeasure, or whom he might single out to murder, for no other reason than a desire to keep his hand in practice.

It may well be imagined that popular superstition went along with the popular dread of these wolf-and-bear-skinned rovers, and that they were believed to be endued with the force, as they certainly were with the ferocity, of the beasts whose skins they wore.

Nor would superstition stop there, but the imagination of the trembling peasants would speedily invest these unscrupulous disturbers of the public peace with the attributes hitherto appropriated to trolls and jøtuns.

The incident mentioned in the Vølsung Saga, of the sleeping men being found with their wolf-skins hanging to the wall above their heads, is divested of its improbability, if we regard these skins as worn over their armour, and the marvellous in the whole story is reduced to a minimum, when we suppose that Sigmund and Sinfjøtli stole these for the purpose of disguising themselves, whilst they lived a life of violence and robbery.

In a similar manner the story of the northern "Beauty and Beast," in Hrolf's Saga Kraka, is rendered less improbable, on the supposition that Bjørn was living as an outlaw among the mountain fastnesses in a bearskin dress, which would effectually disguise him—*all but his eyes*—which would gleam out of the sockets in his hideous visor, unmistakably human. His very name, Bjørn, signifies a bear; and these two circumstances may well have invested a kernel of historic fact with all the romance of fable; and if divested of these supernatural embellishments, the story would resolve itself into the very simple fact of there having been a King Hring of the Updales, who was at variance with his son, and whose son took to the woods, and lived a berserkr life, in company with his mistress, till he was captured and slain by his father.

I think that the circumstance insisted on by the Saga-writers, of the eyes of the person remaining unchanged, is very significant, and points to the fact that the skin was merely drawn over the body as a disguise.

But there was other ground for superstition to fasten on the berserkir, and invest them with supernatural attributes.

No fact in connection with the history of the Northmen is more firmly established, on reliable evidence, than that of the berserkr rage being a species of diabolical possession. The berserkir were said to work themselves up into a state of frenzy, in which a demoniacal power came over them, impelling them to acts from which in their sober senses they would have recoiled. They acquired superhuman force, and were as invulnerable and as insensible to pain as the Jansenist convulsionists of St. Medard. No sword would wound them, no fire would burn them, a club alone could destroy them, by breaking their bones, or crushing in their skulls. Their eyes glared as though a flame burned in the sockets, they ground their teeth, and frothed at the mouth; they gnawed at their shield rims, and are said to have sometimes bitten them through, and as they rushed into conflict they yelped as dogs or howled as wolves. [1]

[1. Hic (Syraldus) septem filios habebat, tanto veneficiorum usu callentes, ut sépe subitis furoris viribus instincti solerent ore torvum infremere, scuta morsibus attrectare, torridas fauce prunas absumere, extructa quévis incendia penetrare, nec posset conceptis dementié motus alio remedii genere quam aut vinculorum injuriis aut cédis humané piaculo temperari. Tantam illis rabiem site sévitia ingenii sive furiaram ferocitas inspirabat.—*Saxo Gramm*. VII.]

According to the unanimous testimony of the old Norse historians, the berserkr rage was extinguished by baptism, and as Christianity advanced, the number of these berserkir decreased.

But it must not be supposed that this madness or possession came only on those persons who predisposed themselves to be attacked by it; others were afflicted with it, who vainly struggled against its influence, and who deeply lamented their own liability to be seized with these terrible accesses of frenzy. Such was Thorir Ingimund's son, of whom it is said, in the *Vatnsdéla Saga*, that "at times there came over Thorir berserkr fits, and it was considered a sad misfortune to such a man, as they were quite beyond control."

The manner in which he was cured is remarkable; pointing as it does to the craving in the heathen mind for a better and more merciful creed:—

"Thorgrim of Korns· had a child by his concubine Vereydr, and, by order of his wife, the child was carried out to perish.

"The brothers (Thorsteinn and Thorir) often met, and it was now the turn of Thorsteinn to visit Thorir, and Thorir accompanied him homeward. On their way Thorsteinn asked Thorir which he thought was the first among the brethren; Thorir answered that the reply was easy, for 'you are above us all in discretion and talent; Jøkull is the best in all perilous adventures, but I,' he added, 'I am the least worth of us brothers, because the berserkr fits come over me, quite against my will, and I wish that you, my brother, with your shrewdness, would devise some help for me.'

"Thorsteinn said,—'I have heard that our kinsman, Thorgrim, has just suffered his little babe to be carried out, at the instigation of his wife. That is ill done. I think also that it is a grievous matter for you to be different in nature from other men.'

"Thorir asked how he could obtain release from his affliction . . . . Then said Thorsteinn, 'Now will I make a vow to Him who created the sun, for I ween that he is most able to take the ban of you, and I will undertake for His sake, in return, to rescue the babe and to bring it up for him, till He who created man shall take it to Himself-for this I reckon He will do!' After this they left their horses and sought the child, and a thrall of Thorir had found it near the Marram river. They saw that a kerchief had been spread over its face, but it had rumpled it up over its nose; the little thing was all but dead, but they took it up and flitted it home to Thorir's house, and he brought the lad up, and called him Thorkell Rumple; as for the berserkr fits, they came on him no more." (c. 37)

But the most remarkable passages bearing on our subject will be found in the *Aigla*.

There was a man, Ulf (the wolf) by name, son of Bj·lfi and Hallbera. Ulf was a man so tall and strong that the like of him was not to be seen in the land at that time. And when he was young he was out viking expeditions and harrying . . . He was a great landed proprietor. It was his wont to rise early, and to go about the men's work, or to the smithies, and inspect all his goods and his acres; and sometimes he talked with those men who wanted his advice; for he was a good adviser, he was so clear-headed; however, every day, when it drew towards dusk, he became so savage that few dared exchange a word with him, for he was given to dozing in the afternoon.

"People said that he was much given to changing form (*hamrammr*), so he was called the evening-wolf, *kveld'lfr*."—(c. 1.) In this and the following passages, I do not consider *hamrammr* to have its primary signification of actual transformation, but simply to mean subject to fits of diabolical possession, under the influence of which the bodily powers were greatly exaggerated. I shall translate pretty freely from this most interesting Saga, as I consider that the description given in it of Kveldulf in his fits greatly elucidates our subject.

"Kveldulf and Skallagrim got news during summer of an expedition. Skallagrim. was the keenest-sighted of men, and he caught sight of the vessel of Hallvard and his brother, and recognized it at once. He followed their course and marked the haven into which they entered at even. Then he returned to his company, and told Kveldulf of what he had seen . . . . Then they busked them and got ready both their boats; in each they put twenty men, Kveldulf steering one and Skallagrim the other, and they rowed in quest of the ship. Now when they came to the place where it was, they lay to. Hallvard and his men had spread an awning over the deck, and were asleep. Now when Kveldulf and his party came upon them, the watchers who were seated at the end of the bridge sprang up and called to the people on board to wake up, for there was danger in the wind. So Hallvard and his men sprang to arms. Then came Kveldulf over the bridge and Skallagrim with him into the ship. Kveldulf had in his hand a cleaver, and he bade his men go through the vessel and hack away the awning. But he pressed on to the quarter-deck. It is said the were-wolf fit came over him and many of his companions. They slow all the men who were before them. Skallagrim did the same as he went round the vessel. He and his father paused not till they had cleared it. Now when Kveldulf came upon the quarter-deck he raised his cleaver, and smote Hallvard through helm and head, so that the haft was buried in the flesh; but he dragged it to him so violently that he whisked Hallvard into the air., and flung him overboard. Skallagrim cleared the forecastle and slew Sigtrygg. Many men flung themselves overboard, but Skallagrim's men took to the boat and rowed about, killing all they found. Thus perished Hallvard with fifty men. Skallagrim and his party took the ship and all the goods which had belonged to Hallvard . . . and flitted it and the wares to their own vessel, and then exchanged ships, lading their capture, but quitting their own. After which they filled their old ship with stones, brake it up and sank it. A good breeze sprang up, and they stood out to sea.

It is said of these men in the engagement who were were-wolves, or those on whom came the berserkr rage, that as long as the fit was on them no one could oppose them, they were so strong; but when it had passed off they were feebler than usual. It was the same with Kveldulf when the were-wolf fit went off him—he then felt the exhaustion consequent on the fight, and he was so completely 'done up,' that he was obliged to take to his bed."

In like manner Skallagrim had his fits of frenzy, taking after his amiable father.

"Thord and his companion were opposed to Skallagrim in the game, and they were too much for him, he wearied, and the game went better with them. But at dusk, after sunset, it went worse with Egill and Thord, for Skallagrim became so strong that he caught up Thord and cast him down, so that he broke his bones, and that was the death of him. Then he caught at Egill. Thorgerd Brk was the name of a servant of Skallagrim, who had been foster-mother to Egill. She was a woman of great stature, strong as a man and a bit of a witch. Brk exclaimed,—'Skallagrim! are you now falling upon your son?' (hamaz ˙ at syni Ìnum). Then Skallagrim let go his hold of Egill and clutched at her. She started aside and fled. Skallagrim. followed. They ran out upon Digraness, and she sprang off the headland into the water. Skallagrim cast after her a huge stone which struck her between the shoulders, and she never rose after it. The place is now called Brak's Sound."—(c. 40.)

Let it be observed that in these passages from the *Aigla*, the words aæ hamaz, hamrammr, &c. are used without any intention of conveying the idea of a change of bodily shape, though the words taken literally assert it. For they are derived from *hamr*, a skin or habit; a word which has its representatives in other Aryan languages, and is therefore a primitive word expressive of the skin of a beast.

The Sanskrit *carmma*; the Hindustanee *cam*, hide or skin; and *camra*, leather; the Persian *game*, clothing, disguise; the Gothic *ham* or *hams*, skin; and even the Italian *camicia*, and the French *chemise*, are cognate words. [1]

[1. I shall have more to say on this subject in the chapter on the Mythology of Lycanthropy.]

It seems probable accordingly that the verb *aæ hamaz* was first applied to those who wore the skins of savage animals, and went about the country as freebooters; but that popular superstition soon invested them with supernatural powers, and they were supposed to assume the forms of the beasts in whose skins they were disguised. The verb then acquired the significance "to become a were-wolf, to change shape." It did not stop there, but went through another change of meaning, and was finally applied to those who were afflicted with paroxysms of madness or demoniacal possession.

This was not the only word connected with were-wolves which helped on the superstition. The word *vargr*, a wolf, had a double significance, which would be the means of originating many a were-wolf story. *Vargr* is the same as *u-argr*, restless; *argr* being the same as the Anglo-Saxon *earg*. *Vargr* had its double signification in Norse. It signified a wolf, and also a godless man. This *vargr* is the English *were*, in the word were-wolf, and the *garou* or *varou* in French. The Danish word for were-wolf is *var-ulf*, the Gothic *vaira-ulf*. In the *Romans de Garin*, it is *"Leu warou, sanglante beste."* In the *Vie de St. Hildefons* by Gauthier de Coinsi,—

Cil lon desve, cil lou garol, Ce sunt deable, que saul Ne puent estre de nos mordre.

Here the loup-garou is a devil. The Anglo-Saxons regarded him as an evil man: *wearg*, a scoundrel; Gothic *varys*, a fiend. But very often the word meant no more than an outlaw. Pluquet in his *Contes Populaires* tells us that the ancient Norman laws said of the criminals condemned to outlawry for certain offences, *Wargus esto*: be an outlaw!

In like manner the Lex Ripuaria, tit. 87, "Wargus sit, hoe est expulsus." In the laws of Canute, he is called verevulf. (*Leges Canuti*, Schmid, i. 148.) And the Salic Law (tit. 57) orders: "Si quis corpus jam sepultum effoderit, aut expoliaverit, *wargus* sit." "If any one shall have dug up or despoiled an already buried corpse, let him be a varg."

Sidonius Apollinaris. says, "Unam feminam quam forte *vargorum*, hoc enim nomine indigenas latrunculos nuncupant," as though the common name by which those who lived a freebooter life were designated, was varg.

In like manner Palgrave assures us in his *Rise and Progress of the English Commonwealth*, that among the Anglo, Saxons an *utlagh*, or out-law, was said to have the head of a wolf. If then the term *vargr* was applied at one time to a wolf, at another to an outlaw who lived the life of a wild beast, away from the haunts of men "he shall be driven away as a wolf, and chased so far as men chase wolves farthest," was the legal form of sentence—it is certainly no matter of wonder that stories of out-laws should have become surrounded with mythical accounts of their transformation into wolves.

But the very idiom of the Norse was calculated to foster this superstition. The Icelanders had curious expressions which are sufficiently likely to have produced misconceptions.

[1. SIDONIUS APOLLINARIS: Opera, lib. vi. ep. 4.]

Snorri not only relates that Odin changed himself into another form, but he adds that by his spells he turned his enemies into boars. In precisely the same manner does a hag, Ljot, in the Vatnsdéla Saga, say that she could have turned Thorsteinn and Jøkull into boars to run about with the wild beasts (c. xxvi.); and the expression *veræa at gjalti*, or at *gjøltum*, to become a boar, is frequently met with in the Sagas.

"Thereupon came Thorarinn and his men upon them, and Nagli led the way; but when he saw weapons drawn he was frightened, and ran away up the mountain, and became a boar. . . . And Thorarinn and his men took to run, so as to help Nagli, lest he should tumble off the cliffs into the sea" (Eyrbyggja Saga, c. xviii.) A similar expression occurs in the Gisla Saga Surssonar, p. 50. In the Hrolfs Saga

Kraka, we meet with a troll in boar's shape, to whom divine honours are paid; and in the Kjalnessinga Saga, c. xv., men are likened to boars—"Then it began to fare with them as it fares with boars when they fight each other, for in the same manner dropped their foam." The true signification of *veræa at gjalti* is to be in such a state of fear as to lose the senses; but it is sufficiently peculiar to have given rise to superstitious stories.

I have dwelt at some length on the Northern myths relative to were-wolves and animal transformations, because I have considered the investigation of these all-important towards the elucidation of the truth which lies at the bottom of mediéval superstition, and which is nowhere so obtainable as through the Norse literature. As may be seen from the passages quoted above at length, and from an examination of those merely referred to, the result arrived at is pretty conclusive, and may be summed up in very few words.

The whole superstructure of fable and romance relative to transformation into wild beasts, reposes simply on this basis of truth—that among the Scandinavian nations there existed a form of madness or possession, under the influence of which men acted as though they were changed into wild and savage brutes, howling, foaming at the mouth, ravening for blood and slaughter, ready to commit any act of atrocity, and as irresponsible for their actions as the wolves and bears, in whose skins they often equipped themselves.

The manner in which this fact became invested with supernatural adjuncts I have also pointed out, to wit, the change in the significance of the word designating the madness, the double meaning of the word *vargr*, and above all, the habits and appearance of the maniacs. We shall see instances of berserkr rage reappearing in the middle ages, and late down into our own times, not exclusively in the North, but throughout France, Germany, and England, and instead of rejecting the accounts given by chroniclers as fabulous, because there is much connected with them which seems to be fabulous, we shall be able to refer them to their true origin.

It may be accepted as an axiom, that no superstition of general acceptance is destitute of a foundation of truth; and if we discover the myth of the were-wolf to be widely spread, not only throughout Europe, but through the whole world, we may rest assured that there is a solid core of fact, round which popular superstition has crystallized; and that fact is the existence of a species of madness, during the accesses of which the person afflicted believes himself to be a wild beast, and acts like a wild beast.

In some cases this madness amounts apparently to positive possession, and the diabolical acts into which the possessed is impelled are so horrible, that the blood curdles in reading them, and it is impossible to recall them without a shudder.

CHAPTER V
THE WERE-WOLF IN THE MIDDLE-AGES

Olaus Magnus relates that—"In Prussia, Livonia, and Lithuania, although the inhabitants suffer considerably from the rapacity of wolves throughout the year, in that these animals rend their cattle, which are scattered in great numbers through the woods, whenever they stray in the very least, yet this is not regarded by them as such a serious matter as what they endure from men turned into wolves.

"On the feast of the Nativity of Christ, at night, such a multitude of wolves transformed from men gather together in a certain spot, arranged among themselves, and then spread to rage with wondrous ferocity against human beings, and those animals which are not wild, that the natives of these regions suffer more detriment from these, than they do from true and natural wolves; for when a human habitation has been detected by them isolated in the woods, they besiege it with atrocity, striving to break in the doors, and in the event of their doing so, they devour all the human beings, and every animal which is found within. They burst into the beer-cellars, and there they empty the tuns of beer or mead, and pile up the empty casks one above another in the middle of the cellar, thus showing their difference from natural and genuine wolves. . . . Between Lithuania, Livonia, and Courland are the walls of a certain old ruined castle. At this spot congregate thousands, on a fixed occasion, and try their agility in jumping. Those who are unable to bound over the wall, as; is often the case with the fattest, are fallen upon with scourges by the captains and slain." [1] Olaus relates also in c. xlvii. the story of a certain nobleman who was travelling through a large forest with some peasants in his retinue who dabbled in the black art. They found no house where they could lodge for the night, and were well-nigh famished. Then one of the peasants offered, if all the rest would hold their tongues as to what he should do, that he would bring them a lamb from a distant flock.

[1. OLAUS MAGNUS: *Historia de Vent. Septent.* Basil. 15, lib. xviii. cap. 45.]

He thereupon retired into the depths of the forest and changed his form into that of a wolf, fell upon the flock, and brought a lamb to his companions in his mouth. They received it with gratitude. Then he retired once more into the thicket, and transformed himself back again into his human shape.

The wife of a nobleman in Livonia expressed her doubts to one of her slaves whether it were possible for man or woman thus to change shape. The servant at once volunteered to give her evidence of the possibility. He left the room, and in another moment a wolf was observed running over the country. The dogs followed him, and notwithstanding his resistance, tore out one of his eyes. Next day the slave appeared before his mistress blind of an eye.

Bp. Majolus [1] and Caspar Peucer [2] relate the following circumstances of the Livonians:—

[1. MAJOLI *Episc. Vulturoniensis Dier. Canicul.* Helenopolis, 1612, tom. ii. colloq. 3.]

[2. CASPAR PEUCER: *Comment. de Précipuis Divin. Generibus*, 1591, p. 169.]

At Christmas a boy lame of a leg goes round the country summoning the devil's followers, who are countless, to a general conclave. Whoever remains behind, or goes reluctantly, is scourged by another with an iron whip till the blood flows, and his traces are left in blood. The human form vanishes, and the whole multitude become wolves. Many thousands assemble. Foremost goes the leader armed with an iron whip, and the troop follow, "firmly convinced in their imaginations that they are transformed into wolves." They fall upon herds of cattle and flocks of sheep, but they have no power to slay men. When they come to a river, the leader smites the water with his scourge, and it divides, leaving a dry path through the midst, by which the pack may go. The transformation lasts during twelve days, at the expiration of which period the wolf-skin vanishes, and the human form reappears. This superstition was expressly forbidden by the church. "Credidisti, quod quidam credere solent, ut illé qué a vulgo Parcé vocantur, ipsé, vel sint vel possint hoc facere quod creduntur, id est, dum aliquis homo nascitur, et tunc valeant illum designare ad hoc quod velint, ut quandocunque homo ille voluerit, in lupum transformari possit, quod vulgaris stultitia, *werwolf* vocat, aut in aliam aliquam figuram?"—Ap. Burchard. (d. 1024). In like manner did St. Boniface preach against those who believed superstitiously in it strigas et fictos lupos." (*Serm.* apud Mart. et Durand. ix. 217.)

In a dissertation by Müller [1] we learn, on the authority of Cluverius and Dannhaverus (*Acad. Homilet.* p. ii.), that a certain Albertus Pericofcius in Muscovy was wont to tyrannize over and harass his subjects in the most unscrupulous manner. One night when he was absent from home, his whole herd of cattle, acquired by extortion, perished. On his return he was informed of his loss, and the wicked man broke out into the most horrible blasphemies, exclaiming, "Let him who has slain, eat; if God chooses, let him devour me as well."

[1. De {Greek *Lukanærwpìa*}. Lipsié, 1736.]

As he spoke, drops of blood fell to earth, and the nobleman, transformed into a wild dog, rushed upon his dead cattle, tore and mangled the carcasses and began to devour them; possibly he may be devouring them still (*ac forsan hodie que pascitur*). His wife, then near her confinement, died of fear. Of these circumstances there were not only ear but also eye witnesses. (*Non ab auritis tantum, sed et ocidatis accepi, quod narro*). Similarly it is related of a nobleman in the neighbourhood of Prague, that he robbed his subjects of their goods and reduced them to penury through his exactions. He took the last cow from a poor widow with five children, but as a judgment, all his own cattle died. He then broke into fearful oaths, and God transformed him into a dog: his human head, however, remained.

St. Patrick is said to have changed Vereticus, king of Wales, into a wolf, and St. Natalis, the abbot, to have pronounced anathema upon an illustrious family in Ireland; in consequence of which, every male and female take the form of wolves for seven years and live in the forests and career over the bogs, howling mournfully, and appeasing their hunger upon the sheep of the peasants. [1] A duke of Prussia, according to Majolus, had a countryman brought for sentence before him, because he had devoured his neighbour's cattle. The fellow was an ill-favoured, deformed man, with great wounds in his face, which he had received from dogs' bites whilst he had been in his wolf's form. It was believed that he changed shape twice in the year, at Christmas and at Midsummer. He was said to exhibit much uneasiness and discomfort when the wolf-hair began to break out and his bodily shape to change.

[1. PHIL. HARTUNG: *Conciones Tergeminé*, pars ii. p. 367.]

He was kept long in prison and closely watched, lest he should become a werewolf during his confinement and attempt to escape, but nothing remarkable took place. If this is the same individual as that mentioned by Olaus Magnus, as there seems to be a probability, the poor fellow was burned alive.

John of Nüremberg relates the following curious story. [1] A priest was once travelling in a strange country, and lost his way in a forest. Seeing a fire, he made towards it, and beheld a wolf seated over it. The wolf addressed him in human-voice, and bade him not fear, as "he was of the Ossyrian race, of which a man and a woman were doomed to spend a certain number of years in wolf's form. Only after seven years might they return home and resume their former shapes, if they were still alive." He begged the priest to visit and console his sick wife, and to give her the last sacraments. This the priest consented to do, after some hesitation, and only when convinced of the beasts being human beings, by observing that the wolf used his front paws as hands, and when he saw the she-wolf peel off her wolf-skin from her head to her navel, exhibiting the features of an aged woman.

[1. JOHN EUS NIERENBERG *de Miracul. in Europa*, lib. ii. cap. 42.]

Marie de France says in the Lais du Bisclaveret:— [1]

Bisclaveret ad nun en Bretan Garwall Papelent li Norman. * * * * Jadis le poet-hum oir Et souvent suleit avenir, Humes pluseirs Garwall deviendrent E es boscages meisun tindrent

[1. An epitome of this curious were-wolf tale will be found in Ellis's *Early English Metrical Romances*.]

There is an interesting paper by Rhanéus, on the Courland were-wolves, in the Breslauer Sammlung. [2] The author says,—"There are too many examples derived not merely from hearsay, but received on indisputable evidence, for us to dispute the fact, that Satan—if we do not deny that such a being exists, and that he has his work in the children of darkness—holds the Lycanthropists in his net in three ways:—

[2. Supplement III. *Curieuser* und nutzbarer Anmerkungen von Natur und Kunstgeschichten, gesammelt von Kanold. 1728.]

"1. They execute as wolves certain acts, such as seizing a sheep, or destroying cattle, &c., not changed into wolves, which no scientific man in Courland believes, but in their human frames, and with their human limbs, yet in such a state of phantasy and hallucination, that they believe themselves transformed into wolves, and are regarded as such by others suffering under similar hallucination, and in this manner run these people in packs as wolves, though not true wolves.

"2. They imagine, in deep sleep or dream, that they injure the cattle, and this without leaving their conch; but it is their master who does, in their stead, what their fancy points out, or suggests to him.

"3. The evil one drives natural wolves to do some act, and then pictures it so well to the sleeper, immovable in his place, both in dreams and at awaking, that he believes the act to have been committed by himself."

Rhanéus, under these heads, relates three stories, which he believes be has on good authority. The first is of a gentleman starting on a journey, who came upon a wolf engaged in the act of seizing a sheep in his own flock; he fired at it, and wounded it, so that it fled howling to the thicket. When the gentleman returned from his expedition he found the whole neighbourhood impressed with the belief that he had, on a given day and hour, shot at one of his tenants, a publican, Mickel. On inquiry, the man's Wife, called Lebba, related the following circumstances, which were fully corroborated by numerous witnesses:—When her husband had sown his rye he had consulted with his wife how he was to get some meat, so as to have a good feast. The woman urged him on no account to steal from his landlord's flock, because it was guarded by fierce dogs. He, however, rejected her advice, and Mickel fell upon his landlord's sheep, but he had suffered and had come limping home, and in his rage at the ill success of his attempt, had fallen upon his own horse and had bitten its throat completely through. This took place in the year 1684.

In 1684, a man was about to fire upon a pack of wolves, when he heard from among the troop a voice exclaiming—"Gossip! Gossip! don't fire. No good will come of it."

The third story is as follows:—A lycanthropist was brought before a judge and accused of witchcraft, but as nothing could be proved against him, the judge ordered one of his peasants to visit the man in his prison, and to worm the truth out of him, and to persuade the prisoner to assist him in revenging himself upon another peasant who had injured him; and this was to be effected by destroying one of the man's cows; but the peasant was to urge the prisoner to do it secretly, and, if possible, in the disguise of a wolf. The fellow undertook the task, but he had great difficulty in persuading the prisoner to fall in with his wishes: eventually, however, he succeeded. Next morning the cow was found in its stall frightfully mangled, but the prisoner had not left his cell: for the watch, who had been placed to observe him, declared that he had spent the night in profound sleep, and that he had only at one time made a slight motion with his head and hands and feet.

Wierius and Forestus quote Gulielmus Brabantinus as an authority for the fact, that a man of high position had been so possessed by the evil one, that often during the year he fell into a condition in which he believed himself to be turned into a wolf, and at that time he roved in the woods and tried to seize and devour little children, but that at last, by God's mercy, he recovered his senses.

Certainly the famous Pierre Vidal, the Don Quixote of ProvenÁal troubadours, must have had a touch of this madness, when, after having fallen in love with a lady of Carcassone, named Loba, or the Wolfess, the excess of his passion drove him over the country, howling like a wolf, and demeaning himself more like an irrational beast than a rational man.

He commemorates his lupine madness in the poem *A tal Donna*:—[1]
[1. BRUCE WHYTE: *Histoire des Langues Romaines*, tom. ii. p. 248.]

Crowned with immortal joys I mount The proudest emperors above, For I am honoured with the love Of the fair daughter of a count. A lace from Na Raymbauda's hand I value more than all the land Of Richard, with his Poüctou, His rich Touraine and famed Anjou. When *loup-garou* the rabble call me, When vagrant shepherds hoot, Pursue, and buffet me to boot, It doth not for a moment gall me; I seek not palaces or halls, Or refuge when the winter falls; Exposed to winds and frosts at night, My soul is ravished with delight. Me claims my she-wolf (*Loba*) so divine: And justly she that claim prefers, For, by my troth, my life is hers More than another's, more than mine.

Job Fincelius [1] relates the sad story of a farmer of Pavia, who, as a wolf, fell upon many men in the open country and tore them to pieces. After much trouble the maniac was caught, and he then assured his captors that the only difference which existed between himself and a natural wolf, was that in a true wolf the hair grew outward, whilst in him it struck inward. In order to put this assertion to the proof, the magistrates, themselves most certainly cruel and bloodthirsty wolves, cut off his arms and legs; the poor wretch died of the mutilation. This took place in 1541. The idea of the skin being reversed is a very ancient one: *versipellis* occurs as a name of reproach in Petronius, Lucilius, and Plautus, and resembles the Norse *hamrammr*.

[1. FINCELIUS *de Mirabilibus*, lib. xi.]

Fincelius relates also that, in 1542, there was such a multitude of were-wolves about Constantinople that the Emperor, accompanied by his guard, left the city to give them a severe correction, and slew one hundred and fifty of them.

Spranger speaks of three young ladies who attacked a labourer, under the form of cats, and were wounded by him. They were found bleeding in their beds next morning.

Majolus relates that a man afflicted with lycanthropy was brought to Pomponatius. The poor fellow had been found buried in hay, and when people approached, he called to them to flee, as he was a were wolf, and would rend them. The country-folk wanted to flay him, to discover whether the hair grew inwards, but Pomponatius rescued the man and cured him.

Bodin tells some were-wolf stories on good authority; it is a pity that the good authorities of Bodin were such liars, but that, by the way. He says that the Royal Procurator-General Bourdin had assured him that he had shot a wolf, and that the arrow had stuck in the beast's thigh. A few hours after, the arrow was found in the thigh of a man in bed. In Vernon, about the year 1566, the witches and warlocks gathered in great multitudes, under the shape of cats. Four or five men were attacked in a lone place by a number of these beasts. The men stood their ground with the utmost heroism, succeeded in slaying one puss, and in wounding many others. Next day a number of wounded women were found in the town, and they gave the judge an accurate account of all the circumstances connected with their wounding.

Bodin quotes Pierre Marner, the author of a treatise on sorcerers, as having witnessed in Savoy the transformation of men into wolves. Nynauld [1] relates that in a village of Switzerland, near Lucerne, a peasant was attacked by a wolf, whilst he was hewing timber; he defended himself, and smote off a fore-leg of the beast. The moment that the blood began to flow the wolf's form changed, and he recognized a woman without her arm. She was burnt alive.

[1. NYNAULD, *De la Lycanthropie*. Paris, 1615, p. 52.]

An evidence that beasts are transformed witches is to be found in their having no tails. When the devil takes human form, however, he keeps his club-foot of the Satyr, as a token by which he may be recognized. So animals deficient in caudal appendages are to be avoided, as they are witches in disguise. The Thingwald should consider the case of the Manx cats in its next session.

Forestus, in his chapter on maladies of the brain, relates a circumstance which came under his own observation, in the middle of the sixteenth century, at Alcmaar in the Netherlands. A peasant there was attacked every spring with a fit of insanity; under the influence of this he rushed about the churchyard, ran into the church, jumped over the benches, danced, was filled with fury, climbed up, descended, and never remained quiet. He carried a long staff in his hand, with which he drove away the dogs, which flew at him and wounded him, so that his thighs were covered with scars. His face was pale, his eyes deep sunk in their sockets. Forestus pronounces the man to be a lycanthropist, but he does not say that the poor fellow believed himself to be transformed into a wolf. In reference to this case, however, he mentions that of a Spanish nobleman who believed himself to be changed into a bear, and who wandered filled with fury among the woods.

Donatus of Altomare [1] affirms that he saw a man in the streets of Naples, surrounded by a ring of people, who in his were-wolf frenzy had dug up a corpse and was carrying off the leg upon his shoulders. This was in the middle of the sixteenth century.

[1. *De Medend. Human. Corp_*. lib. i. cap. 9.]

CHAPTER VI
A CHAMBER OF HORRORS

Pierre Bourgot and Michel Verdung—'Me Hermit of St. Bonnot—The Gandillon Family—Thievenne Paget—The Tailor of Ch,lons—Roulet.

IN December, 1521, the Inquisitor-General for the diocese of BesanÁon, Boin by name, heard a case of a sufficiently terrible nature to produce a profound sensation of alarm in the neighbourhood. Two men were under accusation of witchcraft and cannibalism. Their names were Pierre Bourgot, or Peter the Great, as the people had nicknamed him from his stature, and Michel Verdung. Peter had not been long under trial, before he volunteered a full confession of his crimes. It amounted to this:—

About nineteen years before, on the occasion of a New Year's market at Poligny, a terrible storm had broken over the country, and among other mischiefs done by it, was the scattering of Pierre's flock. "In vain," said the prisoner, "did I labour, in company with other peasants, to find the sheep and bring them together. I went everywhere in search of them.

"Then there rode up three black horsemen, and the last said to me: 'Whither away? you seem to be in trouble?'

"I related to him my misfortune with my flock. He bade me pluck up my spirits, and promised that his master would henceforth take charge of and protect my flock., if I would only rely upon him. He told me, as well, that I should find my strayed sheep very shortly, and he promised to provide me with money. We agreed to meet again in four or five days. My flock I soon found collected together. At my second meeting I learned of the stranger that he was a servant of the devil. I forswore God and our Lady and all saints and dwellers in Paradise. I renounced Christianity, kissed his left hand, which was black and ice-cold as that of a corpse. Then I fell on my knees and gave in my allegiance to Satan. I remained in the service of the devil for two years, and never entered a church before the end of mass, or at all events till the holy water had been sprinkled, according to the desire of my master, whose name I afterwards learned was Moyset.

"All anxiety about my flock was removed, for the devil had undertaken to protect it and to keep off the wolves.

"This freedom from care, however, made me begin to tire of the devil's service, and I recommenced my attendance at church, till I was brought back into obedience to the evil one by Michel Verdung, when I renewed my compact on the understanding that I should be supplied with money.

"In a wood near Chastel Charnon we met with many others whom I did not recognize; we danced, and each had in his or her hand a green taper with a blue flame. Still under the delusion that I should obtain money, Michel persuaded me to move with the greatest celerity, and in order to do this, after I had stripped myself, he smeared me with a salve, and I believed myself then to be transformed into a wolf. I was at first somewhat horrified at my four wolf's feet, and the fur with which I was covered all at once, but I found that I could now travel with the speed of the wind. This could not have taken place without the help of our powerful master, who was present during our excursion, though I did not perceive him till I had recovered my human form. Michel did the same as myself.

"When we had been one or two hours in this condition of metamorphosis, Michel smeared us again, and quick as thought we resumed our human forms. The salve was given us by our masters; to me it was given by Moyset, to Michel by his own master, Guillemin."

Pierre declared that he felt no exhaustion after his excursions, though the judge inquired particularly whether he felt that prostration after his unusual exertion, of which witches usually complained. Indeed the exhaustion consequent on a werewolf raid was so great that the lycanthropist was often confined to his bed for days, and could hardly move hand or foot, much in the same way as the berserkir and *ham rammir* in the North were utterly prostrated after their fit had left them.

In one of his were-wolf runs, Pierre fell upon a boy of six or seven years old, with his teeth, intending to rend and devour him, but the lad screamed so loud that he was obliged to beat a retreat to his clothes, and smear himself again, in order to recover his form and escape detection. He and Michel, however, one day tore to pieces a woman as she was gathering peas; and a M. de Chusnée, who came to her rescue, was attacked by them and killed.

On another occasion they fell upon a little girl of four years old, and ate her up, with the exception of one arm. Michel thought the flesh most delicious.

Another girl was strangled by them, and her blood lapped up. Of a third they ate merely a portion of the stomach. One evening at dusk, Pierre leaped over a garden wall, and came upon a little maiden of nine years old, engaged upon the weeding of the garden beds. She fell on her knees and entreated Pierre to spare her; but he snapped the neck, and left her a corpse, lying among her flowers. On this occasion he does not seem to have been in his wolf's shape. He fell upon a goat which he found in the field of Pierre Lerugen, and bit it in the throat, but he killed it with a knife.

Michel was transformed in his clothes into a wolf, but Pierre was obliged to strip, and the metamorphosis could not take place with him unless he were stark naked.

He was unable to account for the manner in which the hair vanished when he recovered his natural condition.

The statements of Pierre Bourgot were fully corroborated by Michel Verdung.

Towards the close of the autumn of 1573, the peasants of the neighbourhood of Düle, in Franche Comté, were authorized by the Court of Parliament at DÙle, to hunt down the were-wolves which infested the country. The authorization was as follows:— "According to the advertisement made to the sovereign Court of Parliament at Dole, that, in the territories of Espagny, Salvange, Courchapon, and the neighbouring villages, has often been seen and met, for some time past, a were-wolf, who, it is said, has already seized and carried off several little children, so that they have not been seen since, and since he has attacked and done injury in the country to some horsemen, who kept him of only with great difficulty and danger to their persons: the said Court, desiring to prevent any greater danger, has permitted, and does permit, those who are abiding or dwelling in the said places and others, notwithstanding all edicts concerning the chase, to assemble with pikes, halberts, arquebuses, and sticks, to chase and to pursue the said were-wolf in every place where they may find or seize him; to tie and to kill, without incurring any pains or penalties. . . . Given at the meeting of the said Court, on the thirteenth day of the month September, 1573." It was some time, however, before the loup-garou was caught.

In a retired spot near Amanges, half shrouded in trees, stood a small hovel of the rudest construction; its roof was of turf, and its walls were blotched with lichen. The garden to this cot was run to waste, and the fence round it broken through. As the hovel was far from any road, and was only reached by a path over moorland and through forest, it was seldom visited, and the couple who lived in it were not such as would make many friends. The man, Gilles Garnier, was a sombre, ill-looking fellow, who walked in a stooping attitude, and whose pale face, livid complexion, and deep-set eyes under a pair of coarse and bushy brows, which met across the forehead, were sufficient to repel any one from seeking his acquaintance. Gilles seldom spoke, and when he did it was in the broadest patois of his country. His long grey beard and retiring habits procured for him the name of the Hermit of St. Bonnot, though no one for a moment attributed to him any extraordinary amount of sanctity.

The hermit does not seem to have been suspected for some time, but one day, as some of the peasants of Chastenoy were returning home from their work, through the forest, the screams of a child and the deep baying of a wolf, attracted their notice, and on running in the direction whence the cries sounded, they found a little girl defending herself against a monstrous creature, which was attacking her tooth and nail, and had already wounded her severely in five places. As the peasants came up, the creature fled on all fours into the gloom of the thicket; it was so dark that it could not be identified with certainty, and whilst some affirmed that it was a wolf, others thought they had recognized the features of the hermit. This took place on the 8th November.

On the 14th a little boy of ten years old was missing, who had been last seen at a short distance from the gates of Dole.

The hermit of St. Bonnot was now seized and brought to trial at Dole, when the following evidence was extracted from him and his wife, and substantiated in many particulars by witnesses.

On the last day of Michaelmas, under the form of a wolf, at a mile from Dole, in the farm of Gorge, a vineyard belonging to Chastenoy, near the wood of La Serre, Gilles Gamier had attacked a little maiden of ten or twelve years old, and had slain her with his teeth and claws; he had then drawn her into the wood, stripped her, gnawed the flesh from her legs and arms, and had enjoyed his meal so much, that, inspired with conjugal affection, he had brought some of the flesh home for his wife Apolline.

Eight days after the feast of All Saints, again in the form of a were-wolf, he had seized another girl, near the meadow land of La Pouppe, on the territory of Athume and Chastenoy, and was on the point of slaying and devouring her, when three persons came up, and he was compelled to escape. On the fourteenth day after All Saints, also as a wolf, he had attacked a boy of ten years old, a mile from DÙle, between Gredisans and Menoté, and had strangled him. On that occasion he had eaten all the flesh off his legs and arms, and had also devoured a great part of the belly; one of the legs he had rent completely from the trunk with his fangs.

On the Friday before the last feast of St. Bartholomew, he had seized a boy of twelve or thirteen, under a large pear-trees near the wood of the village Perrouze, and had drawn him into the thicket and killed him, intending to eat him as he had eaten the other children, but the approach of men hindered him from fulfilling his intention. The boy was, however, quite dead, and the men who came up declared that Gilles appeared as a man and not as a wolf. The hermit of St. Bonnot was sentenced to be dragged to the place of public execution, and there to be burned alive, a sentence which was rigorously carried out.

In this instance the poor maniac fully believed that actual transformation into a wolf took place; he was apparently perfectly reasonable on other points, and quite conscious of the acts he had committed.

We come now to a more remarkable circumstance, the affliction of a whole family with the same form of insanity. Our information is derived from Boguet's *Discours de Sorciers*, 1603-1610.

Pernette Gandillon was a poor girl in the Jura, who in 1598 ran about the country on all fours, in the belief that she was a wolf. One day as she was ranging the country in a fit of lycanthropic madness, she came upon two children who were plucking wild strawberries. Filled with a sudden passion for blood, she flew at the little girl and would have brought her down, had not her brother, a lad of four years old, defended her lustily with a knife. Pernette, however, wrenched the weapon from his tiny hand, flung him down and gashed his throat, so that he died of the wound. Pernette was torn to pieces by the people in their rage and horror.

Directly after, Pierre, the brother of Pernette Gandillon, was accused of witchcraft. He was charged with having led children to the sabbath, having made hail, and having run about the country in the form of a wolf. The transformation was effected by means of a salve which he had received from the devil. He had on one occasion assumed the form of a hare, but usually he appeared as a wolf, and his skin became covered with shaggy grey hair. He readily acknowledged that the charges brought against him were well founded, and he allowed that he had, during the period of his transformation, fallen on, and devoured, both beasts and human beings. When he desired to recover his true form, he rolled himself in the dewy grass. His son Georges asserted that he had also been anointed with the salve, and had gone to the sabbath in the shape of a wolf. According to his own testimony, he had fallen upon two goats in one of his expeditions.

One Maundy-Thursday night he had lain for three hours in his bed in a cataleptic state, and at the end of that time had sprung out of bed. During this period he had been in the form of a wolf to the witches' sabbath.

His sister Antoinnette confessed that she had made hail, and that she had sold herself to the devil, who had appeared to her in the shape of a black he-goat. She had been to the sabbath on several occasions.

Pierre and Georges in prison behaved as maniacs, running on all fours about their cells and howling dismally. Their faces, arms, and legs were frightfully scarred with the wounds they had received from dogs when they had been on their raids. Boguet accounts for the transformation not taking place, by the fact of their not having the necessary salves by them.

All three, Pierre, Georges, and Antoinnette, were hung and burned.

Thievenne Paget, who was a witch of the most unmistakable character, was also frequently changed into a she-wolf, according to her own confession, in which state she had often accompanied the devil over hill and dale, slaying cattle, and falling on and devouring children. The same thing may be said of Clauda Isan Prost, a lame woman, Clauda Isan Guillaume, and Isan Roquet, who owned to the murder of five children.

On the 14th of December, in the same year as the execution of the Gandillon family (1598), a tailor of Ch,lons was sentenced to the flames by the Parliament of Paris for lycanthropy. This wretched man had decoyed children into his shop, or attacked them in the gloaming when they strayed in the woods, had torn them with his teeth, and killed them, after which he seems calmly to have dressed their flesh as ordinary meat, and to have eaten it with great relish. The number of little innocents whom he destroyed is unknown. A whole cask full of bones was discovered in his house. The man was perfectly hardened, and the details of his trial were so full of horrors and abominations of all kinds, that the judges ordered the documents to be burned.

Again in 1598, a year memorable in the annals of lycanthropy, a trial took place in Angers, the details of which are very terrible.

In a wild and unfrequented spot near Caude, some countrymen came one day upon the corpse of a boy of fifteen, horribly mutilated and bespattered with blood. As the men approached, two wolves, which had been rending the body, bounded away into the thicket. The men gave chase immediately, following their bloody tracks till they lost them; when suddenly crouching among the bushes, his teeth chattering with fear, they found a man half naked, with long hair and beard, and with his hands dyed in blood. His nails were long as claws, and were clotted with fresh gore, and shreds of human flesh.

This is one of the most puzzling and peculiar cases which come under our notice.

The wretched man, whose name was Roulet, of his own accord stated that he had fallen upon the lad and had killed him by smothering him, and that he had been prevented from devouring the body completely by the arrival of men on the spot.

Roulet proved on investigation to be a beggar from house to house, in the most abject state of poverty. His companions in mendicity were his brother John and his cousin Julien. He had been given lodging out of charity in a neighbouring village, but before his apprehension he had been absent for eight days.

Before the judges, Roulet acknowledged that he was able to transform himself into a wolf by means of a salve which his parents had given him. When questioned about the two wolves which had been seen leaving the corpse, he said that he knew perfectly well who they were, for they were his companions, Jean and Julian, who possessed the same secret as himself. He was shown the clothes he had worn on the day of his seizure, and he recognized them immediately; he described the boy whom he had murdered, gave the date correctly, indicated the precise spot where the deed had been done, and recognized the father of the boy as the man who had first run up when the screams of the lad had been heard. In prison, Roulet behaved like an idiot. When seized, his belly was distended and hard; in prison he drank one evening a whole pailful of water, and from that moment refused to eat or drink.

His parents, on inquiry, proved to be respectable and pious people, and they proved that his brother John and his cousin Julien had been engaged at a distance on the day of Roulet's apprehension.

"What is your name, and what your estate?" asked the judge, Pierre Hérault.

"My name is Jacques Roulet, my age thirty-five; I am poor, and a mendicant."

"What are you accused of having done?"

"Of being a thief—of having offended God. My parents gave me an ointment; I do not know its composition."

"When rubbed with this ointment do you become a wolf?"

"No; but for all that, I killed and ate the child Cornier: I was a wolf."

"Were you dressed as a wolf?"

"I was dressed as I am now. I had my hands and my face bloody, because I had been eating the flesh of the said child."

"Do your hands and feet become paws of a wolf?"

"Yes, they do."

"Does your head become like that of a wolf-your mouth become larger?"

"I do not know how my head was at the time; I used my teeth; my head was as it is to-day. I have wounded and eaten many other little children; I have also been to the sabbath."

The *lieutenant criminel* sentenced Roulet to death. He, however, appealed to the Parliament at Paris; and this decided that as there was more folly in the poor idiot than malice and witchcraft, his sentence of death should be commuted to two years' imprisonment in a madhouse, that he might be instructed in the knowledge of God, whom he had forgotten in his utter poverty. [1]

[1. "La cour du Parliament, par arrÍt, mist l'appellation et la sentence dont il avoit esté appel au néant, et, néanmoins, ordonna que le dit Roulet serait mis ‡ l'hospital Saint Germain des Prés, o˘ on a accoustumé de mettre les folz, pour y demeurer l'espace de deux ans, afin d'y estre instruit et redressé tant de son esprit, que ramené ‡ la cognoissance de Dieu, que l'extrÍme pauvreté lui avoit fait mescognoistre."]

CHAPTER VII
JEAN GRENIER
On the Sand-dunes
A Wolf attacks Marguerite Poirier
Jean Grenier brought to Trial
His Confessions
Charges of Cannibalism proved
His Sentence
Behaviour in the Monastery
Visit of Del'ancre.

One fine afternoon in the spring, some village girls were tending their sheep on the sand-dunes which intervene between the vast forests of pine covering the greater portion of the present department of *Landes* in the south of France, and the sea.

The brightness of the sky, the freshness of the air puffing up off the blue twinkling Bay of Biscay, the hum or song of the wind as it made rich music among the pines which stood like a green uplifted wave on the East, the beauty of the sandhills speckled with golden cistus, or patched with gentian-blue, by the low growing *Gremille couchée*, the charm of the forest-skirts, tinted variously with the foliage of cork-trees, pines, and acacia, the latter in full bloom, a pile of rose-coloured or snowy flowers,—all conspired to fill the peasant maidens with joy, and to make their voices rise in song and laughter, which rung merrily over the hills, and through the dark avenues of evergreen trees.

Now a gorgeous butterfly attracted their attention, then a flight of quails skimming the surface.

"Ah!" exclaimed Jacquiline Auzun," ah, if I had my stilts and bats, I would strike the little birds down, and we should have a fine supper."

"Now, if they would fly ready cooked into one's mouth, as they do in foreign parts!" said another girl.

"Have you got any new clothes for the St. Jean?" asked a third; "my mother has laid by to purchase me a smart cap with gold lace."

"You will turn the head of Etienne altogether, Annette!" said Jeanne Gaboriant. "But what is the matter with the sheep?"

She asked because the sheep which had been quietly browsing before her, on reaching a small depression in the dune, had started away as though frightened at something. At the same time one of the dogs began to growl and show his fangs.

The girls ran to the spot, and saw a little fall in the ground, in which, seated on a log of fir, was a boy of thirteen. The appearance of the lad was peculiar. His hair was of a tawny red and thickly matted, falling over his shoulders and completely covering his narrow brow. His small pale-grey eyes twinkled with an expression of horrible ferocity and cunning, from deep sunken hollows. The complexion was of a dark olive colour; the teeth were strong and white, and the canine teeth protruded over the lower lip when the mouth was closed. The boy's hands were large and powerful, the nails black and pointed like bird's talons. He was ill clothed, and seemed to be in the most abject poverty. The few garments he had on him were in tatters, and through the rents the emaciation of his limbs was plainly visible.

The girls stood round him, half frightened and much surprised, but the boy showed no symptoms of astonishment. His face relaxed into a ghastly leer, which showed the whole range of his glittering white fangs.

"Well, my maidens," said he in a harsh voice, "which of you is the prettiest, I should like to know; can you decide among you?"

"What do you want to know for?" asked Jeanne Gaboriant, the eldest of the girls, aged eighteen, who took upon herself to be spokesman for the rest.

"Because I shall marry the prettiest," was the answer.

"Ah!" said Jeanne jokingly; "that is if she will have you, which is not very likely, as we none of us know you, or anything about you."

"I am the son of a priest," replied the boy curtly.

"Is that why you look so dingy and black?"

"No, I am dark-coloured, because I wear a wolf-skin sometimes."

"A wolf-skin!" echoed the girl; "and pray who gave it you?"

"One called Pierre Labourant."

"There is no man of that name hereabouts. Where does he live?"

A scream of laughter mingled with howls, and breaking into strange gulping bursts of fiendlike merriment from the strange boy.

The little girls recoiled, and the youngest took refuge behind Jeanne.

"Do you want to know Pierre Labourant, lass? Hey, he is a man with an iron chain about his neck, which he is ever engaged in gnawing. Do you want to know where he lives, lass? Ha., in a place of gloom and fire, where there are many companions, some seated on iron chairs, burning, burning; others stretched on glowing beds, burning too. Some cast men upon blazing coals, others roast men before fierce flames, others again plunge them into caldrons of liquid fire."

The girls trembled and looked at each other with scared faces, and then again at the hideous being which crouched before them.

"You want to know about the wolf-skin cape?" continued he. "Pierre Labourant gave me that; he wraps it round me, and every Monday, Friday, and Sunday, and for about an hour at dusk every other day, I am a wolf, a were-wolf. I have killed dogs and drunk their blood; but little girls taste better, their flesh is tender and sweet, their blood rich and warm. I have eaten many a maiden, as I have been on my raids together with my nine companions. I am a were-wolf! Ah, ha! if the sun were to set I would soon fall on one of you and make a meal of you!" Again he burst into one of his frightful paroxysms of laughter, and the girls unable to endure it any longer, fled with precipitation.

Near the village of St. Antoine de Pizon, a little girl of the name of Marguerite Poirier, thirteen years old, was in the habit of tending her sheep, in company with a lad of the same age, whose name was Jean Grenier. The same lad whom Jeanne Gaboriant had questioned.

The little girl often complained to her parents of the conduct of the boy: she said that he frightened her with his horrible stories; but her father and mother thought little of her complaints, till one day she returned home before her usual time so thoroughly alarmed that she had deserted her flock. Her parents now took the matter up and investigated it. Her story was as follows:—

Jean had often told her that he had sold himself to the devil, and that he had acquired the power of ranging the country after dusk, and sometimes in broad day, in the form of a wolf. He had assured her that he had killed and devoured many dogs, but that he found their flesh less palatable than the flesh of little girls, which he regarded as a supreme delicacy. He had told her that this had been tasted by him not unfrequently, but he had specified only two instances: in one he had eaten as much as he could, and had thrown the rest to a wolf, which had come up during the repast. In the other instance he had bitten to death another little girl, had lapped her blood, and, being in a famished condition at the time, had devoured every portion of her, with the exception of the arms and shoulders.

The child told her parents, on the occasion of her return home in a fit of terror, that she had been guiding her sheep as usual, but Grenier had not been present. Hearing a rustle in the bushes she had looked round, and a wild beast had leaped upon her, and torn her clothes on her left side with its sharp fangs. She added that she had defended herself lustily with her shepherd's staff, and had beaten the creature off. It had then retreated a few paces, had seated itself on its hind legs like a dog when it is begging, and had regarded her with such a look of rage, that she had fled in terror. She described the animal as resembling a wolf, but as being shorter and stouter; its hair was red, its tail stumpy, and the head smaller than that of a genuine wolf.

The statement of the child produced general consternation in the parish. It was well known that several little girls had vanished in a most mysterious way of late, and the parents of these little ones were thrown into an agony of terror lest their children had become the prey of the wretched boy accused by Marguerite Poirier. The case was now taken up by the authorities and brought before the parliament of Bordeaux.

The investigation which followed was as complete as could be desired.

Jean Grenier was the son of a poor labourer in the village of St. Antoine do Pizon, and not the son of a priest, as he had asserted. Three months before his seizure he had left home, and had been with several masters doing odd work, or wandering about the country begging. He had been engaged several times to take charge of the flocks belonging to farmers, and had as often been discharged for neglect of his duties. The lad exhibited no reluctance to communicate all he knew about himself, and his statements were tested one by one, and were often proved to be correct.

The story he related of himself before the court was as follows:—

"When I was ten or eleven years old, my neighbour, Duthillaire, introduced me, in the depths of the forest, to a M. de la Forest, a black man, who signed me with his nail, and then gave to me and Duthillaire a salve and a wolf-skin. From that time have I run about the country as a wolf.

"The charge of Marguerite Poirier is correct. My intention was to have killed and devoured her, but she kept me off with a stick. I have only killed one dog, a white one, and I did not drink its blood."

When questioned touching the children, whom he said he had killed and eaten as a wolf, he allowed that he had once entered an empty house on the way between St. Coutras and St. Anlaye, in a small village, the name of which he did not remember, and had found a child asleep in its cradle; and as no one was within to hinder him, he dragged the baby out of its cradle, carried it into the garden, leaped the hedge, and devoured as much of it as satisfied his hunger. What remained he had given to a wolf. In the parish of St. Antoine do Pizon he had attacked a little girl, as she was keeping sheep. She was dressed in a black frock; he did not know her name. He tore her with his nails and teeth, and ate her. Six weeks before his capture he had fallen upon another child, near the stone-bridge, in the same parish. In Eparon he had assaulted the hound of a certain M. Millon, and would have killed the beast, had not the owner come out with his rapier in his hand.

Jean said that he had the wolf-skin in his possession, and that he went out hunting for children, at the command of his master, the Lord of the Forest. Before transformation he smeared himself with the salve, which be preserved in a small pot, and hid his clothes in the thicket.

He usually ran his courses from one to two hours in the day, when the moon was at the wane, but very often he made his expeditions at night. On one occasion he had accompanied Duthillaire, but they had killed no one.

He accused his father of having assisted him, and of possessing a wolf-skin; he charged him also with having accompanied him on one occasion, when he attacked and ate a girl in the village of Grilland, whom he had found tending a flock of geese. He said that his stepmother was separated from his father. He believed the reason to be, because she had seen him once vomit the paws of a dog and the fingers of a child. He added that the Lord of the Forest had strictly forbidden him to bite the thumb-nail of his left hand, which nail was thicker and longer than the others, and had warned him never to lose sight of it, as long as he was in his were-wolf disguise.

Duthillaire was apprehended, and the father of Jean Grenier himself claimed to be heard by examination.

The account given by the father and stepmother of Jean coincided in many particulars with the statements made by their son.

The localities where Grenier declared he had fallen on children were identified, the times when he said the deeds had been done accorded with the dates given by the parents of the missing little ones, when their losses had occurred.

The wounds which Jean affirmed that he had made, and the manner in which he had dealt them, coincided with the descriptions given by the children he had assaulted.

He was confronted with Marguerite Poirier, and he singled her out from among five other girls, pointed to the still open gashes in her body, and stated that he had made them with his teeth, when he attacked her in wolf-form, and she had beaten him off with a stick. He described an attack he had made on a little boy whom he would have slain, had not a man come to the rescue, and exclaimed, "I'll have you presently."

The man who saved the child was found, and proved to be the uncle of the rescued lad, and he corroborated the statement of Grenier, that he had used the words mentioned above.

Jean was then confronted with his father. He now began to falter in his story, and to change his statements. The examination had lasted long, and it was seen that the feeble intellect of the boy was wearied out, so the case was adjourned. When next confronted with the elder Grenier, Jean told his story as at first, without changing it in any important particular.

The fact of Jean Grenier having killed and eaten several children, and of his having attacked and wounded others, with intent to take their life, were fully established; but there was no proof whatever of the father having had the least hand in any of the murders, so that he was dismissed the court without a shadow of guilt upon him.

The only witness who corroborated the assertion of Jean that he changed his shape into that of a wolf was Marguerite Poirier.

Before the court gave judgment, the first president of assize, in an eloquent speech, put on one side all questions of witchcraft and diabolical compact, and bestial transformation, and boldly stated that the court had only to consider the age and the imbecility of the child, who was so dull and idiotic—that children of seven or eight years old have usually a larger amount of reason than he. The president went on to say that Lycanthropy and Kuanthropy were mere hallucinations, and that the change of shape existed only in the disorganized brain of the insane, consequently it was not a crime which could be punished. The tender age of the boy must be taken into consideration, and the utter neglect of his education and moral development. The court sentenced Grenier to perpetual imprisonment within the walls of a monastery at Bordeaux, where he might be instructed in his Christian and moral obligations; but any attempt to escape would be punished with death.

A pleasant companion for the monks! a promising pupil for them to instruct! No sooner was he admitted into the precincts of the religious house, than he ran frantically about the cloister and gardens upon all fours, and finding a heap of bloody and raw offal, fell upon it and devoured it in an incredibly short space of time.

Delancre visited him seven years after, and found him diminutive in stature, very shy, and unwilling to look any one in the face. His eyes were deep set and restless; his teeth long and protruding; his nails black, and in places worn away; his mind was completely barren; he seemed unable to comprehend the smallest things. He related his story to Delancre, and told him how he had run about formerly in the woods as a wolf, and he said that he still felt a craving for raw flesh, especially for that of little girls, which he said was delicious, and he added that but for his confinement it would not be long before he tasted it again. He said that the Lord of the Forest had visited him twice in the prison, but that he had driven him off with the sign of the cross. The account be then gave of his murders coincided exactly with what had come out in his trial; and beside this, his story of the compact he had made with the Black One, and the manner in which his transformation was effected, also coincided with his former statements.

He died at the age of twenty, after an imprisonment of seven years, shortly after Delancre's visit. [1]

[1. DELANCRE: *Tableau de l'linconstance*, p 305.]

In the two cases of Roulet and Grenier the courts referred the whole matter of Lycanthropy, or animal transformation, to its true and legitimate cause, an aberration of the brain. From this time medical men seem to have regarded it as a form of mental malady to be brought under their treatment, rather than as a crime to be punished by law. But it is very fearful to contemplate that there may still exist persons in the world filled with a morbid craving for human blood, which is ready to impel them to commit the most horrible atrocities, should they escape the vigilante of their guards, or break the bars of the madhouse which restrains them.

CHAPTER VIII
FOLK-LORE RELATING TO WERE-WOLVES
Barrenness of English Folk-lore
Devonshire Traditions
Derivation of Were-wolf
Cannibalism in Scotland
The Angus Robber
The Carle of Perth
French Superstitions
Norwegian Traditions
Danish Tales of Were-wolves
Holstein Stories
The Werewolf in the Netherlands
Among the Greeks; the Serbs; the White Russians; the Poles; the Russians
A Russian Receipt for becoming a Were-wolf
The Bohemian Vlkodlak
Armenian Story
Indian Tales
Abyssinian Budas
American Transformation Tales
A Slovakian Household Tale
Similar Greek, Béarnais, and Icelandic Tales.

ENGLISH folk-lore is singularly barren of were-wolf stories, the reason being that wolves had been extirpated from England under the Anglo-Saxon kings, and therefore ceased to be objects of dread to the people. The traditional belief in were-wolfism must, however, have remained long in the popular mind, though at present it has disappeared, for the word occurs in old ballads and romances. Thus in Kempion—

O was it war-wolf in the wood? Or was it mermaid in the sea? Or was it man, or vile woman, My ain true love, that mis-shaped thee?

There is also the romance of *William and the Were-wolf* in Hartshorn; [1] but this professes to be a translation from the French:—

[1. HARTSHORN: *Ancient Metrical Tales*, p. 256. See also "The Witch Cake," in CRUMEK'S *Remains of Nithsdale Song*.]

For he of Frenche this fayre tale ferst dede translate, In ese of Englysch men in Englysch speche.

In the popular mind the cat or the hare have taken the place of the wolf for witches' transformation, and we hear often of the hags attending the devil's Sabbath in these forms.

In Devonshire they range the moors in the shape of black dogs, and I know a story of two such creatures appearing in an inn and nightly drinking the cider, till the publican shot a silver button over their heads, when they were instantly transformed into two ill-favoured old ladies of his acquaintance. On Heathfield, near Tavistock, the wild huntsman rides by full moon with his "wush hounds;" and a white hare which they pursued was once rescued by a goody returning from market, and discovered to be a transformed young lady.

Gervaise of Tilbury says in his *Otia Imperalia*—

"Vidimus frequenter in Anglia, per lunationes, homines in lupos mutari, quod hominum genus *gerulfos* Galli vocant, Angli vero *wer-wlf*, dicunt: *wer* enim Anglice virum sonat, *wlf*, lupum." Gervaise may be right in his derivation of the name, and were-wolf may mean man-wolf, though I have elsewhere given a different derivation, and one which I suspect is truer. But Gervaise has grounds for his assertion that wér signifies man; it is so in Anglo-Saxon, *vair* in Gothic, *vir* in Latin, *verr*, in Icelandic, *vÓra*, Zend, *wirs*, old Prussian, *wirs*, Lettish, *vÓra*, Sanskrit, *bÓr*, Bengalee.

There have been cases of cannibalism in Scotland, but no bestial transformation is hinted at in connection with them.

Thus Bthius, in his history of Scotland, tells us of a robber and his daughter who devoured children, and Lindsay of Pitscottie gives a full account.

"About this time (1460) there was ane brigand ta'en with his haill family, who haunted a place in Angus. This mischievous man had ane execrable fashion to take all young men and children he could steal away quietly, or tak' away without knowledge, and eat them, and the younger they were, esteemed them the mair tender and delicious. For the whilk cause and damnable abuse, he with his wife and bairns were all burnt, except ane young wench of a year old who was saved and brought to Dandee, where she was brought up and fostered; and when she came to a woman's years, she was condemned and burnt quick for that crime. It is said that when she was coming to the place of execution, there gathered ane huge multitude of people, and specially of women, cursing her that she was so unhappy to commit so damnable deeds. To whom she turned about with an ireful countenance, saying:—'Wherefore chide ye with me, as if I had committed ane unworthy act? Give me credence and trow me, if ye had experience of eating men and women's flesh, ye wold think it so delicious that ye wold never forbear it again.' So, but any sign of repentance, this unhappy traitor died in the sight of the people." [1]

[1. LINDSAY'S *Chronicles of Scotland*, 1814, p. 163.]

Wyntoun also has a passage in his metrical chronicle regarding a cannibal who lived shortly before his own time, and he may easily have heard about him from surviving contemporaries. It was about the year 1340, when a large portion of Scotland had been devastated by the arms of Edward III.

About Perth thare was the countrie Sae waste, that wonder wes to see;

For intill well-great space thereby, Wes nother house left nor herb'ry. Of deer thare wes then sic foison (profusion), That they wold near come to the town, Sae great default was near that stead, That mony were in hunger dead. A carle they said was near thereby, That wold act settis (traps) commonly, Children and women for to slay, And swains that he might over-ta; And ate them all that he get might; Chwsten Cleek till name behight. That sa'ry life continued he, While waste but folk was the countrie. [1]

[1. WYNTOUN'S *Chronicle*, ii. 236.]

We have only to compare these two cases with those recorded in the last two chapters, and we see at once how the popular mind in Great Britain had lost the idea of connecting change of form with cannibalism. A man guilty of the crimes committed by the Angus brigand, or the carle of Perth, would have been regarded as a were-wolf in France or Germany, and would have been tried for Lycanthropy.

St. Jerome, by the way, brought a sweeping charge against the Scots. He visited Gaul in his youth, about 880, and he writes:—"When I was a young man in Gaul, I may have seen the Attacotti, a British people who live upon human flesh; and when they find herds of pigs, droves of cattle, or flocks of sheep in the woods, they cut off the haunches of the men and the breasts of the women, and these they regard as great dainties;" in other words they prefer the shepherd to his flock. Gibbon who quotes this passage says on it: "If in the neighbourhood of the commercial and literary town of Glasgow, a race of cannibals has really existed, we may contemplate, in the period of the Scottish history, the opposite extremes of savage and civilized life. Such reflections tend to enlarge the circle of our ideas, and to encourage the pleasing hope that New Zealand may produce in a future age, the Hume of the Southern hemisphere."

If traditions of were-wolves are scanty in England, it is quite the reverse if we cross the water.

In the south of France, it is still believed that fate has destined certain men to be lycanthropists—that they are transformed into wolves at full moon. The desire to run comes upon them at night. They leave their beds, jump out of a window, and plunge into a fountain. After the bath, they come out covered with dense fur, walking on all fours, and commence a raid over fields and meadows, through woods and villages, biting all beasts and human beings that come in their way. At the approach of dawn, they return to the spring, plunge into it, lose their furry skins, and regain their deserted beds. Sometimes the loup-garou is said to appear under the form of a white dog, or to be loaded with chains; but there is probably a confusion of ideas between the were-wolf and the church-dog, bar-ghest, pad-foit, wush-hound, or by whatever name the animal supposed to haunt a church-yard is designated.

In the Périgord, the were-wolf is called louléerou. Certain men, especially bastards, are obliged at each full moon to transform themselves into these diabolic beasts.

It is always at night that the fit comes on. The lycanthropist dashes out of a window, springs into a well, and, after having struggled in the water for a few moments, rises from it, dripping, and invested with a goatskin which the devil has given him. In this condition, the louléerous run upon four legs, pass the night in ranging over the country, and in biting and devouring all the dogs they meet. At break of day they lay aside their goatskins and return home. Often they are ill in consequence of having eaten tough old hounds, and they vomit up their undigested paws. One great nuisance to them is the fact that they may be wounded or killed in their louléerou state. With the first effusion of blood their diabolic covering vanishes, and they are recognized, to the disgrace of their families.

A were-wolf may easily be detected, even when devoid of his skin; for his hands are broad, and his fingers short, and there are always some hairs in the hollow of his hand.

In Normandy, those who are doomed to be loups-garoux, clothe themselves every evening with a skin called their *héüre* or *hure*, which is a loan from the devil. When they run in their transformed state, the evil one accompanies them and scourges them at the foot of every cross they pass. The only way in which a werewolf can be liberated from this cruel bondage, is by stabbing him three times in the forehead with a knife. However, some people less addicted to allopathic treatment, consider that three drops of blood drawn by a needle, will be sufficient to procure release.

According to an opinion of the vulgar in the same province, the loup-garou is sometimes a metamorphosis forced upon the body of a damned person, who, after having been tormented in his grave, has torn his way out of it. The first stage in the process consists in his devouring the cerecloth which enveloped his face; then his moans and muffled howls ring from the tomb, through the gloom of night, the earth of the grave begins to heave, and at last, with a scream, surrounded by a phosphorescent glare, and exhaling a ftid odour, he bursts away as a wolf.

In Le Bessin, they attribute to sorcerers the power of metamorphosing certain men into beasts, but the form of a dog is that principally affected by them.

In Norway it is believed that there are persons who can assume the form of a wolf or a bear (Huse-bjørn), and again resume their own; this property is either imparted to them by the Trollmen, or those possessing it are themselves Trolls.

In a hamlet in the midst of a forest, there dwelt a cottager named Lasse, and his wife. One day he went out in the forest to fell a tree, but had forgot to cross himself and say his paternoster, so that some troll or wolf-witch (varga mor) obtained power over him and transformed him into a wolf. His wife mourned him for many years, but, one Christmas-eve, there came a beggar-woman, very poor and ragged, to the door, and the good woman of the house took her in, fed her well, and entreated her kindly. At her departure the beggar-woman said that the wife would probably see her husband again, as he was not dead, but was wandering in the forest as a wolf. Towards night-fall the wife went to her pantry to place in it a piece of meat for the morrow, when, on turning to go out, she perceived a wolf standing before her, raising itself with its paws on the pantry steps, regarding her with sorrowful and hungry looks. Seeing this she exclaimed, "If I were sure that thou wert my own Lasse, I would give thee a bit of meat." At that instant the wolf-skin fell off, and her husband stood before her in the clothes he wore on the unlucky morning when she had last beheld him.

Finns, Lapps, and Russians are held in particular aversion, because the Swedes believe that they have power to change people into wild beasts. During the last year of the war with Russia, when Calmar was overrun with an unusual number of wolves, it was generally said that the Russians had transformed their Swedish prisoners into wolves, and sent them home to invest the country.

In Denmark the following stories are told:—

A man, who from his childhood had been a were-wolf, when returning one night with his wife from a merrymaking, observed that the hour was at hand when the evil usually came upon him; giving therefore the reins to his wife, he descended from the vehicle, saying to her, "If anything comes to thee, only strike at it with thine apron." He then withdrew, but immediately after, the woman, as she was sitting in the vehicle, was attached by a were-wolf. She did as the man had enjoined her, and struck it with her apron, from which it rived a portion, and then ran away. After some time the man returned, holding in his mouth the rent portion of his wife's apron, on seeing which, she cried out in terror,—"Good Lord, man, why, thou art a were-wolf!" "Thank thee, wife," said he, "now I am free." And from that time he was no more afflicted.

If a female at midnight stretches between four sticks the membrane which envelopes the foal when it is brought forth, and creeps through it, naked, she will bear children without pain; but all the boys will be were-wolves, and all the girls maras. By day the were-wolf has the human form, though he may be known by the meeting of his eyebrows above the nose. At a certain time of the night he has the form of a dog on three legs. It is only when another person tells him that he is a were-wolf, or reproaches him with being such, that a man can be freed from the ban.

According to a Danish popular song, a hero transformed by his step-mother into a bear, fights with a knight:—

For 'tis she who bath bewitched me, A woman false and fell, Bound an iron girdle round me, If thou can'st not break this belt, Knight, I'll thee destroy!

The noble made the Christian sign, The girdle snapped, the bear was changed, And see! he was a lusty knight, His father's realm regained.

Kjémpeviser, p. 147.

When an old bear in Ofodens Priestegjeld was killed, after it had caused the death of six men und sixty horses, it was found to be girded with a similar girdle.

In Schleswig and Holstein they say that if the were-wolf be thrice addressed by his baptismal name, he resumes his human form.

On a hot harvest day some reapers lay down in the field to take their noontide sleep, when one who could not sleep observed that the fellow next to him rose softly, and having girded himself with a strap, became a were-wolf.

A young man belonging to Jœgerup returning late one night from Billund, was attacked, when near Jœgerup, by three were-wolves, and would probably have been torn to pieces, had he not saved himself by leaping into a rye-field, for there they had no more power over him.

At Caseburg, on the isle of Usedom, a man and his wife were busy in the field making hay, when after some time the woman said to the man that she had no more peace, she could stay no longer, and went away. But she had previously desired her husband to promise, that if perchance a wild beast should come that way, he would cast his hat at it and then run away, and it would do him no injury. She had been gone but a short while, when a wolf came swimming across the Swine, and ran directly towards the haymakers. The man threw his hat at it, which the animal instantly tore to rags. But in the meantime a boy had run up with a pitchfork, and he dabbed the wolf from behind: in the same moment it became changed, and all saw that the boy had killed the man's wife.

Formerly there were individuals in the neighbourhood of Steina, who, by putting on a certain girdle, could transform themselves into were-wolves. A man of the neighbourhood, who had such a girdle, forgot one day when going out to lock it up, as was his wont. During his absence, his little son chanced to find it; he buckled it round him., and was instantaneously turned into an animal, to all outward appearance like a bundle of peat-straw, and he rolled about like an unwieldy bear. When those who were in the room perceived this, they hastened in search of the father, who was found in time to come and unbuckle the belt, before the child had done any mischief. The boy afterwards said, that when he had put on the girdle, he was seized with such a raging hunger, that he was ready to tear in pieces and devour all that came in his way.

The girdle is supposed to be made of human skin, and to be three finger-breadths wide.

In East Friesland, it is believed, when seven girls succeed each other in one family, that among them one is of necessity a were-wolf, so that youths are slow in seeking one of seven sisters in marriage.

According to a curious Lithuanian story related by Schleicher in his *Litauische Mœrchen*, a person who is a were-wolf or bear has to remain kneeling in one spot for one hundred years before he can hope to obtain release from his bestial form.

In the Netherlands they relate the following tale:—A man had once gone out with his bow to attend a shooting match at Rousse, but when about half way to the place, he saw on a sudden, a large wolf spring from a thicket, and rush towards a young girl, who was sitting in a meadow by the roadside watching cows. The man did not long hesitate, but quickly drawing forth an arrow, took aim, and luckily hit the wolf in the right side, so that the arrow remained sticking in the wound, and the animal fled howling to the wood.

On the following day he heard that a serving-man of the burgomaster's household lay at the point of death, in consequence of having been shot in the right side, on the preceding day. This so excited the archer's curiosity, that he went to the wounded man, and requested to see the arrow. He recognized it immediately as one of his own. Then, having desired all present to leave the room, he persuaded the man to confess that he was a were-wolf and that he had devoured little children. On the following day he died.

Among the Bulgarians and Sloyakians the were-wolf is called *vrkolak*, a name resembling that given it by the modern Greeks {Greek *br'kolakas*}. The Greek were-wolf is closely related to the vampire. The lycanthropist falls into a cataleptic trance, during which his soul leaves his body, enters that of a wolf and ravens for blood. On the return of the soul, the body is exhausted and aches as though it had been put through violent exercise. After death lycanthropists become vampires. They are believed to frequent battlefields in wolf or hyéna shapes, and to suck the breath from dying soldiers, or to enter houses and steal the infants from their cradles. Modern Greeks call any savage-looking man, with dark complexion, and with distorted, misshapen limbs, a {Greek *br'kolakas*}, and suppose him to be invested with power of running in wolf-form.

The Serbs connect the vampire and the were-wolf together, and call them by one name *vlkoslak*. These rage chiefly in the depths of winter: they hold their annual gatherings, and at them divest themselves of their wolf-skins, which they hang on the trees around them. If any one succeeds in obtaining the skin and burning it, the vlkoslak is thenceforth disenchanted.

The power to become a were-wolf is obtained by drinking the water which settles in a foot-print left in clay by a wolf.

Among the White Russians the *wawkalak* is a man who has incurred the wrath of the devil, and the evil one punishes him by transforming him into a wolf and sending him among his relations, who recognize him and feed him well. He is a most amiably disposed were-wolf, for he does no mischief, and testifies his affection for his kindred by licking their hands. He cannot, however, remain long in any place, but is driven from house to house, and from hamlet to hamlet, by an irresistible passion for change of scene. This is an ugly superstition, for it sets a premium on standing well with the evil one.

The Sloyakians merrily term a drunkard a vlkodlak, because, forsooth, he makes a beast of himself. A Slovakian household were-wolf tale closes this chapter.

The Poles have their were-wolves, which rage twice in the year—at Christmas and at midsummer.

According to a Polish story, if a witch lays a girdle of human skin on the threshold of a house in which a marriage is being celebrated, the bride and bridegroom, and bridesmaids and groomsmen, should they step across it, are transformed into wolves. After three years, however, the witch will cover them with skins with the hair. turned outward; immediately they will recover their natural form. On one occasion, a witch cast a skin of too scanty dimensions over the bridegroom, so that his tail was left uncovered: he resumed his human form, but retained his lupine caudal appendage {*i.e. tail—jbh*}.

The Russians call the were-wolf *oborot*, which signifies "one transformed." The following receipt is given by them for becoming one.

"He who desires to become an oborot, let him seek in the forest a hewn-down tree; let him stab it with a small copper knife, and walk round the tree, repeating the following incantation:—

On the sea, on the ocean, on the island, on Bujan, On the empty pasture gleams the moon, on an ashstock lying In a green wood, in a gloomy vale. Toward the stock wandereth a shaggy wolf. Horned cattle seeking for his sharp white fangs; But the wolf enters not the forest, But the wolf dives not into the shadowy vale, Moon, moon, gold-horned moon, Cheek the flight of bullets, blunt the hunters' knives, Break the shepherds' cudgels, Cast wild fear upon all cattle, On men, on all creeping things, That they may not catch the grey wolf, That they may not rend his warm skin My word is binding, more binding than sleep, More binding than the promise of a hero!

"Then he springs thrice over the tree and runs into the forest, transformed into a wolf." [1]

[1. SACHAROW: *Inland*, 1838, No. 17.]

In the ancient Bohemian Lexicon of Vacerad (A. D. 1202) the were-wolf is called vilkodlak, and is explained as faunus. Safarik says under that head,-

"Incubi sepe improbi existunt mulieribus, et earum peragunt concubitum, quos demones Galli *dusios* nuncupant." And in another place: "Vilkodlaci, incubi, sive invidi, ab inviando passim cum animalibus, unde et incubi dicuntur ab incubando homines, i. e. stuprando, quos Romani faunos ficarios dicunt."

That the same belief in lycanthropy exists in Armenia is evident from the following story told by Haxthausen, in his *Trans-Caucasia* (Leipzig, i. 322):—"A man once saw a wolf, which had carried off a child, dash past him. He pursued it hastily, but was unable to overtake it. At last he came upon the hands and feet of a child, and a little further on he found a cave, in which lay a wolf-skin. This he cast into a fire, and immediately a woman appeared, who howled and tried to rescue the skin from the flames. The man, however, resisted, and, as soon as the hide was consumed, the woman had vanished in the smoke."

In India, on account of the prevalence of the doctrine of metempsychosis, the belief in transformation is widely diffused. Traces of genuine lycanthropy are abundant in all regions whither Buddhism has reached. In Ceylon, in Thibet, and in China, we find it still forming a portion of the national creed.

In the Pantschatantra is a story of an enchanted Brahmin's son, who by day was a serpent, by night a man.

Vikram,ditya's father, the son of Indra, was condemned to be an ass by day and a man by night.

A modern Indian tale is to this effect:—A prince marries a female ape, but his brothers wed handsome princesses. At a feast given by the queen to her step-daughters, there appears an exquisitely beautiful lady in gorgeous robes. This is none other than the she-ape, who has laid aside her skin for the occasion: the prince slips out of the room and burns the skin, so that his wife is prevented from resuming her favourite appearance.

Nathaniel Pierce [1] gives an account of an Abyssinian superstition very similar to that prevalent in Europe.

[1. *Life and Adventures of Nathaniel Pierce*, written by himself during a residence in Abyssinia from 1810-19. London, 1831.]

He says that in Abyssinia the gold. and silversmiths are highly regarded, but that the ironworkers are looked upon with contempt, as an inferior grade of beings. Their kinsmen even ascribe to them the power of transforming themselves into hyénas, or other savage beasts. All convulsions and hysterical disorders are attributed to the effect of their evil eye. The Amhara call them *Buda*, the Tigré, *Tebbib*. There are also Mahomedan and Jewish Budas. It is difficult to explain the origin of this strange superstition. These Budas are distinguished from other people by wearing gold ear-rings, and Coffin declares that he has often found hyénas with these rings in their ears, even among the beasts which he has shot or speared himself. But how the rings got into their ears is more than Coffin was able to ascertain.

Beside their power to transform themselves into hyénas or other wild beasts, all sorts of other strange things are ascribed to them; and the Abyssinians are firmly persuaded that they rob the graves by midnight, and no one would venture to touch what is called *quanter*, or dried meat in their houses, though they would not object to partake of fresh meat, if they had seen the animal, from which it came, killed before them. Coffin relates, as eye-witness of the fact, the following story:—

Among his servants was a Buda, who, one evening, whilst it was still light, came to his master and asked leave of absence till the following morning. He obtained the required leave and departed; but scarcely had Coffin turned his head, when one of his men exclaimed,—"Look! there he is, changing himself into hyéna," pointing in the direction taken by the Buda. Coffin turned to look, and although he did not witness the process of transformation, the young man had vanished from the spot on which he had been standing, not a hundred paces distant, and in his place was a hyéna running away. The place was a plain without either bush or tree to impede the view. Next morning the young man returned, and was charged by his companions with the transformation: this he rather acknowledged than denied, for he excused himself on the plea that it was the habit of his class. This statement of Pierce is corroborated by a note contributed by Sir Gardner Wilkinson to Rawlinson's *Herodotus* (book iv. chap. 105). "A class of people in Abyssinia are believed to change themselves into hyénas when they like. On my appearing to discredit it, I was told by one who lived for years there, that no well-informed person doubted it, and that he was once walking with one of them, when he happened to look away for a moment, and on turning again towards his companion, he saw him trotting off in the shape of a hyéna. He met him afterwards in his old form. These worthies are blacksmiths.—G. W."

A precisely similar superstition seems to have existed in America, for Joseph Acosta (*Hist. Nat. des Indes*) relates that the ruler of a city in Mexico, who was sent for by the predecessor of Montezuma, transformed himself, before the eyes of those who were sent to seize him, into an eagle, a tiger, and an enormous serpent. He yielded at last, and was condemned to death. No longer in his own house, he was unable to work miracles so as to save his life. The Bishop of Chiapa, a province of Guatemala, in a writing published in 1702, ascribes the same power to the Naguals, or national priests, who laboured to bring back to the religion of their ancestors, the children brought up as Christians by the government. After various ceremonies, when the child instructed advanced to embrace him, the Nagual suddenly assumed a frightful aspect, and under the form of a lion or tiger, appeared chained to the young Christian convert.—(*Recueil de Voyages*, tom. ii. 187.)

Among the North American Indians, the belief in transformation is very prevalent. The following story closely resembles one very prevalent all over the world.

"One Indian fixed his residence on the borders of the Great Bear lake, taking with him only a dog big with young. In due time, this dog brought forth eight pups. Whenever the Indian went out to fish, he tied up the pups, to prevent the straying of the litter. Several times, as he approached his tent, he heard noises proceeding from it, which sounded like the talking, the laughing, the crying, the wail, and the merriment of children; but, on entering it, he only perceived the pups tied up as usual. His curiosity being excited by the noises he had heard, he determined to watch and learn whence these sounds proceeded, and what they were. One day he pretended to go out to fish, but, instead of doing so, he concealed himself in a convenient place. In a short time he again heard -voices, and, rushing suddenly into the tent, beheld some beautiful children sporting and laughing, with the dog-skins lying by their side. He threw the dog-skins into the fire, and the children, retaining their proper forms, grew up, and were the ancestors of the dog-rib nation."—(*Traditions of the North American Indians*, by T. A. Jones, 1830, Vol. ii. p. 18.)

In the same work is a curious story entitled *The Mother of the World*, which bears a close analogy to another world-wide myth: a woman marries a dog, by night the dog lays aside its skin, and appears as a man. This may be compared with the tale of Bjørn and Bera already given.

I shall close this chapter with a Slovakian household tale given by T. T. Hanush in the third volume of *Zeitschrift für Deutsche Mythologie*.

The Daughter of the Vlkolak

"There was once a father, who had nine daughters, and they were all marriageable, but the youngest was the most beautiful. The father was a were-wolf. One day it came into his head: 'What is the good of having to support so many girls?' so he determined to put them all out of the way.

"He went accordingly into the forest to hew wood, and he ordered his daughters to let one of them bring him his dinner. It was the eldest who brought it.

"'Why, how come you so early with the food?' asked the woodcutter.

"'Truly, father, I wished to strengthen you, lest you should fall upon us, if famished!'

"'A good lass! Sit down whilst I eat.' He ate, and whilst he ate he thought of a scheme. He rose and said: "My girl, come, and I will show you a pit I have been digging.'

"'And what is the pit for? '

"'That we may be buried in it when we die, for poor folk will not be cared for much after they are dead and gone.'

"So the girl went with him to the side of the deep pit. 'Now hear,' said the were-wolf, 'you must die and be cast in there.'

"She begged for her life, but all in vain, so he laid hold of her and cast her into the grave. Then he took a great stone and flung it in upon her and crushed her head, so the poor thing breathed out her soul. When the were-wolf had done this he went back to his work, and as dusk came on, the second daughter arrived, bringing him food. He told her of the pit, and brought her to it, and cast her in, and killed her as the first. And so he dealt with all his girls up to the last. The youngest knew well that her father was a were-wolf, and she was grieved that her sisters did not return; she thought, 'Now where can they be? Has my father kept them for companionship; or to help him in his work?' So she made the food which she was to take him, and crept cautiously through the wood. When she came near the place where her father worked, she heard his strokes felling timber, and smelt smoke. She saw presently a large fire and two human heads roasting at it. Turning from the fire, she went in the direction of the axe-strokes, and found her father.

"See,' said she, 'father, I have brought you food.'

"'That is a good lass,' said he. 'Now stack the wood for me whilst I eat.'

"'But where are my sisters?' she asked.

"'Down in yon valley drawing wood,' he replied 'follow me, and I will bring you to them.'

"They came to the pit; then he told her that he had dug it for a grave. 'Now,' said he, 'you must die, and be cast into the pit with your sisters. '

"'Turn aside, father,' she asked, 'whilst I strip of my clothes, and then slay me if you will.'

"He turned aside as she requested, and then—tchich! she gave him a push, and he tumbled headlong into the hole he had dug for her.

"She fled for her life, for the were-wolf was not injured, and he soon would scramble out of the pit.

"Now she hears his howls resounding through the gloomy alleys of the forest, and swift as the wind she runs. She hears the tramp of his approaching feet, and the snuffle of his breath. Then she casts behind her her handkerchief. The were-wolf seizes this with teeth and nails, and rends it till it is reduced to tiny ribands. In another moment he is again in pursuit foaming at the mouth, and howling dismally, whilst his red eyes gleam like burning coals. As he gains on her, she casts behind her her gown, and bids him tear that. He seizes the gown and rives it to shreds, then again he pursues. This time she casts behind her her apron, next her petticoat, then her shift, and at last rums much in the condition in which she was born. Again the were-wolf approaches; she bounds out of the forest into a hay-field, and hides herself in the smallest heap of hay. Her father enters the field, runs howling about it in search of her, cannot find her, and begins to upset the different haycocks, all the while growling and gnashing his gleaming white fangs in his rage at her having escaped him. The foam flakes drop at every step from his mouth, and his skin is reeking with sweat. Before he has reached the smallest bundle of hay his strength leaves him, he feels exhaustion begin to creep over him, and he retires to the forest.

"The king goes out hunting every clay; one of his dogs carries food to the hay-field, which has most unaccountably been neglected by the hay-makers for three days. The king, following the dog, discovers the fair damsel, not exactly 'in the straw,' but up to her neck in hay. She is carried, hay and all, to the palace, where she becomes his wife, making only one stipulation before becoming his bride, and that is, that no beggar shall be permitted to enter the palace.

"After some years a beggar does get in, the beggar being, of course, none other than her were-wolf father. He steals upstairs, enters the nursery, cuts the throats of the two children borne by the queen to her lord, and lays the knife under her pillow.

"In the morning, the king, supposing his wife to be the murderess, drives her from home, with the dead princes hung about her neck. A hermit comes to the rescue, and restores the babies to life. The king finds out his mistake, is reunited to the lady out of the hay, and the were-wolf is cast off a high cliff into the sea, and that is the end of him. The king, the queen, and the princes live happily, and may be living yet, for no notice of their death has appeared in the newspaper."

This story bears some resemblance to one told by Von Hahn in his *Griechische und Albanesische Mœrchen*; I remember having heard a very similar one in the Pyrenees; but the man who flies from the were-wolf is one who, after having stripped off all his clothes, rushes into a cottage and jumps into a bed. The were-wolf dares not, or cannot, follow. The cause of his flight was also different. He was a freemason who had divulged the secret, and the were-wolf was the master of his lodge in pursuit of him. In the Bearnais story, there is nothing similar to the last part of the Slovakian tale, and in the Greek one the transformation and the pursuit are omitted, though the woman-eater is called "dog's-head," much as an outlaw in the north of Europe was said to be wolf-headed.

It is worthy of notice in the tale of *The Daughter of the Ulkolak*, that the were-wolf fit is followed by great exhaustion, [1] and that the wolf is given clothes to tear, much as in the Danish stories already related. There does not seem to be any indication of his Laving changed his shape, at least no change is mentioned, his hands are spoken of, and he swears and curses his daughter in broad Slovakian. The fit very closely resembles that to which Skallagrim, the Icelander, was subject. It is a pity that the maid Br‡k in the Icelandic tale did not fall upon her legs like the young lady in the hay.

[1. Compare this with the exhaustion following a Berserkir fit, and that which succeeded the attacks to which M. Bertrand was subject.]

CHAPTER IX
NATURAL CAUSES OF LYCANTHROPY
Innate Cruelty
Its Three Forms
Dumollard
Andreas Bichel
A Dutch Priest
Other instances of Inherent Cruelty
Cruelty united to Refinement
A Hungarian Bather in Blood
Suddenness with which the Passion is developed
Cannibalism; in pregnant Women; in Maniacs
Hallucination; how Produced
Salves
The Story of Lucius
Self-deception.

WHAT I have related from the chronicles of antiquity, or from the traditional lore of the people, is veiled under the form of myth or legend; and it is only from Scandinavian descriptions of those afflicted with the wolf-madness, and from the trials of those charged with the crime of lycanthropy in the later Middle Ages, that we can arrive at the truth respecting that form of madness which was invested by the superstitious with so much mystery.

It was not till the close of the Middle Ages that lycanthropy was recognized as a disease; but it is one which has so much that is ghastly and revolting in its form, and it is so remote from all our ordinary experience, that it is not surprising that the casual observer should leave the consideration of it, as a subject isolated and perplexing, and be disposed to regard as a myth that which the feared investigation might prove a reality.

In this chapter I purpose briefly examining the conditions under which men have been regarded as werewolves.

Startling though the assertion may be, it is a matter of fact, that man, naturally, in common with other carnivora, is actuated by an impulse to kill, and by a love of destroying life.

It is positively true that there are many to whom the sight of suffering causes genuine pleasure, and in whom the passion to kill or torture is as strong as any other passion. Witness the number of boys who assemble around a sheep or pig when it is about to be killed, and who watch the struggle of the dying brute with hearts beating fast with pleasure, and eyes sparkling with delight. Often have I seen an eager crowd of children assembled around the slaughterhouses of French towns, absorbed in the expiring agonies of the sheep and cattle, and hushed into silence as they watched the flow of blood.

The propensity, however, exists in different degrees. In some it is manifest simply as indifference to suffering, in others it appears as simple pleasure in seeing killed, and in others again it is dominant as an irresistible desire to torture and destroy.

This propensity is widely diffused; it exists in children and adults, in the gross-minded and the refined., in the well-educated and the ignorant, in those who have never had the opportunity of gratifying it, and those who gratify it habitually, in spite of morality, religion, laws, so that it can only depend on constitutional causes.

The sportsman and the fisherman follow a natural instinct to destroy, when they make wax on bird, beast, and fish: the pretence that the spoil is sought for the table cannot be made with justice, as the sportsman cares little for the game he has obtained, when once it is consigned to his pouch. The motive for his eager pursuit of bird or beast must be sought elsewhere; it will be found in the natural craving to extinguish life, which exists in his soul. Why does a child impulsively strike at a butterfly as it flits past him? He cares nothing for the insect when once it is beaten down at his feet, unless it be quivering in its agony, when he will watch it with interest. The child strikes at the fluttering creature because it has _life_ in it, and he has an instinct within him impelling him to destroy life wherever he finds it.

Parents and nurses know well that children by nature are cruel, and that humanity has to be acquired by education. A child will gloat over the sufferings of a wounded animal till his mother bids him "put it out of its misery." An unsophisticated child would not dream of terminating the poor creature's agonies abruptly, any more than he would swallow whole a bon-bon till he had well sucked it. Inherent cruelty may be obscured by after impressions, or may be kept under moral restraint; the person who is constitutionally a Nero, may scarcely know his own nature, till by some accident the master passion becomes dominant, and sweeps all before it. A relaxation of the moral check, a shock to the controlling intellect, an abnormal condition of body, are sufficient to allow the passion to assert itself.

As I have already observed, this passion exists in different persons in different degrees.

In some it is exhibited in simple want of feeling for other people's sufferings. This temperament may lead to crime, for the individual who is regardless of pain in another, will be ready to destroy that other, if it suit his own purposes. Such an one was the pauper Dumollard, who was the murderer of at least six poor girls, and who attempted to kill several others. He seems not to have felt much gratification in murdering them, but to have been so utterly indifferent to their sufferings, that he killed them solely for the sake of their clothes, which were of the poorest description. He was sentenced to the guillotine, and executed in 1862. [1]

[1. A full account of this man's trial is given by one who was present, in *All the Year Round*, No. 162.]

In others, the passion for blood is developed alongside with indifference to suffering.

Thus Andreas Bichel enticed young women into his house, under the pretence that he was possessed of a magic mirror, in which he would show them their future husbands; when he had them in his power he bound their hands behind their backs, and stunned them with a blow. He then stabbed them and despoiled them of their clothes, for the sake of which he committed the murders; but as he killed the young women the passion of cruelty took possession of him, and he hacked the poor girls to pieces whilst they were still alive, in his anxiety to examine their insides. Catherine Seidel he opened with a hammer and a wedge, from her breast downwards, whilst still breathing. "I may say," he remarked at his trial, "that during the operation I was so eager, that I trembled all over, and I longed to rive off a piece and eat it."

Andreas Bichel was executed in 1809. [1]

[1. The case of Andreas Bichel is given in Lady Duff Gordon's *Remarkable Criminal Trials*.]

Again, a third class of persons are cruel and bloodthirsty, because in them bloodthirstiness is a raging insatiable passion. In a civilized country those possessed by this passion are forced to control it through fear of the consequences, or to gratify it upon the brute creation. But in earlier days, when feudal lords were supreme in their domains, there have been frightful instances of their excesses, and the extent to which some of the Roman emperors indulged their passion for blood is matter of history.

Gall gives several authentic instances of bloodthirstiness. [1] A Dutch priest had such a desire to kill and to see killed, that he became chaplain to a regiment that he might have the satisfaction of seeing deaths occurring wholesale in engagements. The same man kept a large collection of various kinds of domestic animals, that he might be able to torture their young. He killed the animals for his kitchen, and was acquainted with all the hangmen in the country, who sent him notice of executions, and he would walk for days that he might have the gratification of seeing a man executed.

[1. GALL: *Sur les Fonctions du Cerveau*, tom. iv.]

In the field of battle the passion is variously developed; some feel positive delight in slaying, others are indifferent. An old soldier, who had been in Waterloo, informed me that to his mind there was no pleasure equal to running a man through the body, and that he could lie awake at night musing on the pleasurable sensations afforded him by that act.

Highwaymen are frequently not content with robbery, but manifest a bloody inclination to torment and kill. John Rosbeck, for instance, is well known to have invented and exercised the most atrocious cruelties, merely that he might witness the sufferings of his victims, who were especially women and children. Neither fear nor torture could break him of the dreadful passion till he was executed.

Gall tells of a violin-player, who, being arrested, confessed to thirty-four murders, all of which he had committed, not from enmity or intent to rob, but solely because it afforded him an intense pleasure to kill.

Spurzheim [1] tells of a priest at Strasbourg, who, though rich, and uninfluenced by envy or revenge, from exactly the same motive, killed three persons.

[1. *Doctrine of the Mind*, p. 158.]

Gall relates the case of a brother of the Duke of Bourbon, Condé, Count of Charlois, who, from infancy, had an inveterate pleasure in torturing animals: growing older, he lived to shed the blood of human beings, and to exercise various kinds of cruelty. He also murdered many from no other motive, and shot at slaters for the pleasure of seeing them fall from the roofs of houses.

Louis XI. of France caused the death of 4,000 people during his reign; he used to watch their executions from a neighbouring lattice. He had gibbets placed outside his own palace, and himself conducted the executions.

It must not be supposed that cruelty exists merely in the coarse and rude; it is quite as frequently observed in the refined and educated. Among the former it is manifest chiefly in insensibility to the sufferings of others; in the latter it appears as a passion, the indulgence of which causes intense pleasure.

Those bloody tyrants, Nero and Caligula, Alexander Borgia, and Robespierre, whose highest enjoyment consisted in witnessing the agonies of their fellow-men, were full of delicate sensibilities and great refinement of taste and manner.

I have seen an accomplished young woman of considerable refinement and of a highly strung nervous temperament, string flies with her needle on a piece of thread, and watch complacently their flutterings. Cruelty may remain latent till, by some accident. it is aroused, and then it will break forth in a devouring flame.

It is the same with the passion for blood as with the passions of love and hate; we have no conception of the violence with which they can rage till circumstances occur which call them into action. Love or hate will be dominant in a breast which has been in serenity, till suddenly the spark falls, passion blazes forth, and the serenity of the quiet breast is shattered for ever. A word, a glance, a touch, are sufficient to fire the magazine of passion in the heart, and to desolate for ever an existence. It is the same with bloodthirstiness. It may lurk in the deeps of some heart very dear to us. It may smoulder in the bosom which is most cherished by us, and we may be perfectly unconscious of its existence there. Perhaps circumstances will not cause its development; perhaps moral principle may have bound it down with fetters it can never break.

Michael Wagener [1] relates a horrible story which occurred in Hungary, suppressing the name of the person, as it was that of a still powerful family in the country. It illustrates what I have been saying, and shows how trifling a matter may develope the passion in its most hideous proportions.

[1. *Beitrage zur philosophischen Anthropologie*, Wien, 1796.]

"Elizabeth ——— was wont to dress well in order to please her husband, and she spent half the day over her toilet. On one occasion, a lady's-maid saw something wrong in her head-dress, and as a recompence for observing it, received such a severe box on the ears that the blood gushed from her nose, and spirted on to her mistress's face. When the blood drops were washed off her face, her skin appeared much more beautiful—whiter and more transparent on the spots where the blood had been.

"Elizabeth formed the resolution to bathe her face and her whole body in human blood so as to enhance her beauty. Two old women and a certain Fitzko assisted her in her undertaking. This monster used to kill the luckless victim, and the old women caught the blood, in which Elizabeth was wont to bathe at the hour of four in the morning. After the bath she appeared more beautiful than before.

"She continued this habit after the death of her husband (1604) in the hopes of gaining new suitors. The unhappy girls who were allured to the castle, under the plea that they were to be taken into service there, were locked up in a cellar. Here they were beaten till their bodies were swollen. Elizabeth not unfrequently tortured the victims herself; often she changed their clothes which dripped with blood, and then renewed her cruelties. The swollen bodies were then cut up with razors.

"Occasionally she had the girls burned, and then cut up, but the great majority were beaten to death.

"At last her cruelty became so great, that she would stick needles into those who sat with her in a carriage, especially if they were of her own sex. One of her servant-girls she stripped naked, smeared her with honey, and so drove her out of the house.

"When she was ill, and could not indulge her cruelty, she bit a person who came near her sick bed as though she were a wild beast.

"She caused, in all, the death of 650 girls, some in Tscheita, on the neutral ground, where she had a cellar constructed for the purpose; others in different localities; for murder and bloodshed became with her a necessity.

"When at last the parents of the lost children could no longer be cajoled, the castle was seized, and the traces of the murders were discovered. Her accomplices were executed, and she was imprisoned for life."

An equally remarkable example will be found in the account of the Mareschal de Retz given at some length in the sequel. He vas an accomplished man, a scholar, an able general, and a courtier; but suddenly the impulse to murder and destroy came upon him whilst sitting in the library reading Suetonius; he yielded to the impulse, and became one of the greatest monsters of cruelty the world has produced.

The case of Sviatek, the Gallician cannibal, is also to the purpose. This man was a harmless pauper, till one day accident brought him to the scene of a conflagration. Hunger impelled him to taste of the roast fragments of a human being who had perished in the fire, and from that moment he ravened for man's flesh.

M. Bertrand was a French gentleman of taste and education. He one day lounged over the churchyard wall in a quiet country village and watched a funeral. Instantly an overwhelming desire to dig up and rend the corpse which he had seen committed to the ground came upon him, and for years he lived as a human hyéna, preying upon the dead. His story is given in detail in the fifteenth chapter.

An abnormal condition of body sometimes produces this desire for blood. It is manifest in certain cases of pregnancy, when the constitution loses its balance, and the appetite becomes diseased. Schenk [1] gives instances.

[1. *Observationes Medic*. lib. iv. De Gravidis.]

A pregnant woman saw a baker carrying loaves on his bare shoulder. She was at once filled with such a craving for his flesh that she refused to taste any food till her husband persuaded the baker, by the offer of a large sum, to allow his wife to bite him. The man yielded, and the woman fleshed her teeth in his shoulder twice; but he held out no longer. The wife bore twins on three occasions, twice living, the third time dead.

A woman in an interesting condition, near Andernach on the Rhine, murdered her husband, to whom she was warmly attached, ate half his body, and salted the rest. When the passion left her she became conscious of the horrible nature of her act, and she gave herself up to justice.

In 1553, a wife cut her husband's throat, and gnawed the nose and the left arm, whilst the body was yet warm. She then gutted the corpse, and salted it for future consumption. Shortly after, she gave birth to three children, and she only became conscious of what she had done when her neighbours asked after the father, that they might announce to him the arrival of the little ones.

In the summer of 1845, the Greek papers contained an account of a pregnant woman murdering her husband for the purpose of roasting and eating his liver.

That the passion to destroy is prevalent in certain maniacs is well known; this is sometimes accompanied by cannibalism.

Gruner [1] gives an account of a shepherd who was evidently deranged, who killed and ate two men. Marc [2] relates that a woman of Unterelsas, during the absence of her husband, a poor labourer, murdered her son, a lad fifteen months old. She chopped of his legs and stewed them with cabbage. She ate a portion, and offered the rest to her husband. It is true that the family were very poor, but there was food in the house at the time. In prison the woman gave evident signs of derangement.

[1. *De Anthropophago Bucano*. Jen. 1792.]

[2. *Die Geistes Krankheiten*. Berlin, 1844.]

The cases in which bloodthirstiness and cannibalism are united with insanity are those which properly fall under the head of Lycanthropy. The instances recorded in the preceding chapter point unmistakably to hallucination accompanying the lust for blood. Jean Grenier, Roulet, and others, were firmly convinced that they had undergone transformation. A disordered condition of mind or body may produce hallucination in a form depending on the character and instincts of the individual. Thus, an ambitious man labouring under monomania will imagine himself to be a king; a covetous man will be plunged in despair, believing himself to be penniless, or exult at the vastness of the treasure which he imagines that he has discovered.

The old man suffering from rheumatism or gout conceives himself to be formed of china or glass, and the foxhunter tallyhos! at each new moon, as though he were following a pack. In like manner, the naturally cruel man, if the least affected in his brain, will suppose himself to be transformed into the most cruel and bloodthirsty animal with which he is acquainted.

The hallucinations under which lycanthropists suffered may have arisen from various causes. The older writers, as Forestus and Burton, regard the were-wolf mania as a species of melancholy madness, and some do not deem it necessary for the patient to believe in his transformation for them to regard him as a lycanthropist.

In the present state of medical knowledge, we know that very different conditions may give rise to hallucinations.

In fever cases the sensibility is so disturbed that the patient is often deceived as to the space occupied by his limbs, and he supposes them to be preternaturally distended or contracted. In the case of typhus, it is not uncommon for the sick person, with deranged nervous system, to believe himself to be double in the bed, or to be severed in half, or to have lost his limbs. He may regard his members as composed of foreign and often fragile materials, as glass, or he may so lose his personality as to suppose himself to have become a woman.

A monomaniac who believes himself to be some one else, seeks to enter into the feelings, thoughts, and habits of the assumed personality, and from the facility with which this is effected, he draws an argument, conclusive to himself, of the reality of the change. He thenceforth speaks of himself under the assumed character, and experiences all its needs, wishes, passions, and the like. The closer the identification becomes, the more confirmed is the monomaniac in his madness, the character of which varies with the temperament of the individual. If the person's mind be weak, or rude and uncultivated, the tenacity with which he clings to his metamorphosis is feebler, and it becomes more difficult to draw the line between his lucid and insane utterances. Thus Jean Grenier, who laboured under this form of mania, said in his trial much that was true, but it was mixed with the ramblings of insanity.

Hallucination may also be produced by artificial means, and there are evidences afforded by the confessions of those tried for lycanthropy, that these artificial means were employed by them. I refer to the salve so frequently mentioned in witch and were-wolf trials. The following passage is from the charming *Golden Ass of Apuleius*; it proves that salves were extensively used by witches for the purpose of transformation, even in his day:—

"Fotis showed me a crack in the door, and bade me look through it, upon which I looked and saw Pamphile first divest herself of all her garments, and then, having unlocked a chest, take from it several little boxes, and open one of the latter, which contained a certain ointment. Rubbing this ointment a good while previously between the palms of her hands, she anointed her whole body, from the very nails of her toes to the hair on the crown of her head, and when she was anointed all over, she whispered many magic words to a lamp, as if she were talking to it. Then she began to move her arms, first with tremulous jerks, and afterwards by a gentle undulating motion, till a glittering, downy surface by degrees overspread her body, feathers and strong quills burst forth suddenly, her nose became a hard crooked beak, her toes changed to curved talons, and Pamphile was no longer Pamphile, but it was an owl I saw before me. And now, uttering a harsh, querulous scream, leaping from the ground by little and little, in order to try her powers, and presently poising herself aloft on her pinions, she stretched forth her wings on either Side to their full extent, and flew straight away.

"Having now been actually a witness of the performance of the magical art, and of the metamorphosis of Pamphile, I remained for some time in a stupefied state of astonishment. . . . At last, after I had rubbed my eyes some time, had recovered a little from the amazement and abstraction of mind, and begun to feel a consciousness of the reality of things about me, I took hold of the hand of Fotis and said,— 'Sweet damsel, bring me, I beseech thee, a portion of the ointment with which thy mistress hath just now anointed, and when thou hast made me a bird, I will be thy slave, and even wait upon thee like a winged Cupid.' Accordingly she crept gently into the apartment, quickly returned with the box of ointment, hastily placed it in my hands, and then immediately departed.

"Elated to an extraordinary degree at the sight of the precious treasure, I kissed the box several times successively; and uttering repeated aspirations in hopes of a prosperous flight, I stripped off my clothes as quick as possible, dipped my fingers greedily into the box, and having thence extracted a good large lump of ointment, rubbed it all over my body and limbs. When I was thoroughly anointed, I swung my arms up and down, in imitation of the movement of a bird's pinions, and continued to do so a little while, when instead of any perceptible token of feathers or wings making their appearance, my own thin skin, alas! grew into a hard leathern hide, covered with bristly hair, my fingers and toes disappeared, the palms of my hands and the soles of my feet became four solid hoofs, and from the end of my spine a long tail projected. My face was enormous, my mouth wide, my nostrils gaping, my lips pendulous, and I had a pair of immoderately long, rough, hairy ears. In short, when I came to contemplate my transformation to its full extent, I found that, instead of a bird, I had become—an ASSt." [1]

[1. APULEIUS, Sir George Head's translation, bk. iii.]

Of what these magical salves were composed we know. They were composed of narcotics, to wit, *Solanum somniferum*, aconite, hyoscyamus, belladonna, opium, *acorus vulgaris*, *sium*. These were boiled down with oil, or the fat of little children who were murdered for the purpose. The blood of a bat was added, but its effects could have been *nil*. To these may have been added other foreign narcotics, the names of which have not transpired.

Whatever may have been the cause of the hallucination, it is not surprising that the lycanthropist should have imagined himself transformed into a beast. The cases I have instanced are those of shepherds, who were by nature of their employment, brought into collision with wolves; and it is not surprising that these persons, in a condition liable to hallucinations, should imagine themselves to be transformed into wild beasts, and that their minds reverting to the injuries sustained from these animals, they should, in their state of temporary insanity, accuse themselves of the acts of rapacity committed by the beasts into which they believed themselves to be transformed. It is a well-known fact that men, whose minds are unhinged, will deliver themselves up to justice, accusing themselves of having committed crimes which have actually taken place, and it is only on investigation that their self-accusation proves to be false; and yet they will describe the circumstances with the greatest minuteness, and be thoroughly convinced of their own criminality. I need give but a single instance.

In the war of the French Revolution, the *Hermione* frigate was commanded by Capt. Pigot, a harsh man and a severe commander. His crew mutinied, and carried the ship into an enemy's port, having murdered the captain and several of the officers, under circumstances of extreme barbarity. One midshipman escaped, by whom many of the criminals, who were afterwards taken and delivered over to justice, one by one, were identified. Mr. Finlayson, the Government actuary, who at that time held an official situation in the Admiralty, states:—"In my own experience I have known, on separate occasions, *more than six sailors* who voluntarily confessed to having struck the first blow at Capt. Pigot. These men detailed all the horrid circumstances of the mutiny with extreme minuteness and perfect accuracy; nevertheless, not one of them had ever been in the ship, nor had so much as seen Capt. Pigot in their lives. They had obtained by tradition, from their messmates, the particulars of the story. When long on a foreign station, hungering and thirsting for home, their minds became enfeebled; at length they actually believed themselves guilty of the crime over which they had so long brooded, and submitted with a gloomy pleasure to being sent to England in irons, for judgment. At the Admiralty we were always able to detect and establish their innocence, in defiance of their own solemn asseverations."—(*London Judicial Gazette*, January, 1803.)

CHAPTER X
MYTHOLOGICAL ORIGIN OF THE WERE-WOLF MYTH

Transformation into beasts forms an integral portion of all mythological systems. The gods of Greece were wont to change themselves into animals in order to carry out their designs with greater speed, security, and secrecy, than in human forms. In Scandinavian mythology, Odin changed himself into the shape of an eagle, Loki into that of a salmon. Eastern religions abound in stories of transformation.

The line of demarcation between this and the translation of a beast's soul into man, or a man's soul into a beast's (metempsychosis) is very narrow.

The doctrine of metempsychosis is founded on the consciousness of gradation between beasts and men. The belief in a soul-endowed animal world was present among the ancients, and the laws of intelligence and instinct were misconstrued, or were regarded as a puzzle, which no man might solve.

The human soul with its consciousness seemed to be something already perfected in a pre-existing state, and, in the myth of metempsychosis, we trace the yearnings and gropings of the soul after the source whence its own consciousness was derived, counting its dreams and hallucinations as gleams of memory, recording acts which had taken place in a former state of existence.

Modern philosophy has resumed the same thread of conjecture, and thinks to see in man the perfected development of lower organisms.

After death the translation of the soul was supposed to continue. It became either absorbed into the *nous*, into Brahma, into the deity, or it sank in the scale of creation, and was degraded to animate a brute. Thus the doctrine of metempsychosis was emphatically one of rewards and punishments, for the condition of the soul after death depended on its training during life. A savage and bloodthirsty man was exiled, as in the case of Lycaon, into the body of a wild beast: the soul of a timorous man entered a hare, and drunkards or gluttons became swine.

The intelligence which was manifest in the beasts bore such a close resemblance to that of man, in the childhood and youth of the world, that it is not to be wondered at, if our forefathers failed to detect the line of demarcation drawn between instinct and reason. And failing to distinguish this, they naturally fell into the belief in metempsychosis.

It was not merely a fancied external resemblance between the beast and man, but it was the perception of skill, pursuits, desires, sufferings, and griefs like his own, in the animal creation, which led man to detect within the beast something analogous to the soul within himself; and this, notwithstanding the points of contrast existing between them, elicited in his mind so strong a sympathy that, without a great stretch of imagination, he invested the beast with his own attributes, and with the full powers of his own understanding. He regarded it as actuated by the same motives, as subject to the same laws of honour, as moved by the same prejudices, and the higher the beast was in the scale, the more he regarded it as an equal. A singular illustration of this will be found in the Finnboga Saga, c. xi.

"Now we must relate about Finnbog. Afterward in the evening, when men slept, he rose, took his weapons, and went forth, following the tracks which led to the dairy farm. As was his wont, he stepped out briskly along the spoor till he came to the dairy. There he found the bear lying down, and he had slain the sheep, and he was lying on them lapping their blood. Then said Finnbog: 'Stand up, Brain! make ready against me; that becomes you more than crouching over those sheep's carcases.'

"The bear sat up, looked at him, and lay down again. Finnbog said, 'If you think that I am too fully armed to match with you, I will do this,' and he took of his helmet and laid aside his shield. Then he said, Stand up now, if you dare! '

"The bear sat up, shook his head, and then cast himself down again. "Finnbog exclaimed, 'I see, you want us both to be *boune* alike!' so he flung aside his sword and said, 'Be it as you will; now stand up if you have the heart that I believe you have, rather than one such as was possessed by these rent sheep.'

"Then Bruin stood up and prepared to fight."

The following story taken from the mouth of an Osage Indian by J. A. Jones, and published in his *Traditions of the North American Indians*, shows how thoroughly the savage mind misses the line of demarcation between instinct and reason, and how the man of the woods looks upon beasts as standing on an equality with himself.

An Osage warrior is in search of a wife: he admires the tidy and shrewd habits of the beaver. He accordingly goes to a beaver-hut to obtain one of that race for a bride. "In one corner of the room sat a beaver-woman combing the heads of some little beavers, whose ears she boxed very soundly when they would not lie still.

151

The warrior, *i. e.* the beaver-chief, whispered the Osage that she was his second wife, and was very apt to be cross when there was work to be done, which prevented her from going to see her neighbours. Those whose heads she was combing were her children, he said, and she who had made them rub their noses against each other and be friends, was his eldest daughter. Then calling aloud, 'Wife,' said he, 'what have you to eat? The stranger is undoubtedly hungry; see, he is pale, his eye has no fire, and his step is like that of a moose.'

"Without replying to him, for it was a sulky day with her, she called aloud, and a dirty-looking beaver entered. 'Go,' said she, 'and fetch the stranger something to eat.' With that the beaver girl passed through a small door into another room, from which she soon returned, bringing some large pieces of willow-bark, which she laid at the feet of the warrior and his guest. While the warrior-beaver was chewing the willow, and the Osage was pretending to do so, they fell to talking over many matters, particularly the wars of the beavers with the otters, and their frequent victories over them. He told our father by what means the beavers felled large trees, and moved them to the places where they wished to make dams; how they raised to an erect position the poles for their lodges, and how they plastered them so as to keep out rain. Then he spoke of their employments when they had buried the hatchet; of the peace and happiness and tranquillity they enjoyed when gathered into companies, they rested from their labours, and passed their time in talking and feasting, and bathing, and playing the game of bones, and making love. All the while the young beaver-maiden sat with her eyes fixed upon the Osage, at every pause moving a little nearer, till at length she was at his side with her forepaw upon his arm; a minute more and she had placed it around his neck, and was rubbing her soft furry cheek against his. Our ancestor, on his part, betrayed no disinclination to receive her caresses, but returned them with equal ardour. The old beaver seeing what was going on, turned his back upon them, and suffered them to be as kind to each other as they pleased. At last, turning quickly round, while the maiden, suspecting what was coming, and pretending to be abashed, ran behind her mother, he said, 'To end this foolery, what say you to marrying my daughter? She is well brought up, and is the most industrious girl in the village. She will flap more wall with her tail in a day than any maiden in the nation; she will gnaw down a larger tree betwixt the rising of the sun and the coming of the shadows than many a smart beaver of the other sex. As for her wit, try her at the game of the dish, and see who gets up master; and for cleanliness, look at her petticoat?' Our father answered that he did not doubt that she was industrious and cleanly, able to gnaw down a very large tree, and to use her tail to very good purpose; that he loved her much, and wished to make her the mother of his children. And thereupon the bargain was concluded."

These two stories, the one taken from Icelandic saga, the other from American Indian tradition, shew clearly the oneness which the uncultivated mind believes to exist between the soul of man and the soul of beast. The same sentiments actuate both man and brute, and if their actions are unlike, it is because of the difference in their formation. The soul within is identical, but the external accidents of body are unlike.

Among many rude as well as cultivated people, the body is regarded as a mere garment wrapped around the soul. The Buddist looks upon identity as existing in the soul alone, and the body as no more constituting identity, than the clothes he puts on or takes off. He exists as a spirit; for convenience he vests himself in a body; sometimes that body is human, sometimes it is bestial. As his soul rises in the spiritual scale, the nobler is the animal form which it tenants. Budda himself passed through various stages of existence; in one he was a hare, and his soul being noble, led him to immolate himself, in order that he might offer hospitality to Indra, who, in the form of an old man, craved of him food and shelter. The Buddist regards animals with reverence; an ancestor may be tenanting the body of the ox he is driving, or a descendant may be running at his side barking, and wagging his tail. When he falls into an ecstasy, his soul is leaving his body for a little while, it is laying aside its raiment of flesh and blood and bone, to return to it once more when the trance is over. But this idea is not confined to Buddists, it is common everywhere. The spirit or soul is supposed to be imprisoned in the body, the body is but the lantern through which the spirit shines, "the corruptible body" is believed to "press down the soul," and the soul is unable to attain to perfect happiness till it has shuffled off this earthy coil. Butler regards the members of the body as so many instruments used by the soul for the purpose of seeing, hearing, feeling, &c., just as we use telescopes or crutches, and which may be rejected without injury to our individuality.

The late Mr. J. Holloway, of the Bank of England, brother to the engraver of that name, related of himself that, being one night in bed, and unable to sleep, he had fixed his eyes and thoughts with uncommon intensity on a beautiful star that was shining in at the window, when he suddenly found his spirit released from his body and soaring into space. But instantly seized with anxiety for the anguish of his wife, if she discovered his body apparently dead beside her, he returned, and re-entered it with difficulty. He described that returning as a returning from light into darkness, and that whilst the spirit was free, he was alternately in the light or the dark, accordingly as his thoughts were with his wife or with the star. Popular mythology in most lands regards the soul as oppressed by the body, and its liberation is considered a deliverance from the "burden" of the flesh. Whether the soul is at all able to act or express itself without a body, any more than a fire is able to make cloth without the apparatus of boiler and machinery, is a question which has not commended itself to the popular mind. But it may be remarked that the Christian religion alone is that which raises the body to a dignity equal to that of the soul, and gives it a hope of ennoblement and resurrection never dreamed of in any mythological system.

But the popular creed, in spite of the most emphatic testimony of Scripture, is that the soul is in bondage so long as it is united to a body, a creed entirely in accordance with that of Buddism.

If the body be but the cage, as a poet [1] of our own has been pleased to call it, in which dwells the imprisoned soul, it is quite possible for the soul to change its cage. If the body be but a vesture clothing the soul, as the Buddist asserts, it is not improbable that it may occasionally change its vesture.

[1. VAUGHN, *Sitex Scintillans*.]

This is self-evident, and thus have arisen the countless tales of transformation and transmigration which are found all over the world. That the same view of the body as a mere clothing of the soul was taken by our Teutonic and Scandinavian ancestors, is evident even from the etymology of the words *leichnam, loekhama*, used to express the soulless body.

I have already spoken of the Norse word *hamr*, I wish now to make some further remarks upon it. *Hamr* is represented in Anglo-Saxon by *hama, homa*, in Saxon by *hamo*, in old High German by *hamo*, in old French by *homa, hama*, to which are related the Gothic *gahamon, ufar-hamon, ana-hamon*, {Greek eℑnd˙esæai}, {Greek eℑpend˙esæai}; *and-hamon, af-hamon*, {Greek aℑpekd˙ein} {Greek eℑkd˙esæaiℑ} thence also the old High German *hemidi*, and the modern *Hemde*, garment. In composition we find this word, as *loek-hagnr*, in old Norse; in old High German *loek-hamo*, Anglo-Saxon *loek-hama*, and *flésc-hama*, Old Saxon, *loek-hamo*, modern German *Leich-nam*, a body, *i. e.* a garment of flesh, precisely as the bodies of birds are called in old Norse *fjaær-hamr*, in Anglo-Saxon *feæerhoma*, in Old Saxon *fetherhamo*, or feather-dresses and the bodies of wolves are called in old Norse °*lfshamr*, and seals' bodies in FaroÎse *küpahamr*. The significance of the old verb *aæ hamaz* is now evident; it is to migrate from one body to another, and *hama-skipti* is a transmigration of the soul. The method of this transmigration consisted in simply investing the body with the skin of the animal into which the soul was to migrate. When Loki, the Northern god of evil, went in quest of the stolen Idunn, he borrowed of Freyja her falcon dress, and at once became, to all intents and purposes, a falcon. Thiassi pursued him as he left Thrymheimr, having first taken upon him an eagle's dress, and thereby become an eagle.

In order to seek Thor's lost hammer, Loki borrowed again of Freyja her feather dress, and as be flew away in it, the feathers sounded as they winnowed the breeze (*fjaærhamr dunæi*).

In like manner Cédmon speaks of an evil spirit flying away in feather-dress: "‚œt he mid feæerhomon fleÙgan meahte, windan on wolkne" (Gen. ed. Gr. 417), and of an angel, "‚uo ‚ar suogan quam engil ‚es alowaldon obhana fun radure faran an feæerhamon" (HÍlj. 171, 23), the very expression made use of when speaking of a bird: "farad an feæarhamun" (HÍlj. 50,11).

The soul, in certain cases, is able to free itself from the body and to enter that of beast or man—in this form stood the myth in various theological systems.

Among the Finns and Lapps it is not uncommon for a magician to fall into a cataleptic condition, and during the period his soul is believed to travel very frequently in bodily form, having assumed that of any animal most suitable for its purpose. I have given instances in a former chapter. The same doctrine is evident in most cases of lycanthropy. The patient is in a state of trance, his body is watched, and it remains motionless, but his soul has migrated into the carcase of a wolf, which it vivifies, and in which it runs its course. A curious Basque story shows that among this strange Turanian people, cut off by such a flood of Aryan nations from any other members of its family, the same superstition remains. A huntsman was once engaged in the chase of it bear among the Pyreneean peaks, when Bruin turned suddenly on him and hugged him to death, but not before he had dealt the brute its mortal wound. As the huntsman expired, he breathed his soul into the body of the bear, and thenceforward ranged the mountains as a beast.

One of the tales of the Sanskrit book of fables, the *Pantschatantra*, affords such a remarkable testimony to the Indian belief in metempsychosis, that I am tempted to give it in abstract.

A king was one day passing through the marketplace of his city, when he observed a hunchbacked merryandrew, whose contortions and jokes kept the bystanders in a roar of laughter. Amused with the fellow, the king brought him to his palace. Shortly after, in the hearing of the clown, a necromancer taught the monarch the art of sending his soul into a body not his own.

Some little while after this, the monarch, anxious to put in practice his newly acquired knowledge, rode into the forest accompanied by his fool, who, he believed, had not heard, or, at all events comprehended, the lesson. They came upon the corpse of a Brahmin lying in the depth of the jungle, where he had died of thirst. The king, leaving his horse, performed the requisite ceremony, and instantly his soul had migrated into the body of the, Brahmin, and his own lay as dead upon the ground. At the same moment, however, the hunchback deserted his body, and possessed himself of that which had been the king's, and shouting farewell to the dismayed monarch, he rode back to the palace, where he was received with royal honours. But it was not long before the queen and one of the ministers discovered that a screw was somewhere loose, and when the quondam king, but now Brahmin, arrived and told his tale, a plot was laid for the recovery of his body. The queen asked her false husband whether it were possible to make her parrot talk, and he in a moment of uxorious weakness promised to make it speak. He laid his body aside, and sent his soul into the parrot. Immediately the true king jumped out of his Brahmin body and resumed that which was legitimately his own, and then proceeded, with the queen, to wring the neck of the parrot.

But besides the doctrine of metempsychosis, which proved such a fertile mother of fable, there was another article of popular mythology which gave rise to stories of transformation. Among the abundant superstitions existing relative to transformation, three shapes seem to have been pre-eminently affected—that of the swan, that of the wolf, and that of the serpent. In many of the stories of those transformed, it is evident that the individual who changes shape is regarded with superstitious reverence, as a being of a higher order—of a divine nature. In Christian countries, everything relating to heathen mythology was regarded with a suspicious eye by the clergy, and any miraculous powers not sanctioned by the church were attributed to the evil one. The heathen gods became devils, and the marvels related of them were supposed to be effected by diabolic agency. A case of transformation which had shown the power of an ancient god, was in Christian times considered as an instance of witchcraft. Thus stories of transformation fell into bad odour, and those who changed shapes were no longer regarded as heavenly beings, commanding reverence, but as miserable witches deserving the stake.

In the infancy of the world, when natural phenomena were ill-understood, expressions which to us are poetical were of a real significance. When we speak of thunder rolling, we use an expression which conveys no further idea than a certain likeness observed between the detonations and the roll of a vehicle; but to the uninstructed mind it was more. The priméval savage knew not what caused thunder, and tracing the resemblance between it and the sound of wheels, he at once concluded that the chariot of the gods was going abroad, or that the celestial spirits were enjoying a game of bowls.

We speak of fleecy clouds, because they appear to us soft and light as wool, but the first men tracing the same resemblance, believed the light vapours to be flocks of heavenly sheep. Or we say that the clouds are flying: the savage used the same expression, as he looked up at the mackerel sky, and saw in it flights of swans coursing over the heavenly lake. Once more, we creep nearer to the winter fire, shivering at the wind, which we remark is howling around the house, and yet we do not suppose that the wind has a voice. The wild priméval men thought that it had, and because dogs and wolves howl, and the wind howled, and because they had seen dogs and wolves, they concluded that the storm-wind was a night-hound, or a monstrous wolf, racing over the country in the darkness of the winter night, ravening for prey.

Along with the rise of this system of explaining the operations of nature by analogies in the bestial world, another conclusion forced itself on the untaught mind. The flocks which strayed in heaven were no earthly sheep, but were the property of spiritual beings, and were themselves perhaps spiritual; the swans which flew aloft, far above the topmost peak of the Himalaya, were no ordinary swans, but were divine and heavenly. The wolf which howled so wildly in the long winter night, the hounds, whose bay sounded so. dismally through the shaking black forest, were no mundane wolves and hounds, but issued from the home of a divine hunter, and were themselves wondrous, supernatural beings of godlike race.

And so, the clouds having become swans, the swan-clouds were next believed to be divine beings, valkyries, apsaras, and the like, seen by mortals in their feather-dresses, but appearing among the gods as damsels. The storm-wind having been supposed to be a wolf, next was taken to be a tempestuous god, who delighted to hunt on earth in lupine form.

I have mentioned also the serpent shape, as being one very favourite in mythology. The ancient people saw the forked and writhing lightning, and supposed it to be a heavenly fiery serpent, a serpent which had godlike powers, which was in fact a divine being, manifesting himself to mortals under that form. Among the North American Indians, the lightning is still regarded as the great serpent, and the thunder is supposed to be his hissing.

"Ah!" exclaimed a Magdeburg peasant to a German professor, during a thunder-storm, as a vivid forked gleam shot to earth, "what a glorious snake was that!" And this resemblance did not escape the Greeks.

{Greek _é!likes d? e?kłmpousi steroph~s kspuroi_}.

Asch. Prom. 1064.

{Greek _drkonta pursünwton, ü!s·?platon a?mfeliktÚs é!lik? e?fro rei, ktanw'n_}.
Eurip. Herc. F. 395.

And according to Aristotle, {Greek _e!likÌai_} are the lightnings, {Greek _grammoeidw~s ferümenoi_}.

It is so difficult for us to unlearn all we know of the nature of meteorological phenomena, so hard for us to look upon atmospheric changes as though we knew nothing of the laws that govern them, that we are disposed to treat such explanations of popular myths as I have given above, as fantastic and improbable.

But among the ancients all solutions of natural problems were tentative, and it is only after the failure of every attempt made to explain these phenomena on supernatural grounds that we have been driven to the discovery of the true interpretation. Yet among the vulgar a vast amount of mythology remains, and is used still to explain atmospheric mysteries. The other day a Yorkshire girl, when asked why she was not afraid of thunder, replied because it was only her Father's voice; what knew she of the rushing together of air to fill the vacuum caused by the transit of the electric fluid? to her the thunder-clap was the utterance of the Almighty. Still in North Germany does the peasant say of thunder, that the angels are playing skittles aloft, and of the snow, that they are shaking up the feather-beds in heaven.

The myth of the dragon is one which admits, perhaps more than any other, of identification with a meteorological phenomenon, and presents to us as well the phase of transition from theriomorphosis to anthropomorphosis.

The dragon of popular mythology is nothing else than the thunderstorm, rising at the horizon, rushing with expanded, winnowing, black pennons across the sky, darting out its forked fiery tongue, and belching fire. In a Slovakian legend, the dragon sleeps in a mountain cave through the winter months, but, at the equinox, bursts forth—"In a moment the heaven was darkened and became black as pitch, only illumined by the fire which flashed from dragon's jaws and eyes. The earth shuddered, the stones rattled down the mountain sides into the glens. Right and left, left and right, did the dragon lash his tail, overthrowing pines and beeches, snapping them as rods. He evacuated such floods of water that the mountain torrents were full. But after a while his power was exhausted, he lashed no more with his tail, ejected no more water, and spat no more fire."

I think it is impossible not to see in this description, a spring-tide thunderstorm. But to make it more evident that the untaught mind did regard such a storm as a dragon, I think the following quotation from *John of Brompton's Chronicle* will convince the most sceptical: "Another remarkable thing is this, that took place during a certain month in the Gulf of Satalia (on the coast of Pamphylia). There appeared a great and black dragon which came in clouds, and let down his head into the water, whilst his tail seemed turned to the sky; and the dragon drew the water to him by drinking, with such avidity, that, if any ship, even though laden with men or any other heavy articles, had been near him when drinking, it would nevertheless have been sucked up and carried on high. In order however to avoid this danger, it is necessary, when people see it, at once to make a great uproar, and to shout and hammer tables, so that the dragon, hearing the noise, and the voices of those shouting, may withdraw himself far off. Some people, however, assert that this is not a dragon, but the sun drawing up the waters of the sea; which seems more probable." [1] Such is John of Brompton's account of a waterspout. In Greek mythology the dragon of the storm has begun to undergo anthropomorphosis. Typhus is the son of Tartarus and Terra; the storm rising from the horizon may well be supposed to issue from the earth's womb, and its characteristics are sufficient to decide its paternity. Typhus, the whirlwind or typhoon, has a hundred dragon or serpent heads, the long writhing strive of vapour which run before the hurricane cloud. He belches fire, that is, lightnings issue from the clouds, and his roaring is like the howling of wild dogs. Typhus ascends to heaven to make war on the gods, who fly from him in various fantastic shapes; who cannot see in this ascent the hurricane climbing up the vault of sky, and in the flying gods, the many fleeting fragments of white cloud which are seen drifting across the heavens before the gale!

[1. Apud TWYSDEN, Hist. Anglicé Script. x. 1652. p. 1216.]

Typhus, according to Hesiod, is the father of all bad winds, which destroy with rain and tempest, all in fact which went among the Greeks by the name of {Greek *laĺlaps*}, bringing injury to the agriculturist and peril to the voyager.

{Greek _?Ek dË Tufwéos é?st? a?némwn ménos u!grÚn ·?eptwn, nüsfi Nütou Boréw te, kaÏ a?rgéstew Zef'rou te. oÌ! ge mËn e?n æeüfin geneh', ænhtoÔs még? ü?neiar. ai! d? ·?llai mapsau~rai e?pipneÌousi æalassan. ai! d? h?'toi pÌptousai e?s heroeide· pünton, ph~ma méga ænhtoi~si, kakh~j æ·ousin a?éllhj. ·?llote d? ·?llai a?eÌsi, diaskidna~si te nh~as, na·tas te fæeÌrousi. kakou~ d? ou? gÌgnetai a?lkh' a?ndrsin, oÌ! keÌnhjsi sin·ntwntai kat‡ pünton. ai! d? a°? kaÏ kat‡ gai~an a?peÌriton, a?næemüessan é?rg? e?rat‡ fæeÌrousi xamaigenéwn a?nærw'pwn, pimpleu~sai küniüs te kaÏ a?rgaléou kolosurtou~ _ }

Hesiod. Theog. 870, _seq._

In both modern Greek and Lithuanian household mythology the dragon or drake has become an ogre, a gigantic man with few of the dracontine attributes remaining. Von Hahn, in his *Griechische und Albanesische Mœrchen*, tells many tales of drakes, and in all, the old characteristics have been lost, and the drake is simply a gigantic man with magical and superhuman powers.

It is the same among the Lithuanian peasantry. A dragon walks on two legs, talks, flirts with a lady, and marries her. He retains his evil disposition, but has sloughed off his scales and wings.

Such is the change which has taken place in the popular conception of the dragon, which is an impersonification of the thunderstorm. A similar change has taken place in the swan-maiden and were-wolf myths.

In ancient Indian Vedaic mythology the apsaras were heavenly damsels who dwelt in the tether, between earth and sun. Their name, which signifies "the shapeless," or "those who go in the water "—it is uncertain which. is the correct derivation—is expressive of the white cirrus, constantly changing form, and apparently floating swan-like on the blue heaven-sea. These apsaras, according to the Vedaic creed, were fond of changing their shapes, appearing generally as ducks or swans, occasionally as human beings. The souls of heroes were given to them for lovers and husbands. One of the most graceful of the early Indian myths is the story of the apsaras, Urvaåø. Urvaåø loved Puravaras and became his 'wife, on the condition that she was n-ever to behold him in a state of nudity. They remained together for years, till the heavenly companions of Urvaåø determined to secure her return to them. They accordingly beguiled Puravaras into leaving his bed in the darkness of night, and then with a lightning flash they disclosed him, in his nudity, to his wife, who was thereupon constrained to leave him. He pursued her, full of sorrow at his loss, and found her at length swimming in a large lotus pond, in swan's shape.

That this story is not a mere invention, but rests on some mythological explanation of natural phenomena, I think more than probable, as it is found all over the world with few variations. As every Aryan branch retains the story, or traces of it, there can be no doubt that the belief in swan-maidens, who swam in the heavenly sea, and who sometimes became the wives of those fortunate men who managed to steal from them their feather dresses, formed an integral portion of the old mythological system of the Aryan family, before it was broken up into Indian, Persian, Greek, Latin, Russian, Scandinavian, Teutonic, and other races. But more, as the same myth is found. in tribes not Aryan, and far removed from contact with European or Indian superstition,—as, for instance, among Samoyeds and American Indians,—it is even possible that this story may be a tradition of the first priméval stock of men.

But it is time for me to leave the summer cirrus and turn to the tempest-born rain-cloud. It is represented in ancient Indian mythology by the Vritra or R,kshasas. At first the form of these démons was uncertain and obscure. Vritra is often used as an appellative for a cloud, and kabhanda, an old name for a rain-cloud, in later times became the name of a devil. Of Vritra, who envelopes the mountains with vapour, it is said, "The darkness stood retaining the water, the mountains lay in the belly of Vritra." By degrees Vritra stood out more prominently as a démon, and he is described as a "devourer" of gigantic proportions. In the same way R,kshasas obtained corporeal form and individuality. He is a misshapen giant "like to a cloud," with a red beard and red hair, with pointed protruding teeth, ready to lacerate and devour human flesh. His body is covered with coarse bristling hair, his huge mouth is open, he looks from side to side as he walks, lusting after the flesh and blood of men, to satisfy his raging hunger, and quench his consuming thirst. Towards nightfall his strength increases manifold. He can change his shape at will. He haunts the woods, and roams howling through the jungle; in short, he is to the Hindoo what the were-wolf is to the European.

A certain wood was haunted by a R,kschasa; he one day came across a Brahmin, and with a bound reached his shoulders, and clung to them, exclaiming, "Heh! go on with you!" And the Brahmin, quaking with fear, advanced with him. But when he observed that the feet of the R,kschasa were as delicate as the stamens of the lotus, he asked him, How is it that you have such weak and slender feet? The R,kschasa replied, "I never walk nor touch the earth with my feet. I have made a vow not to do so." Presently they came to a large pond. Then the R,kschasa bade the Brahmin wait at the edge whilst he bathed and prayed to the gods. But the Brahmin thought: "As soon as these prayers and ablutions are over, he will tear me to pieces with his fangs and eat me. He has vowed not to walk; I will be off post haste!" so he ran away, and the R,kschasa dared not follow him for fear of breaking his VOW. (*Pantschatantra*, v. 13.) There is a similar story in the Mah,bh,rata, xiii., and in the Kath, Sarit S,gara, v. 49-53.

I have said sufficient to show that natural phenomena gave rise to mythological stories, and that these stories have gradually deteriorated, and have been degraded into vulgar superstitions. And I have shown that both the doctrine of metempsychosis and the mythological explanations of meteorological changes have given rise to abundant fable, and among others to the popular and widespread superstition of lycanthropy. I shall now pass from myth to history, and shall give instances of bloodthirstiness, cruelty, and cannibalism.

CHAPTER XI

THE MAR...CHAL DE RETZ.-I. THE INVESTIGATION OF CHARGES

The history of the man whose name heads this chapter I purpose giving in detail, as the circumstances I shall narrate have, I believe, never before been given with accuracy to the English public. The name of Gilles de Laval may be well known, as sketches of his bloody career have appeared in many biographies, but these sketches have been very incomplete, as the material from which they were composed was meagre. M. Michelet alone ventured to give the public an idea of the crimes which brought a marshal of France to the gallows, and his revelations were such that, in the words of M. Henri

Martin, "this iron age, which seemed unable to feel surprise at any amount of evil, was struck with dismay."

M. Michelet derived his information from the abstract of the papers relating, to the case, made by order of Ann of Brittany, in the Imperial Library. The original documents were in the library at Nantes, and a great portion of them were destroyed in the Revolution of 1789. But a careful analysis had been made of them, and this valuable abridgment, which was inaccessible to M. Michelet, came into the hands of M. Lacroix, the eminent French antiquarian, who published a memoir of the marshal from the information he had thus obtained, and it is his work, by far the most complete and circumstantial which has appeared, that I condense into the following chapters.

"The most monstrously depraved imagination," says M. Henri Martin, "never could have conceived what the trial reveals." M. Lacroix has been obliged to draw a veil over much that transpired, and I must draw it closer still. I have, however, said enough to show that this memorable trial presents horrors probably unsurpassed in the whole volume of the world's history.

During the year 1440, a terrible rumour spread through Brittany, and especially through the ancient *pays de Retz*, which extends along the south of the Loire from Nantes to Paimbuf, to the effect that one of the most famous and powerful noblemen in Brittany, Gilles de Laval, Maréchal de Retz, was guilty of crimes of the most diabolical nature.

Gilles de Laval, eldest son of Gay de Laval, second of his name, Sire de Retz, had raised the junior branch of the illustrious house of Laval above the elder branch, which was related to the reigning family of Brittany. He lost his father when he was aged twenty, and remained master of a vast territorial inheritance, which was increased by his marriage with Catharine de Thouars in 1420. He employed a portion of their fortune in the cause of Charles VII., and in strengthening the French crown. During seven consecutive years, from 1426 to 1433, he was engaged in military enterprises against the English; his name is always cited along with those of Dunois, Xaintrailles, Florent d'Illiers, Gaucourt, Richemont, and the most faithful servants of the king. His services were speedily acknowledged by the king creating him Marshal of France. In 1427, he assaulted the Castle of Lude, and carried it by storm; he killed with his own hand the commander of the place; next year he captured from the English the fortress of Rennefort, and the Castle of Malicorne; in 1429, he took an active part in the expedition of Joan of Arc for the deliverance of Orleans, and the occupation of Jargeau, and he was with her in the moat, when she was wounded by an arrow under the walls of Paris.

The marshal, councillor, and chamberlain of the king participated in the direction of public affairs, and soon obtained the entire confidence of his master. He accompanied Charles to Rheims on the occasion of his coronation, and had the honour of bearing the oriflamme, brought for the occasion from the abbey of St. Remi. His intrepidity on the field of battle was as remarkable as his sagacity in council, and he proved himself to be both an excellent warrior and a shrewd politician.

Suddenly, to the surprise of every one, he quitted the service of Charles VII., and sheathed for ever his sword, in the retirement of the country. The death of his maternal grandfather, Jean de Craon, in 1432, made him so enormously wealthy, that his revenues were estimated at 800,000 livres; nevertheless, in two years, by his excessive prodigality, he managed to lose a considerable portion of his inheritance. Mauléon, St. Etienne de Malemort, Loroux-Botereau, Pornic, and Chantolé, he sold to John V., Duke of Brittany, his kinsman, and other lands and seigneurial rights he ceded to the Bishop of Nantes, and to the chapter of the cathedral in that city.

The rumour soon spread that these extensive cessions of territory were sops thrown to the duke and to the bishop, to restrain the one from confiscating his goods, and the other from pronouncing excommunication, for the crimes of which the people whisperingly accused him; but these rumours were probably without foundation, for eventually it was found hard to persuade the duke of the guilt of his kinsman, and the bishop was the most determined instigator of the trial.

The marshal seldom visited the ducal court, but he often appeared in the city of Nantes, where he inhabited the Hùtel de la Suze, with a princely retinue. He had, always accompanying him, a guard of two hundred men at arms, and a numerous suit of pages, esquires, chaplains, singers, astrologers, &c., all of whom he paid handsomely.

Whenever he left the town, or moved to one of his other seats, the cries of the poor, which had been restrained during the time of his presence, broke forth. Tears flowed, curses were uttered, a long-continued wail rose to heaven, the moment that the last of the marshal's party had left the neighbourhood. Mothers had lost their children, babes had been snatched from the cradle, infants had been spirited away almost from the maternal arms, and it was known by sad experience that the vanished little ones would never be seen again.

But on no part of the country did the shadow of this great fear fall so deeply as on the villages in the neighbourhood of the Castle of Machecoul, a gloomy ch,teau, composed of huge towers, and surrounded by deep moats, a residence much frequented by Do Retz, notwithstanding its sombre and repulsive appearance. This fortress was always in a condition to resist a siege: the drawbridge was raised, the portcullis down, the gates closed, the men under arms, the culverins on the bastion always loaded. No one, except the servants, had penetrated into this mysterious asylum and had come forth alive. In the surrounding country strange tales of horror and devilry circulated in whispers, and yet it was observed that the chapel of the castle was gorgeously decked with tapestries of silk and cloth of gold, that the sacred vessels were encrusted with gems, and that the vestments of the priests were of the most sumptuous character. The excessive devotion of the marshal was also noticed; he was said to hear mass thrice daily, and to be passionately fond of ecclesiastical music. He was said to have asked permission of the pope, that a crucifer should precede him in processions. But when dusk settled down over the forest, and one by one the windows of the castle became illumined, peasants would point to one casement high up in an isolated tower, from which a clear light streamed through the gloom of night; they spoke of a fierce red glare which irradiated the chamber at times, and of sharp cries ringing out of it, through the hushed woods, to be answered only by the howl of the wolf as it rose from its lair to begin its nocturnal rambles.

On certain days, at fixed hours, the drawbridge sank, and the servants of De Retz stood in the gateway distributing clothes, money, and food to the mendicants who crowded round them soliciting alms. It often happened that children were among the beggars: as often one of the servants would promise them some dainty if they would go to the kitchen for it. Those children who accepted the offer were never seen again.

In 1440 the long-pent-up exasperation of the people broke all bounds, and with one voice they charged the marshal with the murder of their children, whom they said he had sacrificed to the devil.

This charge came to the ears of the Duke of Brittany, but he pooh-poohed it, and would have taken no steps to investigate the truth, had not one of his nobles insisted on his doing so. At the same time Jean do Ch,teaugiron, bishop of Nantes, and the noble and sage Pierre de l'Hospital, grand-seneschal of Brittany, wrote to the duke, expressing very decidedly their views, that the charge demanded thorough investigation.

John V., reluctant to move against a relation, a man who had served his country so well, and was in such a high position, at last yielded to their request, and authorized them to seize the persons of the Sire de Retz and his accomplices. A *serjent d'armes*, Jean Labbé, was charged with this difficult commission. He picked a band of resolute fellows, twenty in all, and in the middle of September they presented themselves at the gate of the castle, and summoned the Sire do Retz to surrender. As soon as Gilles heard that a troop in the livery of Brittany was at the gate, he inquired who was their leader? On receiving the answer "Labbé," he started, turned pale, crossed himself, and prepared to surrender, observing that it was impossible to resist fate.

Years before, one of his astrologers had assured him that he would one day pass into the hands of an Abbé, and, till this moment, De Retz had supposed that the prophecy signified that he should eventually become a monk.

Gilles de Sillé, Roger de Briqueville, and other of the accomplices of the marshal, took to flight, but Henriet and Pontou remained with him.

The drawbridge was lowered and the marshal offered his sword to Jean Labbé. The gallant serjeant approached, knelt to the marshal, and unrolled before him a parchment sealed with the seal of Brittany.

"Tell me the tenor of this parchment?" said Gilles de Retz with dignity.

"Our good Sire of Brittany enjoins you, my lord, by these presents, to follow me to the good town of Nantes, there to clear yourself of certain criminal charges brought against you."

"I will follow immediately, my friend, glad to obey the will of my lord of Brittany: but, that it may not be said that the Seigneur de Retz has received a message without largess, I order my treasurer, Henriet, to hand over to you and your followers twenty gold crowns."

"Grand-merci, monseigneur! I pray God that he may give you good and long life."

"Pray God only to have mercy upon me, and to pardon my sins."

The marshal had his horses saddled, and left Machecoul with Pontou and Henriet, who had thrown in their lot with him.

It was with lively emotion that the people in the villages traversed by the little troop, saw the redoubted Gilles de Laval ride through their streets, surrounded by soldiers in the livery of the Duke of Brittany, and unaccompanied by a single soldier of his own. The roads and streets were thronged, peasants left the fields, women their kitchens, labourers deserted their cattle at the plough, to throng the road to Nantes. The cavalcade proceeded in silence. The very crowd which had gathered to see it, was hushed. Presently a shrill woman's voice was raised:—

"My child! restore my child!"

Then a wild, wrathful howl broke from the lips of the throng, rang along the Nantes road, and only died away, as the great gates of the Chateau de Bouffay closed on the prisoner.

The whole population of Nantes was in commotion, and it was said that the investigation would be fictitious, that the duke would screen his kinsman, and that the object of general execration would escape with the surrender of some of his lands.

And such would probably have been the event of the trial, had not the Bishop of Nantes and the grand-seneschal taken a very decided course in the matter. They gave the duke no peace till he had yielded to their demand for a thorough investigation and a public trial.

John V. nominated Jean de Toucheronde to collect information, and to take down the charges brought against the marshal. At the same time he was given to understand that the matter was not to be pressed, and that the charges upon which the marshal was to be tried were to be softened down as much as possible.

The commissioner, Jean de Toucheronde, opened the investigation on the 18th September, assisted only by his clerk, Jean Thomas. The witnesses were introduced either singly, or in groups, if they were relations. On entering, the witness knelt before the commissioner, kissed the crucifix, and swore with his hand on the Gospels that he would speak the truth, and nothing but the truth: after this he related all the facts referring to the charge, which came under his cognizance, without being interrupted or interrogated.

The first to present herself was Perrine Loessard, living at la Roche-Bernard.

She related, with tears in her eyes, that two years ago, in the month of September, the Sire de Retz had passed with all his retinue through la Roche-Bernard, on his way from Vannes, and had lodged with Jean Collin. She lived opposite the house in which the nobleman was staying.

Her child, the finest in the village, a lad aged ten, had attracted the notice of Pontou, and perhaps of the marshal himself, who stood at a window, leaning on his squire's shoulder.

Pontou spoke to the child, and asked him whether he would like to be a chorister; the boy replied that his ambition was to be a soldier.

"Well, then," said the squire, "I will equip you."

The lad then laid hold of Pontou's dagger, and expressed his desire to have such a weapon in his belt. Thereupon the mother had ran up and had made him leave hold of the dagger, saying that the boy was doing very well at school, and was getting on with his letters, for he was one day to be a monk. Pontou had dissuaded her from this project, and had proposed to take the child with him to Machecoul, and to educate him to be a soldier. Thereupon he had paid her clown a hundred sols to buy the lad a dress, and had obtained permission to carry him off.

Next day her son had been mounted on a horse purchased for him from Jean Collin, and had left the village in the retinue of the Sire de Retz. The poor mother at parting had gone in tears to the marshal, and had entreated him to be kind to her child. From that time she had been able to obtain no information regarding her son. She had watched the Sire de Retz whenever he had passed through La Roche Bernard, but had never observed her child among his pages. She had questioned several of the marshal's people, but they had laughed at her; the only answer she had obtained was: "Be not afraid. He is either at Machecoul, or else at Tiffauges, or else at Pornic, or somewhere." Perrine's story was corroborated by Jean Collin, his wife, and his mother-in-law.

Jean Lemegren and his wife, Alain Dulix, Perrot Duponest, Guillaume Guillon, Guillaume Portayer, Etienne de Monclades, and Jean Lefebure, all inhabitants of St. Etienne de Montluc, deposed that a little child, son of Guillaume Brice of the said parish, having lost his father at the age of nine, lived on alms, and went round the country begging.

This child, named Jamet, had vanished suddenly at midsummer, and nothing was known of what had become of him; but strong suspicions were entertained of his having been carried off by an aged hag who had appeared shortly before in the neighbourhood, and who had vanished along with the child.

On the 27th September, Jean de Toucheronde, assisted by Nicolas Chateau, notary of the court at Nantes, received the depositions of several inhabitants of Pont-de-Launay, near Bouvron: to wit, Guillaume Fourage and wife; Jeanne, wife of Jean Leflou; and Richarde, wife of Jean Gandeau.

These depositions, though very vague, afforded sufficient cause for suspicion to rest on the marshal. Two years before, a child of twelve, son of Jean Bernard, and another child of the same age, son of Ménégué, had gone to Machecoul. The son of Ménégué had returned alone in the evening, relating that his companion had asked him to wait for him on the road whilst he begged at the gates of the Sire de Retz. The son of Ménégué said that he had waited three hours, but his companion had not returned. The wife of Guillaume Fourage deposed that she had seen the lad at this time with an old hag, who was leading him by the hand towards Machecoul. That same evening this hag passed over the bridge of Launay, and the wife of Fourage asked her what had become of little Bernard. The old woman neither stopped nor answered further than by saying he was well provided for. The boy had not been seen since. On the 28th September, the Duke of Brittany joined another commissioner, Jean Couppegorge, and a second notary, Michel Estallure, to Toucheronde and Chateau.

The inhabitants of Machecoul, a little town over which the Sire de Retz exercised supreme power, appeared now to depose against their lord. André Barbier, shoemaker, declared that last Easter, a child, son of his neighbour Georges Lebarbier, had disappeared. He was last seen gathering plums behind the hotel Rondeau. This disappearance surprised none in Machecoul, and no one ventured to comment on it. André and his wife were in daily terror of losing their own child. They had been a pilgrimage to St. Jean d'Angely, and had been asked there whether it was the custom at Machecoul to eat children. On their return they had heard of two children having vanished—the son of Jean Gendron, and that of Alexandre Ch,tellier. André Barbier had made some inquiries about the circumstances of their disappearance, and had been advised to hold his tongue, and to shut his ears and eyes, unless he were prepared to be thrown into a dungeon by the lord of Machecoul.

"But, bless me!" he had said, "am I to believe that a fairy spirits off and eats our little ones?"

"Believe what you like," was the advice given to him; "but ask no questions." As this conversation had taken place, one of the marshal's men at arms had passed, when all those who had been speaking took to their heels. André, who had run with the rest, without knowing exactly why he fled, came upon a man near the church of the Holy Trinity, who was weeping bitterly, and crying out,—"O my God, wilt Thou not restore to me my little one?" This man had also been robbed of his child.

Licette, wife of Guillaume Sergent, living at La BoneardiÉre, in the parish of St. Croix de Machecoul, had lost her son two years before, and had not seen him since; she besought the commissioners, with tears in her eyes, to restore him to her.

"I left him," said she, "at home whilst I went into the field with my husband to sow flax. He was a bonny little lad, and he was as good as he was bonny. He had to look after his tiny sister, who was a year and a half old. On my return home, the little girl was found, but she could not tell me what had become of him. Afterwards we found in the marsh a small red woollen cap which had belonged to my poor darling; but it was in vain that we dragged the marsh, nothing was found more, except good evidence that he had not been drowned. A hawker who sold needles and thread passed through Machecoul at the time, and told me that an old woman in grey, with a black hood on her head, had bought of him some children's toys, and had a few moments after passed him, leading a little boy by the hand."

Georges Lebarbier, living near the gate of the ch,telet de Machecoul, gave an account of the manner in which his son had evanesced. The boy was apprenticed to Jean Pelletier, tailor to Mme. de Retz and to the household of the castle. He seemed to be getting on in his profession, when last year, about St. Barnabas' day, he went to play at ball on the castle green. He never returned from the game.

This youth and his master, Jean Pelletier, had been in the habit of eating and drinking at the castle, and bad always laughed at the ominous stories told by the people.

Guillaume Hilaire and his wife confirmed the statements of Lebarbier. They also said that they knew of the loss of the sons of Jean Gendron, Jeanne Rouen, and Alexandre Ch,tellier. The son of Jean Gendron, aged twelve, lived with the said Hilaire and learned of him the trade of skinner. He had been working in the shop for seven or eight years, and was a steady, hardworking lad. One day Messieurs Gilles de Sillé and Roger de Briqueville entered the shop to purchase a pair of hunting gloves. They asked if little Gendron might take a message for them to the castle. Hilaire readily consented, and the boy received beforehand the payment for going—a gold angelus, and he started, promising to be back directly. But he had never returned. That evening Hiliare and his wife, observing Gilles de Sillé and Roger de Briqueville returning to the castle, ran to them and asked what had become of the apprentice. They replied that they had no notion of where he was, as they had been absent hunting, but that it was possible he might have been sent to Tiffauges, another castle of De Retz.

Guillaume Hilaire, whose depositions were more grave and explicit than the others, positively asserted that Jean Dujardin, valet to Roger de Briqueville had told him he knew of a cask secreted in the castle, full of children's corpses. He said that he had often heard people say that children were enticed to the ch,teau and then murdered, but had treated it as an idle tale. He said, moreover, that the marshal was not accused of having any hand in the murders, but that his servants were supposed to be guilty.

Jean Gendron himself deposed to the loss of his son, and he added that his was not the only child which had vanished mysteriously at Machecoul. He knew of thirty that had disappeared.

Jean Chipholon, elder and junior, Jean Aubin, and Clement Doré, all inhabitants of the parish of Thomage, deposed that they had known a poor man of the same parish, named Mathelin Thomas, who had lost his son, aged twelve, and that he had died of grief in consequence.

Jeanne Rouen, of Machecoul, who for nine years had been in a state of uncertainty whether her son were alive or dead, deposed that the child had been carried off whilst keeping sheep. She had thought that he had been devoured of wolves, but two women of Machecoul, now deceased, had seen Gilles de Sillé approach the little shepherd, speak to him, and point to the castle. Shortly after the lad had walked off in that direction. The husband of Jeanne Rouen went to the ch,teau to inquire after his son, but could obtain no information. When next Gilles de Sillé appeared in the town, the disconsolate mother entreated him to restore her child to her. Gilles replied that he knew nothing about him, as he had been to the king at Amboise.

Jeanne, widow of Aymery Hedelin, living at Machecoul, had also lost, eight years before, a little child as he had pursued some butterflies into the wood. At the same time four other children had been carried off, those of Gendron, Rouen, and Macé Sorin. She said that the story circulated through the country was, that Gilles de Sillé stole children to make them over to the English, in order to obtain the ransom of his brother who was a captive. But she added that this report was traced to the servants of Sillé, and that it was propagated by them.

One of the last children to disappear was that of Noîl Aise, living in the parish of St. Croix.

A man from Tiffauges had said to her (Jeanne Hedelin) that for one child stolen at Machecoul, there were seven carried away at Tiffauges.

Macé Sorin confirmed the deposition of the widow Hedelin., and repeated the circumstances connected with the loss of the children of Ch,tellier, Rouen, Gendron, and Lebarbier.

Perrine Rondeau had entered the castle with the company of Jean Labbé. She had entered a stable, and had found a heap of ashes and powder, which had a sickly and peculiar smell. At the bottom of a trough she had found a child's shirt covered with blood.

Several inhabitants of the bourg of Fresnay, to wit, Perrot, Parqueteau, Jean Soreau, Catherine Degrépie, Gilles Garnier, Perrine Viellard, Marguerite Rediern, Marie Carfin, Jeanne Laudais, said that they had heard Guillaume Hamelin, last Easter, lamenting the loss of two children.

Isabeau, wife of Guillaume Hamelin, confirmed these depositions, saving that she had lost them seven years before. She had at that time four children; the eldest aged fifteen, the youngest aged seven, went together to Machecoul to buy some bread, but they did not return. She sat up for them all night and next morning. She heard that another child had been lost, the son of Michaut Bonnel of St. Ciré de Retz.

Guillemette, wife of Michaut Bonnel, said that her son had been carried off whilst guarding cows.

Guillaume Rodigo and his wife, living at Bourg-neuf-en-Retz, deposed that on the eve of last St. Bartholomew's day, the Sire do Retz lodged with Guillaume Plumet in his village.

Pontou, who accompanied the marshal, saw a lad of fifteen, named Bernard Lecanino, servant to Rodigo, standing at the door of his house. The lad could not speak much French, but only bas-Breton. Pontou beckoned to him and spoke to him in a low tone. That evening, at ten o'clock, Bernard left his master's house, Rodigo and his wife being absent. The servant maid, who saw him go out, called to him that the supper table was not yet cleared, but he paid no attention to what she said. Rodigo, annoyed at the loss of his servant, asked some of the marshal's men what had become of him. They replied mockingly that they knew nothing of the little Breton, but that he had probably been sent to Tiffauges to be trained as page to their lord.

Marguerite Sorain, the chambermaid alluded to above, confirmed the statement of Rodigo, adding that Pontou had entered the house and spoken with Bernard. Guillaume Plumet and wife confirmed what Rodigo and Sorain had said.

Thomas Aysée and wife deposed to the loss of their son, aged ten, who had gone to beg at the gate of the castle of Machecoul; and a little girl had seen him drawn by an offer of meat into the ch,teau.

Jamette, wife of Eustache Drouet of St. Léger, had sent two sons, one aged ten, the other seven, to the castle to obtain alms. They had not been seen since.

On the 2nd October the commissioners sat again, and the charges became graver, and the servants of the marshal became more and more implicated.

The disappearance of thirteen other children was substantiated under circumstances throwing strong suspicion on the inmates of the castle. I will not give the details, for they much resemble those of the former depositions. Suffice it to say that before the commissioners closed the inquiry, a herald of the Duke of Brittany in tabard blew three calls on the trumpet, from the steps of the tower of Bouffay, summoning all who had additional charges to bring against the Sire de Retz, to present themselves without delay. As no fresh witnesses arrived, the case was considered to be made out, and the commissioners visited the duke, with the information they had collected, in their hands.

The duke hesitated long as to the steps he should take. Should he judge and sentence a kinsman, the most powerful of his vassals, the bravest of his captains, a councillor of the king, a marshal of France?

Whilst still unsettled in his mind as to the course he should pursue, he received a letter from Gilles de Retz, which produced quite a different effect from that which it had been intended to produce.

"MONSIEUR MY COUSIN AND HONOURED SIRE,—

"IT is quite true that I am perhaps the most detestable of all sinners, having sinned horribly again and again, yet have I never failed in my religious duties. I have heard many masses, vespers, &c., have fasted in Lent and on vigils, have confessed my sins, deploring them heartily, and have received the blood of our Lord at least once in the year.

Since I have been languishing in prison, awaiting your honoured justice, I have been overwhelmed with incomparable repentance for my crimes, which I am ready to acknowledge and to expiate as is suitable.

"Wherefore I supplicate you, M. my cousin, to give me licence to retire into a monastery, and there to lead a good and exemplary life. I care not into what monastery I am sent, but I intend that all my goods, &c., should be distributed among the poor, who are the members of Jesus Christ on earth . . . . Awaiting your glorious clemency, on which I rely, I pray God our Lord to protect you and your kingdom.

He who addresses you is in all earthly humility,"

"FRIAR GILLES, Carmelite in intention."

The duke read this letter to Pierre de l'Hospital, president of Brittany, and to the Bishop of Nantes, who were those most resolute in pressing on the trial. They were horrified at the tone of this dreadful communication, and assured the duke that the case was so clear, and the steps taken had been so decided, that it was impossible for him to allow De Retz to escape trial by such an impious device as he suggested. In the meantime, the bishop and the grand-seneschal had set on foot an investigation at the castle of Machecoul, and had found numerous traces of human remains. But a complete examination could not be made, as the duke was anxious to screen his kinsman as much as possible, and refused to authorize one.

The duke now summoned his principal officers and held a council with them. They unanimously sided with the bishop and de l'Hospital, and when John still hesitated, the Bishop of Nantes rose and said: "Monseigneur, this case is one for the church as much as for your court to take up. Consequently, if your President of Brittany does not bring the case into secular court, by the Judge of heaven and earth! I will cite the author of these execrable crimes to appear before our ecclesiastical tribunal."

The resolution of the bishop compelled the duke to yield, and it was decided that the trial should take its course without let or hindrance.

In the meantime, the unhappy wife of Gilles de Retz, who had been separated from him for some while, and who loathed his crimes, though she still felt for him as her husband, hurried to the duke with her daughter to entreat pardon for the wretched man. But the duke refused to hear her. Thereupon she went to Amboise to intercede with the king for him who bad once been his close friend and adviser.

CHAPTER XII

THE MAR...CHAL DE RETZ.—II. THE TRIAL

On the 10th October, Nicolas Chateau, notary of the duke, went to the Ch,teau of Bouffay, to read to the prisoner the summons to appear in person on the morrow before Messire de l'Hospital, President of Brittany, Seneschal of Rennes, and Chief Justice of the Duchy of Brittany.

The Sire de Retz, who believed himself already a novice in the Carmelite order, had dressed in white, and was engaged in singing litanies. When the summons had been read, he ordered a page to give the notary wine and cake, and then he returned to his prayers with every appearance of compunction and piety.

On the morrow Jean Labbé and four soldiers conducted him to the hall of justice. He asked for Pontou and Henriet to accompany him, but this was not permitted.

He was adorned with all his military insignia, as though to impose on his judges; he had around his neck massive chains of gold, and several collars of knightly orders. His costume, with the exception of his purpoint, was white, in token of his repentance. His purpoint was of pearl-grey silk, studded with gold stars, and girded around his waist by a scarlet belt, from which dangled a poignard in scarlet velvet sheath. His collar, cufs, and the edging of his purpoint were of white ermine, his little round cap or *chapel* was white, surrounded with a belt of ermine—a fur which only the great feudal lords of Brittany had a right to wear. All the rest of his dress, to the shoes which were long and pointed, was white.

No one at a first glance would have thought the Sire do Retz to be by nature so cruel and vicious as he was supposed to be. On the contrary, his physiognomy was calm and phlegmatic, somewhat pale, and expressive of melancholy. His hair and moustache were light brown, and his beard was clipped to a point. This beard, which resembled no other beard, was black, but under certain lights it assumed a blue hue, and it was this peculiarity which obtained for the Sire do Retz the surname of Blue-beard, a name which has attached to him in popular romance, at the same time that his story has undergone strange metamorphoses.

But on closer examination of the countenance of Gilles de Retz, contraction in the muscles of the face, nervous quivering of the mouth, spasmodic twitchings of the brows, and above all, the sinister expression of the eyes, showed that there was something strange and frightful in the man. At intervals he ground his teeth like a wild beast preparing to dash upon his prey, and then his lips became so contracted, as they were drawn in and glued, as it were, to his teeth, that their very colour was indiscernible.

At times also his eyes became fixed, and the pupils dilated to such an extent, with a sombre fire quivering in them, that the iris seemed to fill the whole orbit, which became circular, and sank back into the head. At these moments his complexion became livid and cadaverous; his brow, especially just over the nose, was covered with deep wrinkles, and his beard appeared to bristle, and to assume its bluish hues. But, after a few moments, his features became again serene, with a sweet smile reposing upon them, and his expression relaxed into a vague and tender melancholy.

"Messires," said he, saluting his judges, "I pray you to expedite my matter, and despatch as speedily as possible my unfortunate case; for I am peculiarly anxious to consecrate myself to the service of God, who has pardoned my great sins. I shall not fail, I assure you, to endow several of the churches in Nantes, and I shall distribute the greater portion of my goods among the poor, to secure the salvation of my soul."

"Monseigneur," replied gravely Pierre de l'Hospital: "It is always well to think of the salvation of one's soul; but, if you please, think now that we are concerned with the salvation of your body."

"I have confessed to the father superior of the Carmelites," replied the marshal, with tranquillity; "and through his absolution I have been able to communicate: I am, therefore, guiltless and purified."

"Men's justice is not in common with that of God, monseigneur, and I cannot tell you what will be your sentence. Be ready to make your defence, and listen to the charges brought against you, which M. le lieutenant du Procureur de Nantes will read."

The officer rose, and read the following paper of charges, which I shall condense:—

"Having heard the bitter complaints of several of the inhabitants of the diocese of Nantes, whose names follow hereinafter (here follow the names of the parents of the lost children), we, Philippe do Livron, lieutenant assesseur of Messire le Procureur de Nantes, have invited, and do invite, the very noble and very wise Messire Pierre de l'Hospital, President of Brittany, &c., to bring to trial the very high and very powerful lord, Gilles de Laval, Sire de Retz, Machecoul, Ingrande and other places, Councillor of his Majesty the King, and Marshal of France:

"Forasmuch as the said Sire de Retz has seized and caused to be seized several little children, not only ten or twenty, but thirty, forty, fifty, sixty, one hundred, two hundred, and more, and has murdered and slain them inhumanly, and then burned their bodies to convert them to ashes:

"Forasmuch as persevering in evil, the said Sire, notwithstanding that the powers that be are ordained of God, and that every one should be an obedient subject to his prince, . . . has assaulted Jean Leferon, subject of the Duke of Brittany, the said Jean Leferon being guardian of the fortress of Malemort, in the name of Geoffrey Leferon, his brother, to whom the said lord had made over the possession of the said place:

"Forasmuch as the said Sire forced Jean Leferon to give up to him the said place, and moreover retook the lordship of Malemort in despite of the order of the duke and of justice:

"Forasmuch as the said Sire arrested Master Jean Rousseau, sergeant of the duke, who was sent to him with injunctions from the said duke, and beat his men with their own staves, although their persons were under the protection of his grace:

"We conclude that the said Sire de Retz, homicide in fact and in intent according to the first count, rebel and felon according to the second, should be condemned to suffer corporal punishment, and to pay a fine of his possessions in lands and goods held in fief to the said nobleman, and that these should be confiscated and remitted to the crown of Brittany."

This requisition was evidently drawn up with the view of saving the life of the Sire de Retz; for the crime of homicide was presented without aggravating circumstances, in such a manner that it could be denied or shelved, whilst the crimes of felony and rebellion against the Duke of Brittany were brought into exaggerated prominence.

Gilles de Retz had undoubtedly been forewarned of the course which was to be pursued, and he was prepared to deny totally the charges made in the first count.

"Monseigneur," said Pierre de l'Hospital, whom the form of the requisition had visibly astonished: "What justification have you to make? Take an oath on the Gospels to declare the truth."

"No, messire!" answered the marshal. "The witnesses are bound to declare what they know upon oath, but the accused is never put on his oath."

"Quite so," replied the judge. "Because the accused may be put on the rack and constrained to speak the truth, an' please you."

Gilles de Retz turned pale, bit his lips, and cast a glance of malignant hate at Pierre de l'Hospital; then, composing his countenance, he spoke with an appearance of calm:—

"Messires, I shall not deny that I behaved wrongfully in the case of Jean Rousseau; but, in excuse, let me say that the said Rousseau was full of wine, and he behaved with such indecorum towards me in the presence of my servants, that it was quite intolerable. Nor will I deny my revenge on the brothers Leferon: Jean had declared that the said Grace of Brittany had confiscated my fortress of Malemort, which I had sold to him, and for which I have not yet received payment; and Geoffrey Leferon had announced far and wide that I was about to be expelled Brittany as a traitor and a rebel. To punish them I re-entered my fortress of Malemort.—As for the other charges, I shall say nothing about them, they are simply false and calumnious."

"Indeed exclaimed Pierre de l'Hospital, whose blood boiled with indignation against the wretch who stood before him with such effrontery. "All these witnesses who complain of having lost their children, lied under oath!"

"Undoubtedly, if they accuse me of having anything to do with their loss. What am I to know about them, am I their keeper?"

"The answer of Cain!" exclaimed Pierre de l'Hospital, rising from his seat in the vehemence of his emotion. "However, as you solemnly deny these charges, we must question Henriet and Pontou."

"Henriet, Pontou!" cried the marshal, trembling; "they accuse me of nothing, surely!"

"Not as yet, they have not been questioned, but they are about to be brought into court, and I do not expect that they will lie in the face of justice."

"I demand that my servants be not brought forward as witnesses against their master," said the marshal, his eyes dilating, his brow wrinkling, and his beard bristling blue upon his chin: "a master is above the gossiping tales and charges of his servants."

"Do you think then, messire, that your servants will accuse you?"

"I demand that I, a marshal of France, a baron of the duchy, should be sheltered from the slanders of small folk, whom I disown as my servants if they are untrue to their master."

"Messire, I see we must put you on the rack, or nothing will be got from you."

"Hola! I appeal to his grace the Duke of Brittany, and ask an adjournment, that I may take advice on the charges brought against me, which I have denied, and which I deny still."

"Well, I shall adjourn the case till the 25th of this month, that you may be well prepared to meet the accusations."

On his way back to prison, the marshal passed Henriet and Pontou as they were being conducted to the court. Henriet pretended not to see his master, but Pontou burst into tears on meeting him. The marshal held out his hand, and Pontou kissed it affectionately.

"Remember what I have done for you, and be faithful servants," said Gilles de

Retz. Henriet recoiled from him with a shudder, and the marshal passed on.

"I shall speak," whispered Henriet; "for we have another master beside our poor master of Retz, and we shall soon be with the heavenly one."

The president ordered the clerk to read again the requisition of the lieutenant, that the two presumed accomplices of Gilles de Retz might be informed of the charges brought against their master. Henriet burst into tears, trembled violently, and cried out that he would tell all. Pontou, alarmed, tried to hinder his companion, and said that Henriet was touched in his head, and that what he was about to say would be the ravings of insanity.

Silence was imposed upon him.

"I will speak out," continued Henriet and yet I dare not speak of the horrors which I know have taken place, before that image of my Lord Christ; "and he pointed tremblingly to a large crucifix above the seat of the judge.

"Henriet." moaned Pontou, squeezing his hand, "you will destroy yourself as well as your master."

Pierre de l'Hospital rose, and the figure of our Redeemer was solemnly veiled.

Henriet, who had great difficulty in overcoming his agitation, than began his revelations.

The following is the substance of them:—

On leaving the university of Angers, he had taken the situation of reader in the house of Gilles de Retz. The marshal took a liking to him, and made him his chamberlain and confidant.

On the occasion of the Sire de la Suze, brother of the Sire de Retz, taking possession of the castle of Chantoncé, Charles de Soenne, who had arrived at Chantoncé, assured Henriet that he had found in the oubliettes of a tower a number of dead children, some headless, others frightfully mutilated. Henriet then thought that this was but a calumny invented by the Sire de la Suze.

But when, some while after, the Sire de Retz retook the castle of Chantoncé and had ceded it to the Duke of Brittany, he one evening summoned Henriet, Pontou, and a certain Petit Robin to his room; the two latter were already deep in the secrets of their master. But before confiding anything to Henriet, De Retz made him take a solemn oath never to reveal what he was about to tell him. The oath taken, the Sire de Retz, addressing the three, said that on the morrow an officer of the duke would take possession of the castle in the name of the duke, and that it was necessary, before this took place, that a certain well should be emptied of children's corpses, and that their bodies should be put into boxes and transported to Machecoul.

Henriet, Pontou, and Petit Robin went together, furnished with ropes and hooks, to the tower where were the corpses. They toiled all night in removing the half-decayed bodies, and with them they filled three large cases, which they sent by a boat down the Loire to Machecoul, where they were reduced to ashes.

Henriet counted thirty-six children's heads, but there were more bodies than heads. This night's work, he said, bad produced a profound impression on his imagination, and he was constantly haunted with a vision of these heads rolling as in a game of skittles, and clashing with a mournful wail. Henriet soon began to collect children for his master, and was present whilst he massacred them. They were murdered invariably in one room at Machecoul. The marshal used to bathe in their blood; he was fond of making Gilles do Sillé, Pontou, or Henriet torture them, and he experienced intense pleasure in seeing them in their agonies. But his great passion was to welter in their blood. His servants would stab a child in the jugular vein, and let the blood squirt over him. The room was often steeped in blood. When the horrible deed was done, and the child was dead, the marshal would be filled with grief for what he had done, and would toss weeping and praying on a bed, or recite fervent prayers and litanies on his knees, whilst his servants washed the floor, and burned in the huge fireplace the bodies of the murdered children. With the bodies were burned the clothes and everything that had belonged to the little victims.

An insupportable odour filled the room, but the Maréchal do Retz inhaled it with delight.

Henriet acknowledged that he had seen forty children put to death in this manner, and he was able to give an account of several, so that it was possible to identify them with the children reported to be lost.

"It is quite impossible," said the lieutenant, who had been given the cue to do all that was possible to save the marshal—"It is impossible that bodies could be burned in a chamber fireplace."

"It was done, for all that, messire," replied Henriet. "The fireplace was very large, both at the hotel Suze, and also at Machecoul; we piled up great faggots and logs, and laid the dead children among them. In a few hours the operation was complete, and we flung the ashes out of the window into the moat."

Henriet remembered the case of the two sons of Hamelin; he said that, whilst the one child was being tortured, the other was on its knees sobbing and praying to God, till its own turn came.

"What you have said concerning the excesses of Messire de Retz," exclaimed the lieutenant du procureur, "seems to be pure invention, and destitute of all probability. The greatest monsters of iniquity never committed such crimes, except perhaps some Césars of old Rome."

"Messire, it was the acts of these Césars that my Lord of Retz desired to imitate. I used to read to him the chronicles of Suetonius, and Tacitus, in which their cruelties are recorded. He used to delight in hearing of them, and he said that it gave him greater pleasure to hack off a child's head than to assist at a banquet. Sometimes he would seat himself on the breast of a little one, and with a knife sever the head from the body at a single blow; sometimes he cut the throat half through very gently, that the child might languish, and he would wash his hands and his beard in its blood. Sometimes he had all the limbs chopped off at once from the trunk; at other times he ordered us to hang the infants till they were nearly dead, and then take them down and cut their throats. I remember having brought to him three little girls who were asking charity at the castle gates. He bade me cut their throats whilst he looked on. André Bricket found another little girl crying on the steps of the house at Vannes because she had lost her mother. He brought the little thing—it was but a babe—in his arms to my lord, and it was killed before him. Pontou and I had to make away with the body. We threw it down a privy in one of the towers, but the corpse caught on a nail in the outer wall, so that it would be visible to all who passed. Pontou was let down by a rope, and he disengaged it with great difficulty."

"How many children do you estimate that the Sire de Retz and his servants have killed?"

"The reckoning is long. I, for my part, confess to having killed twelve with my own hand, by my master's orders, and I have brought him about sixty. I knew that things of the kind went on before I was admitted to the secret; for the castle of Machecoul had been occupied a short while by the Sire do la Sage. My lord recovered it speedily, for he knew that there were many children's corpses hidden in a hayloft. There were forty there quite dry and black as coal, because they had been charred. One of the women of Madame de Retz came by chance into the loft and saw the corpses. Roger de Briqueville wanted to kill her, but the maréchal would not let him."

"Have you nothing more to declare?

"Nothing. I ask Pontou, my friend, to corroborate what I have said."

This deposition, so circumstantial and detailed, produced on the judges a profound impression of horror. Human imagination at this time had not penetrated such mysteries of refined cruelty. Several times, as Henriet spake, the president had shown his astonishment and indignation by signing himself with the cross. Several times his face had become scarlet, and his eyes had fallen; he had pressed his hand to his brow, to assure himself that he was not labouring under a hideous dream, and a quiver of horror had run through his whole frame.

Pontou had taken no part in the revelation of Henriet; but when the latter appealed to him he raised his head, looked sadly round the court, and sighed.

"Etienne Cornillant, alias Pontou, I command you in the name of God and of justice, to declare what you know."

This injunction of Pierre do l'Hospital remained unresponded to, and Pontou seemed to strengthen himself in his resolution not to accuse his master.

But Henriet, flinging himself into the arms of his accomplice, implored him, as he valued his soul, no longer to harden his heart to the calls of God; but to bring to light the crimes he had committed along with the Sire do Retz.

The lieutenant du procureur, who hitherto had endeavoured to extenuate or discredit the charges brought against Gilles do Retz, tried a last expedient to counterbalance the damaging confessions of Henriet, and to withhold Pontou from giving way.

"You have heard, monseigneur," said he to the president, "the atrocities which have been acknowledged by Henriet, and you, as I do, consider them to be pure inventions of the aforesaid, made out of bitter hatred and envy with the purpose of ruining his master. I therefore demand that Henriet should be put on the rack, that he may be brought to give the lie to his former statements."

"You forget," replied de l'Hospital, "that the rack is for those who do _not_ confess, and not for those who freely acknowledge their crimes. Therefore I order the second accused, Etienne Cornillant, alias Pontou, to be placed on the rack if he continues silent. Pontou! will you speak or will you not?"

"Monseigneur, he will speak!" exclaimed Henriet. Oh, Pontou, dear friend, resist not God any more."

"Well then, messeigneurs," said Pontou, with emotion; "I will satisfy you; I cannot defend my poor lord against the allegations of Henriet, who has confessed all through dread of eternal damnation."

He then fully substantiated all the statements of the other, adding other facts of the same character, known only to himself.

Notwithstanding the avowal of Pontou and Henriet, the adjourned trial was not hurried on. It would have been easy to have captured some of the accomplices of the wretched man; but the duke, who was informed of the whole of the proceedings, did not wish to augment the scandal by increasing the number of the accused. He even forbade researches to be made in the castles and mansions of the Sire de Retz, fearing lest proofs of fresh crimes, more mysterious and more horrible than those already divulged, should come to light.

The dismay spread through the country by the revelations already made, demanded that religion and morality, which had been so grossly outraged, should be speedily avenged. People wondered at the delay in pronouncing sentence, and it was loudly proclaimed in Nantes that the Sire de Retz was rich enough to purchase his life. It is true that Madame de Retz solicited the king and the duke again to give pardon to her husband; but the duke, counselled by the bishop, refused to extend his authority to interfere with the course of justice; and the king, after having sent one of his councillors to Nantes to investigate the case, determined not to stir in it.

CHAPTER XIII
MAR...CHAL DE RETZ.—III. THE SENTENCE AND EXECUTION

On the 24th October the trial of the Maréchal de Retz was resumed. The prisoner entered in a Carmelite habit, knelt and prayed in silence before the examination began. Then he ran his eye over the court, and the sight of the rack, windlass, and cords made a slight shudder run through him.

"Messire Gilles de Laval," began the president; "you appear before me now for the second time to answer to a certain requisition read by M. le Lieutenant du Procureur de Nantes."

"I shall answer frankly, monseigneur," said the prisoner calmly; "but I reserve the right of appeal to the benign intervention of the very venerated majesty of the King of France, of whom I am, or have been, chamberlain and marshal, as may be proved by my letters patent duly enregistered in the parliament at Paris—"

"This is no affair of the King of France," interrupted Pierre de l'Hospital; "if you were chamberlain and marshal of his Majesty, you are also vassal of his grace the Duke of Brittany."

"I do not deny it; but, on the contrary, I trust to his Grace of Brittany to allow me to retire to a convent of Carmelites, there to repent me of my sins."

"That is as may be; will you confess, or must I send you to the rack?"

"Torture me not!" exclaimed Gilles de Retz "I will confess all. Tell me first, what have Henriet and Pontou said?"

"They have confessed. M. le Lieutenant du Procureur shall read you their allegations."

"Not so," said the lieutenant, who continued to show favour to the accused; "I pronounce them false, unless Messire de Retz confirms them by oath, which God forbid!"

Pierre de l'Hospital made a motion of anger to check this scandalous pleading in favour of the accused, and then nodded to the clerk to read the evidence.

The Sire do Retz, on hearing that his servants had made such explicit avowals of their acts, remained motionless, as though thunderstruck. He saw that it was in vain for him to equivocate, and that he would have to confess all.

"What have you to say?" asked the president, when the confessions of Henriet and Pontou had been read.

"Say what befits you, my lord," interrupted the lieutenant du procureur, as though to indicate to the accused the line he was to take: "are not these abominable lies and calumnies trumped up to ruin you?"

"Alas, no!" replied the Sire do Retz; and his face was pale as death: "Henriet and Pontou have spoken the truth. God has loosened their tongues."

"My lord! relieve yourself of the burden of your crimes by acknowledging them at once," said M. do l'Hospital earnestly.

"Messires!" said the prisoner, after a moment's silence: "it is quite true that I have robbed mothers of their little ones; and that I have killed their children, or caused them to be killed, either by cutting their throats with daggers or knives, or by chopping off their heads with cleavers; or else I have had their skulls broken by hammers or sticks; sometimes I had their limbs hewn off one after another; at other times I have ripped them open, that I might examine their entrails and hearts; I have occasionally strangled them or put them to a slow death; and when the children were dead I had their bodies burned and reduced to ashes."

"When did you begin your execrable practices?" asked Pierre de l'Hospital, staggered by the frankness of these horrible avowals: "the evil one must have possessed you."

"It came to me from myself,—no doubt at the instigation of the devil: but still these acts of cruelty afforded me incomparable delight. The desire to commit these atrocities came upon me eight years ago. I left court to go to Chantoncé, that I might claim the property of my grandfather, deceased. In the library of the castle I found a Latin book—*Suetonius*, I believe—full of accounts of the cruelties of the Roman Emperors. I read the charming history of Tiberius, Caracalla, and other Césars, and the pleasure they took in watching the agonies of tortured children. Thereupon I resolved to imitate and surpass these same Césars, and that very night I began to do so. For some while I confided my secret to no one, but afterwards I communicated it to my cousin, Gilles de Sillé, then to Master Roger de Briqueville, next in succession to Henriet, Pontou, Rossignol, and Robin." He then confirmed all the accounts given by his two servants. He confessed to about one hundred and twenty murders in a single year.

"An average of eight hundred in less than seven years!" exclaimed Pierre de l'Hospital, with a cry of pain: "Ah! messire, you were possessed! "

His confession was too explicit and circumstantial for the Lieutenant du Procureur to say another word in his defence; but he pleaded that the case should be made over to the ecclesiastical court, as there were confessions of invocations of the devil and of witchcraft mixed up with those of murder. Pierre de l'Hospital saw that the object of the lieutenant was to gain time for Mme. de Retz to make a fresh attempt to obtain a pardon; however he was unable to resist, so he consented that the case should be transferred to the bishop's court.

But the bishop was not a man to let the matter slip, and there and then a sergeant of the bishop summoned Gilles de Laval, Sire do Retz, to appear forthwith before the ecclesiastical tribunal. The marshal was staggered by this unexpected citation, and he did not think of appealing against it to the president; he merely signed his readiness to follow, and he was at once conducted into the ecclesiastical court assembled hurriedly to try him.

This new trial lasted only a few hours.

The marshal, now thoroughly cowed, made no attempt to defend himself, but he endeavoured to bribe the bishop into leniency, by promises of the surrender of all his lands and goods to the Church, and begged to be allowed to retire into the Carmelite monastery at Nantes.

His request was peremptorily refused, and sentence of death was pronounced against him.

On the 25th October, the ecclesiastical court having pronounced judgment, the sentence was transmitted to the secular court, which had now no pretext upon which to withhold ratification.

There was some hesitation as to the kind of death the marshal was to suffer. The members of the secular tribunal were not unanimous on this point. The president put it to the vote, and collected the votes himself; then he reseated himself, covered his head, and said in a solemn voice:—

"The court, notwithstanding the quality, dignity, and nobility of the accused, condemns him to be hung and burned. Wherefore I admonish you who are condemned, to ask pardon of God, and grace to die well, in great contrition for having committed the said crimes. And the said sentence shall be carried into execution to-morrow morning between eleven and twelve o'clock." A similar sentence was pronounced upon Henriet and Pontou.

On the morrow, October 26th, at nine o'clock in the morning, a general procession composed of half the people of Nantes, the clergy and the bishop bearing the blessed Sacrament, left the cathedral and went round the city visiting each of the principal churches, where masses were said for the three under sentence.

At eleven the prisoners were conducted to the place of execution, which was in the meadow of Biesse, on the further side of the Loire.

Three gibbets had been erected, one higher than the others, and beneath each was a pile of faggots, tar, and brushwood.

It was a glorious, breezy day, not a cloud was to be seen in the blue heavens; the Loire rolled silently towards the sea its mighty volumes of turbid water, seeming bright and blue as it reflected the brilliancy and colour of the sky. The poplars shivered and whitened in the fresh air with a pleasant rustle, and the willows flickered and wavered above the stream.

A vast crowd had assembled round the gallows; it was with difficulty that a way was made for the condemned, who came on chanting the *De profundis*. The spectators of all ages took up the psalm and chanted it with them, so that the surge of the old Gregorian tone might have been heard by the duke and the bishop, who had shut themselves up in the ch,teau of Nantes during the hour of execution.

After the close of the psalm, which was terminated by the *Requiem éternam* instead of the *Gloria*, the Sire de Retz thanked those who had conducted him, and then embraced Pontou and Henriet, before delivering himself of the following address, or rather sermon:—

"My very dear friends and servants, be strong and courageous against the assaults of the devil, and feel great displeasure and contrition for your ill deeds, without despairing of God's mercy. Believe with me, that there is no sin, however great, in the world, which God, in his grace and loving kindness, will not pardon, when one asks it of Him with contrition of heart. Remember that the Lord God is always more ready to receive the sinner than is the sinner to ask of Him pardon. Moreover, let us very humbly thank Him for his great love to us in letting us die in full possession of our faculties, and not cutting us off suddenly in the midst of our misdeeds. Let us conceive such a love of God, and such repentance, that we shall not fear death, which is only a little pang, without which we could not see God in his glory. Besides we must desire to be freed from this world, in which is only misery, that we may go to everlasting glory. Let us rejoice rather, for although we have sinned grievously here below, yet we shall be united in Paradise, our souls being parted from our bodies, and we shall be together for ever and ever, if only we endure in our pious and honourable contrition to our last sigh." [1] Then the marshal, who was to be executed first, left his companions and placed himself in the hands of his executioners. He took off his cap, knelt, kissed a crucifix, and made a pious oration to the crowd much in the style of his address to his friends Pontou and Henriet.

[1. The case of the Sire de Retz is one to make us see the great danger there is in trusting to feelings in matters of religion. "If thou wilt enter into life, keep the commandments," said our Lord. How many hope to go to heaven because they have pious emotions!]

Then he commenced reciting the prayers of the dying; the executioner passed the cord round his neck, and adjusted the knot. He mounted a tall stool, erected at the foot of the gallows as a last honour paid to the nobility of the criminal. The pile of firewood was lighted before the executioners had left him.

Pontou and Henriet, who were still on their knees, raised their eyes to their master and cried to him, extending their arms,—

"At this last hour, monseigneur, be a good and valiant soldier of God, and remember the passion of Jesus Christ which wrought our redemption. Farewell, we hope soon to meet in Paradise!

The stool was cast down, and the Sire de Retz dropped. The fire roared up, the flames leaped about him, and enveloped him as be swung.

Suddenly, mingling with the deep booming of the cathedral bell, swelled up the wild unearthly wail of the *Dies iré*.

No sound among the crowd, only the growl of the fire, and the solemn strain of the hymn

Lo, the Book, exactly worded, Wherein all hath been recorded; Thence shall judgment be awarded. When the Judge his seat attaineth, And each hidden deed arraigneth, Nothing unavenged remaineth. What shall I, frail man, be pleading? Who for me be interceding? When the just are mercy needing. King of Majesty tremendous, Who dost free salvation send us, Fount of pity! then befriend us.

Low I kneel, with heart-submission; See, like ashes, my contrition—Help me in my last condition! Ah I that day of tears and mourning! From the dust of earth returning, Man for judgment must prepare him! Spare, O, God, in mercy spare him! Lord, who didst our souls redeem, Grant a blessed requiem! AMEN.

Six women, veiled, and robed in white, and six Carmelites advanced. bearing a coffin.

It was whispered that one of the veiled women was Madame de Retz, and that the others were members of the most illustrious houses of Brittany.

The cord by which the marshal was hung was cut, and he fell into a cradle of iron prepared to receive the corpse. The body was removed before the fire had gained any mastery over it. It was placed in the coffin., and the monks and the women transported it to the Carmelite monastery of Nantes, according to the wishes of the deceased.

In the meantime, the sentence had been executed upon Pontou and Henriet; they were hung and burned to dust. Their ashes were cast to the winds; whilst in the Carmelite church of Our Lady were celebrated with pomp the obsequies of the very high, very powerful, very illustrious Seigneur Gilles de Laval, Sire de Retz, late Chamberlain of King Charles VII., and Marshal of France!

CHAPTER XIV
A GALICIAN WERE-WOLF

The inhabitants of Austrian Galicia are quiet, inoffensive people, take them as a whole. The Jews, who number a twelfth of the population, are the most intelligent, energetic, and certainly the most money-making individuals in the province, though the Poles proper, or Mazurs, are not devoid of natural parts.

Perhaps as remarkable a phenomenon as any other in that kingdom—for kingdom of Waldimir it was—is the enormous numerical preponderance of the nobility over the untitled. In 1837 the proportions stood thus: 32,190 nobles to 2,076 tradesmen.

The average of execution for crime is nine a year, out of a population of four and a half millions,—by no means a high figure, considering the peremptory way in which justice is dealt forth in that province. Yet, in the most quiet and well-disposed neighbourhoods, occasionally the most startling atrocities are committed, occurring when least expected, and sometimes perpetrated by the very person who is least suspected.

Just sixteen years ago there happened in the circle of Tornow, in Western Galicia-the province is divided into nine circles-a circumstance which will probably furnish the grandames with a story for their firesides, during their bitter Galician winters, for many a long year.

In the circle of Tornow, in the lordship of Parkost, is a little hamlet called Polomyja, consisting of eight hovels and a Jewish tavern. The inhabitants are mostly woodcutters, hewing down the firs of the dense forest in which their village is situated, and conveying them to the nearest water, down which they are floated to the Vistula. Each tenant pays no rent for his cottage and pitch of field, but is bound to work a fixed number of days for his landlord: a practice universal in Galicia, and often productive of much discontent and injustice, as the proprietor exacts labour from his tenant on those days when the harvest has to be got in, or the land is m best condition for tillage, and just when the peasant would gladly be engaged upon his own small plot. Money is scarce in the province, and this is accordingly the only way in which the landlord can be sure of his dues.

Most of the villagers of Polomyja are miserably poor; but by cultivating a little maize, and keeping a few fowls or a pig, they scrape together sufficient to sustain life. During the summer the men collect resin from the pines, from each of which, once in twelve Years, they strip a slip of bark, leaving the resin to exude and trickle into a small earthenware jar at its roots; and, during the winter, as already stated, they fell the trees and roll them down to the river.

Polomyja is not a cheerful spot—nested among dense masses of pine, which shed a gloom over the little hamlet; yet, on a fine day, it is pleasant enough for the old women to sit at their cottage doors, scenting that matchless pine fragrance, sweeter than the balm of the Spice Islands, for there is nothing cloying in that exquisite and exhilarating odour; listening to the harp-like thrill of the breeze in the old grey tree-tops, and knitting quietly at long stockings, whilst their little grandchildren romp in the heather and tufted fern.

Towards evening, too, there is something indescribably beautiful in the firwood. The sun dives among the trees, and paints their boles with patches of luminous saffron, or falling over a level clearing, glorifies it with its orange dye, so visibly contrasting with the blue-purple shadow on the western rim of unreclaimed forest, deep and luscious as the bloom on a plum. The birds then are hastening to their nests, a ger-falcon, high overhead, is kindled with sunlight; capering and gambolling among the branches, the merry squirrel skips home for the night.

The sun goes down, but the sky is still shining with twilight. The wild cat begins to hiss and squall in the forest, the heron to flap hastily by, the stork on the top of the tavern chimney to poise itself on one leg for sleep. To-whoo! an owl begins to wake up. Hark! the woodcutters are coming home with a song.

Such is Polomyja in summer time, and much resembling it are the hamlets scattered about the forest, at intervals of a few miles; in each, the public-house being the most commodious and best-built edifice, the church, whenever there is one, not remarkable for anything but its bulbous steeple.

You would hardly believe that amidst all this poverty a beggar could have picked up any subsistence, and yet, a few years ago, Sunday after Sunday, there sat a white-bearded venerable man at the church door, asking alms.

Poor people are proverbially compassionate and liberal, so that the old man generally got a few coppers, and often some good woman bade him come into her cottage, and let him have some food.

Occasionally Swiatek—that was the beggar's name, went his rounds selling small pinchbeck ornaments and beads; generally, however, only appealing to charity.

One Sunday, after church, a Mazur and his wife invited the old man into their hut and gave him a crust of pie and some meat. There were several children about, but a little girl, of nine or ten, attracted the old man's attention by her artless tricks.

Swiatek felt in his pocket and produced a ring, enclosing a piece of coloured glass set over foil. This he presented to the child, who ran off delighted to show her acquisition to her companions.

"Is that little maid your daughter?" asked the beggar.

"No," answered the house-wife, "she is an orphan; there was a widow in this place who died, leaving the child, and I have taken charge of her; one mouth more will not matter much, and the good God will bless us."

"Ay, ay! to be sure He will; the orphans and fatherless are under His own peculiar care."

"She's a good little thing, and gives no trouble," observed the woman. "You go back to Polomyja tonight, I reckon."

"I do—ah!" exclaimed Swiatek, as the little girl ran up to him. You like the ring, is it not beautiful? I found it under a big fir to the left of the churchyard, there may be dozens there. You must turn round three times, bow to the moon, and say, 'ZaboÔ!' then look among the tree-roots till you find one."

"Come along!" screamed the child to its comrades; "we will go and look for rings."

"You must seek separately," said Swiatek.

The children scampered off into the wood.

"I have done one good thing for you," laughed the beggar, "in ridding you, for a time, of the noise of those children."

"I am glad of a little quiet now and then," said the woman; "the children will not let the baby sleep at times with their clatter. Are you going?"

"Yes; I must reach Polomyja to-night. I am old and very feeble, and poor"—he began to fall into his customary whine— very poor, but I thank and pray to God for you."

Swiatek left the cottage.

That little orphan was never seen again.

The Austrian Government has, of late years, been vigorously advancing education among the lower orders, and establishing schools throughout the province.

The children were returning from class one day, and were scattered among the trees, some pursuing a field-mouse, others collecting juniper-berries, and some sauntering with their hands in their pockets, whistling.

"Where's Peter?" asked one little boy of another who was beside him. "We three go home the same way, let us go together."

"Peter!" shouted the lad.

"Here I am!" was the answer from among the trees; "I'll be with you directly."

"Oh, I see him!" said the elder boy. "There is some one talking to him."

"Where?"

"Yonder, among the pines. Ah! they have gone further into the shadow, and I cannot see them any more. I wonder who was with him; a man, I think."

The boys waited till they were tired, and then they sauntered home, determined to thrash Peter for having kept them waiting. *But Peter was never seen again.*

Some time after this a servant-girl, belonging to a small store kept by a Russian, disappeared from a village five miles from Polomyja. She had been sent with a parcel of grocery to a cottage at no very great distance, but lying apart from the main cluster of hovels, and surrounded by trees.

The day closed in, and her master waited her return anxiously, but as several hours elapsed without any sign of her, he—assisted by the neighbours—went in search of her.

A slight powdering of snow covered the ground, and her footsteps could be traced at intervals where she had diverged from the beaten track. In that part of the road where the trees were thickest, there were marks of two pair of feet leaving the path; but owing to the density of the trees at that spot and to the slightness of the fall of snow, which did not reach the soil, where shaded by the pines, the footprints were immediately lost. By the following morning a heavy fall had obliterated any further traces which day-light might have discovered.

The servant-girl also was never seen again.

During the winter of 1849 the wolves were supposed to have been particularly ravenous, for thus alone did people account for the mysterious disappearances of children.

A little boy had been sent to a fountain to fetch water; the pitcher was found standing by the well, but *the boy had vanished.* The villagers turned out, and those wolves which could be found were despatched.

We have already introduced our readers to Polomyja, although the occurrences above related did not take place among those eight hovels, but in neighbouring villages. The reason for our having given a more detailed account of this cluster of houses—rude cabins they were—will now become apparent.

In May, 1849, the innkeeper of Polomyja missed a couple of ducks, and his suspicions fell upon the beggar who lived there, and whom he held in no esteem, as he himself was a hard-working industrious man, whilst Swiatek maintained himself, his wife, and children by mendicity, although possessed of sufficient arable land to yield an excellent crop of maize, and produce vegetables, if tilled with ordinary care.

As the publican approached the cottage a fragrant whiff of roast greeted his nostrils.

"I'll catch the fellow in the act," said the innkeeper to himself, stealing up to the door, and taking good care not to be observed.

As he threw open the door, he saw the mendicant hurriedly shuffle something under his feet, and conceal it beneath his long clothes. The publican was on him in an instant, had him by the throat, charged him with theft, and dragged him from his seat. Judge of his sickening horror when from beneath the pauper's clothes rolled forth the head of a girl about the age of fourteen or fifteen years, carefully separated from the trunk.

In a short while the neighbours came up. The venerable Swiatek was locked up, along with his wife, his daughter—a girl of sixteen—and a son, aged five.

The hut was thoroughly examined, and the mutilated remains of the poor girl discovered. In a vat were found the legs and thighs, partly raw, partly stewed or roasted. In a chest were the heart, liver, and entrails, all prepared and cleaned, as neatly as though done by a skilful butcher; and, finally, under the oven was a bowl full of fresh blood. On his way to the magistrate of the district. the wretched man flung himself repeatedly on the ground, struggled with his guards, and endeavoured to suffocate himself by gulping clown clods of earth and stones, but was prevented by his conductors.

When taken before the Protokoll at Dabkow, he stated that he had already killed and—assisted by his family—eaten six persons: his children, however, asserted most positively that the number was much greater than he had represented, and their testimony is borne out by the fact, that the remains of *fourteen* different caps and suits of clothes, male as well as female, were found in his house.

The origin of this horrible and depraved taste was as follows, according to Swiatek's own confession:—

In 1846, three years previous, a Jewish tavern in the neighbourhood had been burned down, and the host had himself perished in the flames. Swiatek, whilst examining the ruins, had found the half-roasted corpse of the publican among the charred rafters of the house. At that time the old man was craving with hunger, having been destitute of food for some time. The scent and the sight of the roasted flesh inspired him with an uncontrollable desire to taste of it. He tore off a portion of the carcase and satiated his hunger upon it, and at the same time he conceived such a liking for it, that he could feel no rest till he had tasted again. His second victim was the orphan above alluded to; since then—that is, during the period of no less than three years—he had frequently subsisted in the same manner, and had actually grown sleek and fat upon his frightful meals.

The excitement roused by the discovery of these atrocities was intense; several poor mothers who had bewailed the loss of their little ones, felt their wounds reopened agonisingly. Popular indignation rose to the highest pitch: there was some fear lest the criminal should be torn in pieces himself by the enraged people, as soon as he was brought to trial: but he saved the necessity of precautions being taken to ensure his safety, for, on the first night of his confinement, he hanged himself from the bars of the prison-window.

CHAPTER XV
ANOMALOUS CASE.—THE HUMAN HYE´NA

It is well known that Oriental romance is full of stories of violators of graves. Eastern superstition attributes to certain individuals a passion for unearthing corpses and mangling them. Of a moonlight night weird forms are seen stealing among the tombs, and burrowing into them with their long nails, desiring to reach the bodies of the dead ere the first streak of dawn compels them to retire. These ghouls, as they are called, are supposed generally to require the flesh of the dead for incantations or magical compositions, but very often they are actuated by the sole desire of rending the sleeping corpse, and disturbing its repose. There is every probability that these ghouls were no mere creations of the imagination, but were actual resurrectionists. Human fat and the hair of a corpse which has grown in the grave, form ingredients in many a necromantic receipt, and the witches who compounded these diabolical mixtures, would unearth corpses in order to obtain the requisite ingredients. It was the same in the middle ages, and to such an extent did the fear of ghouls extend, that it was common in Brittany for churchyards to be provided with lamps, kept burning during the night, that witches might be deterred from venturing under cover of darkness to open the graves.

Fornari gives the following story of a ghoul in his *History of Sorcerers:*—

In the beginning of the 15th century, there lived at Bagdad an aged merchant who had grown wealthy in his business, and who had an only son to whom he was tenderly attached. He resolved to marry him to the daughter of another merchant, a girl of considerable fortune, but without any personal attractions. Abul-Hassan, the merchant's son, on being shown the portrait of the lady, requested his father to delay the marriage till he could reconcile his mind to it. Instead, however, of doing this, he fell in love with another girl, the daughter of a sage, and he gave his father no peace till he consented to the marriage with the object of his affections.

191

The old man stood out as long as he could, but finding that his son was bent on acquiring the hand of the fair Nadilla, and was equally resolute not to accept the rich and ugly lady, he did what most fathers, under such circumstances, are constrained to do, he acquiesced.

The wedding took place with great pomp and ceremony, and a happy honeymoon ensued, which might have been happier but for one little circumstance which led to very serious consequences.

Abul-Hassan noticed that his bride quitted the nuptial couch as soon as she thought her husband was asleep, and did not return to it, till an boar before dawn.

Filled with curiosity, Hassan one night feigned sleep, and saw his wife rise and leave the room as usual. He followed cautiously, and saw her enter a cemetery. By the straggling moonbeams he beheld her go into a tomb; he stepped in after her.

The scene within was horrible. A party of ghouls were assembled with the spoils of the graves they had violated., and were feasting on the flesh of the long-buried corpses. His own wife, who, by the way, never touched supper at home, played no inconsiderable part in the hideous banquet.

As soon as he could safely escape, Abul-Hassan stole back to his bed.

He said nothing to his bride till next evening when supper was laid, and she declined to eat; then he insisted on her partaking, and when she positively refused, he exclaimed wrathfully,—"Yes, you keep your appetite for your feast with the ghouls!" Nadilla was silent; she turned pale and trembled, and without a word sought her bed. At midnight she rose, fell on her husband with her nails and teeth, tore his throat, and having opened a vein, attempted to suck his blood; but Abul-Hassan springing to his feet threw her down, and with a blow killed her. She was buried next day.

Three days after, at midnight, she re-appeared, attacked her husband again, and again attempted to suck his blood. He fled from her, and on the morrow opened her tomb, burned her to ashes, and cast them into the Tigris.

This story connects the ghoul with the vampire. As will be seen by a former chapter, the were-wolf and the vampire are closely related.

That the ancients held the same belief that the witches violate corpses, is evident from the third episode in the *Golden Ass* of Apuleius. I will only quote the words of the crier:—

"I pray thee, tell me," replied I, "of what kind are the duties attached to this funeral guardianship?" "Duties!" quoth the crier; "why, keep wide awake all night, with thine eyes fixed steadily upon the corpse, neither winking nor blinking, nor looking to the right nor looking to the left, either to one side or the other, be it even little; for the witches, infamous wretches that they are! can slip out of their skins in an instant and change themselves into the form of any animal they have a mind; and then they crawl along so slyly, that the eyes of justice, nay, the eyes of the sun himself, are not keen enough to perceive them. At all events, their wicked devices are infinite in number and variety; and whether it be in the shape of a bird, or a dog, or a mouse, or even of a common house-fly, that they exercise their dire incantations, if thou art not vigilant in the extreme, they will deceive thee one way or other, and overwhelm thee with sleep; nevertheless, as regards the reward, 'twill be from four to six aurei; nor, although 'tis a perilous service, wilt thou receive more. Nay, hold! I had almost forgotten to give thee a necessary caution. Clearly understand, that it the corpse be not restored to the relatives entire, the deficient pieces of flesh torn off by the teeth of the witches must be replaced from the face of the sleepy guardian."

Here we have the rending of corpses connected with change of form.

Marcassus relates that after a long war in Syria, during the night, troops of lamias, female evil spirits, appeared upon the field of battle, unearthing the hastily buried bodies of the soldiers, and devouring the flesh off their bones. They were pursued and fired upon, and some young men succeeded in killing a considerable number; but during the day they had all of them the forms of wolves or hyénas. That there is a foundation of truth in these horrible stories, and that it is quite possible for a human being to be possessed of a depraved appetite for rending corpses, is proved by an extraordinary case brought before a court-martial in Paris, so late as July 10th, 1849.

The details are given with fulness in the *Annales Medico-psychologiques* for that month and year. They are too revolting for reproduction. I will, however, give an outline of this remarkable case.

In the autumn of 1848, several of the cemeteries in the neighbourhood of Paris were found to have been entered during the night, and graves to have been rifled. The deeds were not those of medical students, for the bodies had not been carried of, but were found lying about the tombs in fragments. It was at first supposed that the perpetration of these outrages must have been a wild beast, but footprints in the soft earth left no doubt that it was a man. Close watch was kept at Pére la Chaise; but after a few corpses had been mangled there, the outrages ceased.

In the winter, another cemetery was ravaged, and it was not till March in 1849, that a spring gun which had been set in the cemetery of St. Parnasse, went off during the night, and warned the guardians of the place that the mysterious visitor had fallen into their trap. They rushed to the spot, only to see a dark figure in a military mantle leap the wall, and disappear in the gloom. Marks of blood, however, gave evidence that he had been hit by the gun when it had discharged. At the same time, a fragment of blue cloth, torn from the mantle, was obtained, and afforded a clue towards the identification of the ravisher of the tombs.

On the following day, the police went from barrack to barrack, inquiring whether officer or man were suffering from a gun-shot wound. By this means they discovered the person. He was a junior officer in the 1st Infantry regiment, of the name of

Bertrand.

He was taken to the hospital to be cured of his wound, and on his recovery, he was tried by court-martial.

His history was this.

He had been educated in the theological seminary of Langres, till, at the age of twenty, he entered the army. He was a young man of retiring habits, frank and cheerful to his comrades, so as to be greatly beloved by them, of feminine delicacy and refinement, and subject to fits of depression and melancholy. In February, 1847, as he was walking with a friend in the country, he came to a churchyard, the gate of which stood open. The day before a woman had been buried, but the sexton had not completed filling in the grave, and he had been engaged upon it on the present occasion, when a storm of rain had driven him to shelter. Bertrand noticed the spade and pick lying beside the grave, and—to use his own words:— "A cette vue des idées noires me vinrent, j'eus comme un violent mal de tÍte, mon cur battait avec force, je no me possédais plus." He managed by some excuse to get rid of his companion, and then returning to the churchyard, he caught up a spade and began to dig into the grave. "Soon I dragged the corpse out of the earth, and I began to hash it with the spade, without well knowing what I was about. A labourer saw me, and I laid myself flat on the ground till he was out of sight, and then I cast the body back into the grave. I then went away, bathed in a cold sweat, to a little grove, where I reposed for several hours, notwithstanding the cold rain which fell, in a condition of complete exhaustion. When I rose, my limbs were as if broken, and my head weak. The same prostration and sensation followed each attack.

Two days after, I returned to the cemetery, and opened the grave with my hands. My hands bled, but I did not feel the pain; I tore the corpse to shreds, and flung it back into the pit."

He had no further attack for four months, till his regiment came to Paris. As he was one day walking in the gloomy, shadowy, alleys of PËre la Chaise, the same feeling came over him like a flood. In the night he climbed the wall, and dug up a little girl of seven years old. He tore her in half. A few days later, he opened the grave of a woman who had died in childbirth, and had lain in the grave for thirteen days. On the 16th November, he dug up an old woman of fifty, and, ripping her to pieces, rolled among the fragments. He did the same to another corpse on the 12th December. These are only a few of the numerous cases of violation of tombs to which he owned. It was on the night of the 15th March that the spring-gun shot him.

Bertrand declared at his trial, that whilst he was in the hospital he had not felt any desire to renew his attempts, and that he considered himself cured of his horrible propensities, for he had seen men dying in the beds around him, and now: *"Je suis guéri, car aujourd'hui j'ai peur d'un mort."*

194

The fits of exhaustion which followed his accesses are very remarkable, as they precisely resemble those which followed the berserkir rages of the Northmen, and the expeditions of the Lycanthropists.

The case of M. Bertrand is indubitably most singular and anomalous; it scarcely bears the character of insanity, but seems to point rather to a species of diabolical possession. At first the accesses chiefly followed upon his drinking wine, but after a while they came upon him without exciting cause. The manner in which he mutilated the dead was different. Some he chopped with the spade, others he tore and ripped with his teeth and nails. Sometimes he tore the mouth open and rent the face back to the ears, he opened the stomachs, and pulled off the limbs. Although he dug up the bodies of several men he felt no inclination to mutilate them, whereas he delighted in rending female corpses. He was sentenced to a year's imprisonment.

CHAPTER XVI
A SERMON ON WERE-WOLVES

THE following curious specimen of a late mediéval sermon is taken from the old German edition of the discourses of Dr. Johann Geiler von Keysersperg, a famous preacher in Strasbourg. The volume is entitled: "_Die Emeis_. Dis ist das Büch von der Omeissen, und durch Herr der Künnig ich diente gern. Und sagt von Eigenschafft der Omeissen, und gibt underweisung von der Unholden oder Hexen, und von Gespenst, der Geist, und von dem Wütenden Heer Wunderbarlich."

This strange series of sermons was preached at Strasbourg in the year 1508, and was taken down and written out by a barefooted friar, Johann Pauli, and by him published in 1517. The doctor died on Mid-Lent Sunday, 1510. There is a Latin edition of his sermons, but whether of the same series or not I cannot tell, as I have been unable to obtain a sight of the volume. The German edition is illustrated with bold and clever woodcuts. Among other, there are representations of the Witches' Sabbath, the Wild Huntsman, and a Werewolf attacking a Man.

The sermon was preached on the third Sunday in Lent. No text is given, but there is a general reference to the gospel for the day. This is the discourse:— [1]

[1. Headed thus:—"Am drittÎ sontag ‡ fastÍ, occuli, predigt dé doctor vÙ dí Werwølffenn."]

"What shall we say about were-wolves? for there are were-wolves which run about the villages devouring men and children. As men say about them, they run about full gallop, injuring men, and are called *ber-wølff*, or *wer-wølff*. Do you ask me if I know aught about them? I answer, Yes. They are apparently wolves which cat men and children, and that happens on seven accounts:—

1. Esuriem	Hunger.
2. Rabiem	Savageness.
3. Senectutem	Old age.

4. Experientiam	Experience.
5. Insaniem	Madness.
6. Diabolum	The Devil.
7. Deum	God.

The first happens through hunger; when the wolves find nothing to eat in the woods, they must come to people and eat men when hunger drives them to it. You see well, when it is very cold, that the stags come in search of food up to the villages, and the birds actually into the dining-room in search of victuals.

"Under the second head, wolves eat children through their innate savageness, because they are savage, and that is (propter locum coitum ferum). Their savageness arises first from their condition. Wolves which live in cold places are smaller on that account, and more savage than other wolves. Secondly, their savageness depends on the season; they are more savage about Candlemas than at any other time of the year, and men must be more on their guard against them then than at other times. It is a proverb, 'He who seeks a wolf at Candlemas, a peasant on Shrove Tuesday, and a parson in Lent, is a man of pluck.' . . . Thirdly, their savageness depends on their having young. When the wolves have young, they are more savage than when they have not. You see it so in all beasts. A wild duck, when it has young poults, you see what an uproar it makes. A cat fights for its young kittens; the wolves do ditto.

"Under the third head, the wolves do injury on account of their age. When a wolf is old, it is weak and feeble in its leas, so it can't ran fast enough to catch stags, and therefore it rends a man, whom it can catch easier than a wild animal. It also tears children and men easier than wild animals, because of its teeth, for its teeth break off when it is very old; you see it well in old women: how the last teeth wobble, and they have scarcely a tooth left in their heads, and they open their mouths for men to feed them with mash and stewed substances.

"Under the fourth head, the injury the were-wolves do arises from experience. It is said that human flesh is far sweeter than other flesh; so when a wolf has once tasted human flesh, he desires to taste it again. So he acts like old topers, who, when they know the best wine, will not be put off with inferior quality.

"Under the fifth head, the injury arises from ignorance. A dog when it is mad is also inconsiderate, and it bites any man; it does not recognize its own lord: and what is a wolf but a wild dog which is mad and inconsiderate, so that it regards no man.

"Under the sixth head, the injury comes of the Devil, who transforms himself, and takes on him the form of a wolf So writes Vincentius in his *Speculum Historiale*. And he has taken it from Valerius Maximus in the Punic war. When the Romans fought against the men of Africa, when the captain lay asleep, there came a wolf and drew his sword, and carried it off. That was the Devil in a, wolf's form. The like writes William of Paris,—that a wolf will kill and devour children, and do the greatest mischief. There was a man who had the phantasy that he himself was a wolf. And afterwards he was found lying in the wood, and he was dead out of sheer hunger.

"Under the seventh head, the injury comes of God's ordinance. For God will sometimes punish certain lands and villages with wolves. So we read of Elisha,—that when Elisha wanted to go up a mountain out of Jericho, some naughty boys made a mock of him and said, 'O bald head, step up! O glossy pate, step up!' What happened? He cursed them. Then came two bears out of the desert and tore about forty-two of the children. That was God's ordinance. The like we read of a prophet who would set at naught the commands he had received of God, for he was persuaded to eat bread at the house of another. As he went home he rode upon his ass. Then came a lion which slew him and left the ass alone. That was God's ordinance. Therefore must man turn to God when He brings wild beasts to do him a mischief: which same brutes may He not bring now or evermore. Amen."

It will be seen from this extraordinary sermon that Dr. Johann Geiler von Keysersperg did not regard werewolves in any other light than natural wolves filled with a lust for human flesh; and he puts aside altogether the view that they are men in a state of metamorphosis. However, he alludes to this superstition in his sermon on wild-men of the woods, but translates his lycanthropists to Spain.

THE END.

The Werewolf
A Short Story
Clemence Houseman

The great farm hall was ablaze with the fire-light, and noisy with laughter and talk and many-sounding work. None could be idle but the very young and the very old: little Rol, who was hugging a puppy, and old Trella, whose palsied hand fumbled over her knitting. The early evening had closed in, and the farm- servants, come from their outdoor work, had assembled in the ample hall, which gave space for a score or more of workers. Several of the men were engaged in carving, and to these were yielded the best place and light; others made or repaired fishing-tackle and harness, and a great seine net occupied three pairs of hands. Of the women most were sorting and mixing eider feather and chopping straw to add to it. Looms were there, though not in present use, but three wheels whirred emulously, and the finest and swiftest thread of the three ran between the fingers of the house-mistress. Near her were some children, busy too, plaiting wicks for candles and lamps. Each group of workers had a lamp in its centre, and those farthest from the fire had live heat from two braziers filled with glowing wood embers, replenished now and again from the generous hearth. But the flicker of the great fire was manifest to remotest corners, and prevailed beyond the limits of the weaker lights.

Little Rol grew tired of his puppy, dropped it incontinently, and made an on-slaught on Tyr, the old wolf- hound, who basked dozing, whimpering and twitch-ing in his hunting dreams. Prone went Rol beside Tyr, his young arms round the shaggy neck, his curls against the black jowl. Tyr gave a perfunctory lick, and stretched with a sleepy sigh. Rol growled and rolled and shoved invitingly, but could only gain from the old dog placid toleration and a half-observant blink. 'Take that then!' said Rol, indignant at this ignoring of his advances, and sent the puppy sprawling against the dignity that disdained him as playmate. The dog took no notice, and the child wandered off to find amusement elsewhere.

The baskets of white eider feathers caught his eye far off in a distant corner. He slipped under the table, and crept along on all-fours, the ordinary commonplace custom of walking down a room upright not being to his fancy. When close to the women he lay still for a moment watching, with his elbows on the floor and his chin in his palms. One of the women seeing him nodded and smiled, and presently he crept out behind her skirts and passed, hardly noticed, from one to another, till he found opportunity to possess himself of a large handful of feathers. With these he traversed the length of the room, under the table again, and emerged near the spinners. At the feet of the youngest he curled himself round, sheltered by her knees from the observation of the others, and disarmed her of interference by secretly displaying his handful with a confiding smile. A dubious nod satisfied him, and presently he started on the play he had devised. He took a tuft of the white down, and gently shook it free of his fingers close to the whirl of the wheel. The wind of the swift motion took it, spun it round and round in widening circles, till it floated above like a slow white moth. Little Rol's eyes danced, and the row of his small teeth shone in a silent laugh of delight. Another and another of the white tufts was sent whirling round like a winged thing in a spider's web, and floating clear at last. Presently the handful failed.

Rol sprawled forward to survey the room, and contemplate another journey under the table. His shoulder, thrusting forward, checked the wheel for an instant; he shifted hastily. The wheel flew on with a jerk, and the thread snapped. 'Naughty Rol!' said the girl. The swiftest wheel stopped also, and the house- mistress, Rol's aunt, leaned forward, and sighting the low curly head, gave a warning against mischief, and sent him off to old Trella's corner.

Rol obeyed, and after a discreet period of obedience, sidled out again down the length of the room farthest from his aunt's eye. As he slipped in among the men, they looked up to see that their tools might be, as far as possible, out of reach of Rol's hands, and close to their own. Nevertheless, before long he managed to secure a fine chisel and take off its point on the leg of the table. The carver's strong objections to this disconcerted Rol, who for five minutes thereafter effaced himself under the table.

During this seclusion he contemplated the many pairs of legs that surrounded him, and almost shut out the light of the fire. How very odd some of the legs were: some were curved where they should be straight, some were straight where they should be curved, and, as Rol said to himself. 'they all seemed screwed on differently.' Some were tucked away modestly under the benches, others were thrust far out under the table, encroaching on Rol's own particular domain. He stretched out his own short legs and regarded them critically, and, after comparison, favourably. Why were not all legs made like his, or like *his*?

These legs approved by Rol were a little apart from the rest. He crawled opposite and again made comparison. His face grew quite solemn as he thought of the innumerably days to come before his legs could be as long and strong. He hoped they would be just like those, his models, as straight as to bone, as curved as to muscle.

A few moments later Sweyn of the long legs felt a small hand caressing his foot, and looking down, met the upturned eyes of his little cousin Rol. Lying on his back, still softly patting and stroking the young man's foot, the child was quiet and happy for a good while. He watched the movement of the strong deft hands, and the shifting of the bright tools. Now and then, minute chips of wood, puffed off by Sweyn, fell down upon his face. At last he raised himself, very gently, lest a jog should wake impatience in the carver, and crossing his own legs round Sweyn's ankle, clasping with his arms too, laid his head against the knee. Such act is evidence of a child's most wonderful hero-worship. Quite content when Sweyn paused a minute to joke, and pat his head and pull his curls. Quiet he remained, as long as quiescence is possible to limbs young as his. Sweyn forgot he was near, hardly noticed when his leg was gently released, and never saw the stealthy abstraction of one of his tools.

Ten minutes thereafter was a lamentable wail from low on the floor, rising to the full pitch of Rol's healthy lungs; for his hand was gashed across, and the copious bleeding terrified him. Then was there soothing and comforting, washing and binding, and a modicum of scolding, till the loud outcry sank into occasional sobs, and the child, tear-stained and subdued, was returned to the chimney-corner settle, where Trella nodded.

In the reaction after pain and fright, Rol found that the quiet of that fire-lit corner was to his mind. Tyr, too, disdained him no longer, but, roused by his sobs, showed all the concern and sympathy that a dog can by licking and wistful watching. A little shame weighed also upon his spirits. He wished he had not cried quite so much. He remembered how once Sweyn had come home with his arm torn down from the shoulder, and a dead bear; and how he had never winced nor said a word, though his lips turned white with pain. Poor little Rol gave another sighing sob over his own faint-hearted shortcomings.

The light and motion of the great fire began to tell strange stories to the child, and the wind in the chimney roared a corroborative note now and then. The great black mouth of the chimney, impending high over the hearth, received as into a mysterious gulf murky coils of smoke and brightness of aspiring sparks; and beyond, in the high darkness, were muttering and wailing and strange doings, so that sometimes the smoke rushed back in panic, and curled out and up to the roof, and condensed itself to invisibility among the rafters. And then the wind would rage after its lost prey, and rush round the house, rattling and shrieking at window and door.

In a lull, after one such loud gust, Rol lifted his head in surprise and listened. A lull had also come on the babel of talk, and thus could be heard with strange distinctness a sound outside the door—the sound of a child's voice, a child's hands. 'Open, open; let me in!' piped the little voice from low down, lower than the handle, and the latch rattled as though a tiptoe child reached up to it, and soft small knocks were struck. One near the door sprang up and opened it. 'No one is here,' he said. Tyr lifted his head and gave utterance to a howl, loud, prolonged, most dismal.

Sweyn, not able to believe that his ears had deceived him, got up and went to the door. It was a dark night; the clouds were heavy with snow, that had fallen fitfully when the wind lulled. Untrodden snow lay up to the porch; there was no sight nor sound of any human being. Sweyn strained his eyes far and near, only to see dark sky, pure snow, and a line of black fir trees on a hill brow, bowing down before the wind. 'It must have been the wind,' he said, and closed the door.

Many faces looked scared. The sound of a child's voice had been so distinct—and the words 'Open, open; let me in!' The wind might creak the wood, or rattle the latch, but could not speak with a child's voice, nor knock with the soft plain blows that a plump fist gives. And the strange unusual howl of the wolf-hound was an omen to be feared, be the rest what it might. Strange things were said by one and another, till the rebuke of the house-mistress quelled them into far-off whispers. For a time after there was uneasiness, constraint, and silence; then the chill fear thawed by degrees, and the babble of talk flowed on again.

Yet half-an-hour later a very slight noise outside the door sufficed to arrest every hand, every tongue. Every head was raised, every eye fixed in one direction. 'It is Christian; he is late,' said Sweyn.

No, no; this is a feeble shuffle, not a young man's tread. With the sound of uncertain feet came the hard tap-tap of a stick against the door, and the high-pitched voice of eld, 'Open, open; let me in!' Again Tyr flung up his head in a long doleful howl.

Before the echo of the tapping stick and the high voice had fairly died away, Sweyn had sprung across to the door and flung it wide. 'No one again,' he said in a steady voice, though his eyes looked startled as he stared out. He saw the lonely expanse of snow, the clouds swagging low, and between the two the line of dark fir-trees bowing in the wind. He closed the door without a word of comment, and re- crossed the room.

A score of blanched faces were turned to him as though he must be solver of the enigma. He could not be unconscious of this mute eye-questioning, and it disturbed his resolute air of composure. He hesitated, glanced towards his mother, the house-mistress, then back at the frightened folk, and gravely, before them all, made the sign of the cross. There was a flutter of hands as the sign was repeated by all, and the dead silence was stirred as by a huge sigh, for the held breath of many was freed as though the sign gave magic relief.

Even the house-mistress was perturbed. She left her wheel and crossed the room to her son, and spoke with him for a moment in a low tone that none could overhear. But a moment later her voice was high- pitched and loud, so that all might benefit by her rebuke of the 'heathen chatter' of one of the girls. Perhaps she essayed to silence thus her own misgivings and forebodings.

No other voice dared speak now with its natural fulness. Low tones made intermittent murmurs, and now and then silence drifted over the whole room. The handling of tools was as noiseless as might be, and suspended on the instant if the door rattled in a gust of wind. After a time Sweyn left his work, joined the group nearest the door, and loitered there on the pretence of giving advice and help to the unskilful.

A man's tread was heard outside in the porch. 'Christian!' said Sweyn and his mother simultaneously, he confidently, she authoritatively, to set the checked wheels going again. But Tyr flung up his head with an appalling howl.

'Open, open; let me in!'

It was a man's voice, and the door shook and rattled as a man's strength beat against it. Sweyn could feel the planks quivering, as on the instant his hand was upon the door, flinging it open, to face the blank porch, and beyond only snow and sky, and firs aslant in the wind.

He stood for a long minute with the open door in his hand. The bitter wind swept in with its icy chill, but a deadlier chill of fear came swifter, and seemed to freeze the beating of hearts. Sweyn stepped back to snatch up a great bearskin cloak.

'Sweyn, where are you going?'

'No farther than the porch, mother,' and he stepped out and closed the door.

He wrapped himself in the heavy fur, and leaning against the most sheltered wall of the porch, steeled his nerves to face the devil and all his works. No sound of voices came from within; the most distinct sound was the crackle and roar of the fire.

It was bitterly cold. His feet grew numb, but he forbore stamping them into warmth lest the sound should strike panic within; nor would he leave the porch, nor print a foot-mark on the untrodden white that declared so absolutely how no human voices and hands could have approached the door since snow fell two hours or more ago. 'When the wind drops there will be more snow,' thought Sweyn.

For the best part of an hour he kept his watch, and saw no living thing—heard no unwonted sound. 'I will freeze here no longer,' he muttered, and re-entered.

One woman gave a half-suppressed scream as his hand was laid on the latch, and then a gasp of relief as he came in. No one questioned him, only his mother said, in a tone of forced unconcern, 'Could you not see Christain coming?' as though she were made anxious only by the absence of her younger son. Hardly had Sweyn stamped near to the fire than clear knocking was heard at the door. Tyr leapt from the hearth, his eyes red as the fire, his fangs showing white in the black jowl, his neck ridged and bristling; and overleaping Rol, ramped at the door, barking furiously.

Outside the door a clear mellow voice was calling. Tyr's bark made the words undistinguishable.

No one offered to stir towards the door before Sweyn.

He stalked down the room resolutely, lifted the latch, and swung back the door.

A white-robed woman glided in.

No wraith! Living—beautiful—young.

Tyr leapt upon her.

Lithely she baulked the sharp fangs with folds of her long fur robe, and snatching from her girdle a small two-edged axe, whirled it up for a blow of defence.

Sweyn caught the dog by the collar, and dragged him off yelling and struggling.

The stranger stood in the doorway motionless, one foot set forward, one arm flung up, till the house- mistress hurried down the room; and Sweyn, relinquishing to others the furious Tyr, turned again to close the door, and offer excuse for so fierce a greeting. Then she lowered her arm, slung the axe in its place at her waist, loosened the furs about her face, and shook over her shoulders the long white robe—all as it were with the sway of one movement.

She was a maiden, tall and fair. The fashion of her dress was strange, half masculine, yet not unwomanly. A fine fur tunic, reaching but little below the knee, was all the skirt she wore; below were the cross-bound shoes and leggings that a hunter wears. A white fur cap was set low upon the brows, and from its edge strips of fur fell lappet-wise about her shoulders; two of these at her entrance had been drawn forward and crossed about her throat, but now, loosened and thrust back, left unhidden long plaits of fair hair that lay forward on shoulder and breast, down to the ivory-studded girdle where the axe gleamed.

Sweyn and his mother led the stranger to the hearth without question or sign of curiosity, till she voluntarily told her tale of a long journey to distant kindred, a promised guide unmet, and signals and landmarks mistaken.

'Alone!' exclaimed Sweyn in astonishment. 'Have you journeyed thus far, a hundred leagues, alone?'

She answered 'Yes' with a little smile. 'Over the hills and the wastes! Why, the folk there are savage and wild as beasts.'

She dropped her hand upon her axe with a laugh of some scorn.

'I fear neither man nor beast; some few fear me.' And then she told strange tales of fierce attack and defence, and of the bold free huntress life she had led.

Her words came a little slowly and deliberately, as though she spoke in a scarce familiar tongue; now and then she hesitated, and stopped in a phrase, as though for lack of some word.

She became the centre of a group of listeners. The interest she excited dissipated, in some degrees, the dread inspired by the mysterious voices. There was nothing ominous about this young, bright, fair reality, though her aspect was strange.

Little Rol crept near, staring at the stranger with all his might. Unnoticed, he softly stroked and patted a corner of her soft white robe that reached to the floor in ample folds. He laid his cheek against it caressingly, and then edged up close to her knees.

'What is your name?' he asked.

The stranger's smile and ready answer, as she looked down, saved Rol from the rebuke merited by his unmannerly question.

'My real name,' she said, 'would be uncouth to your ears and tongue. The folk of this country have given me another name, and from this' (she laid her hand on the fur robe) 'they call me "White Fell."'

Little Rol repeated it to himself, stroking and patting as before. 'White Fell, White Fell.'

The Fair face, and soft, beautiful dress pleased Rol. He knelt up, with his eyes on her face and an air of uncertain determination, like a robin's on a door-step, and plumped his elbows into her lap with a little gasp at his own audacity.

'Rol!' exclaimed his aunt; but, 'Oh, let him!' said White Fell, smiling and stroking his head; and Rol stayed.

He advanced farther, and panting at his own adventurousness in the face of his aunt's authority, climbed up on to her knees. Her welcoming arms hindered any protest. He nestled happily, fingering the axe head, the ivory studs in her girdle, the ivory clasp at her throat, the plaits of fair hair; rubbing his head against the softness of her fur-clad shoulder, with a child's full confidence in the kindness of beauty.

White Fell had not uncovered her head, only knotted the pendant fur loosely behind her neck. Rol reached up his hand towards it, whispering her name to himself, 'White Fell, White Fell,' then slid his arms round her neck, and kissed her—once—twice. She laughed delightedly, and kissed him again.

'The child plagues you?' said Sweyn.

'No, indeed,' she answered, with an earnestness so intense as to seem disproportionate to the occasion.

Rol settled himself again on her lap, and began to unwind the bandage bound round his hand. He paused a little when he saw where the blood had soaked through; then went on till his hand was bare and the cut displayed, gaping and long, though only skin deep. He held it up towards White Fell, desirous of her pity and sympathy.

At sight of it, and the blood-stained linen, she drew in her breath suddenly, clasped Rol to her—hard, hard—till he began to struggle. Her face was hidden behind the boy, so that none could see its expression. It had lighted up with a most awful glee.

Afar, beyond the fir-grove, beyond the low hill behind, the absent Christian was hastening his return. From daybreak he had been afoot, carrying notice of a bear hunt to all the best hunters of the farms and hamlets that lay within a radius of twelve miles. Nevertheless, having been detained till a late hour, he now broke into a run, going with a long smooth stride of apparent ease that fast made the miles diminish.

He entered the midnight blackness of the fir-grove with scarcely slackened pace, though the path was invisible; and passing through into the open again, sighted the farm lying a furlong off down the slope. Then he sprang out freely, and almost on the instant gave one great sideways leap, and stood still. There in the snow was the track of a great wolf.

His hand went to his knife, his only weapon. He stooped, knelt down, to bring his eyes to the level of a beast, and peered about; his teeth set, his heart beat a little harder than the pace of his running insisted on. A solitary wolf, nearly always savage and of large size, is a formidable beast that will not hesitate to attack a single man. This wolf-track was the largest Christian had ever seen, and, so far as he could judge, recently made. It led from under the fir-trees down the slope. Well for him, he thought, was the delay that had so vexed him before: well for him that he had not passed through the dark fir-grove when that danger of jaws lurked there. Going warily, he followed the track.

It led down the slope, across a broad ice-bound stream, along the level beyond, making towards the farm. A less precise knowledge had doubted, and guessed that here might have come straying big Tyr or his like; but Christian was sure, knowing better than to mistake between footmark of dog and wolf.

Straight on—straight on towards the farm.

Surprised and anxious grew Christian, that a prowling wolf should dare so near. He drew his knife and pressed on, more hastily, more keen-eyed. Oh that Tyr were with him!

Straight on, straight on, even to the very door, where the snow failed. His heart seemed to give a great leap and then stop. There the track ended.

Nothing lurked in the porch, and there was no sign of return. The firs stood straight against the sky, the clouds lay low; for the wind had fallen and a few snowflakes came drifting down. In a horror of surprise, Christian stood dazed a moment: then he lifted the latch and went in. His glance took in all the old familiar forms and faces, and with them that of the stranger, fur-clad and beautiful. The awful truth flashed upon him: he knew what she was.

Only a few were startled by the rattle of the latch as he entered. The room was filled with bustle and movement, for it was the supper hour, when all tools were laid aside, and trestles and tables shifted. Christian had no knowledge of what he said and did; he moved and spoke mechanically, half thinking that soon he must wake from this horrible dream. Sweyn and his mother supposed him to be cold and dead-tired, and spared all unnecessary questions. And he found himself seated beside the hearth, opposite that dreadful Thing that looked like a beautiful girl; watching her every movement, curdling with horror to see her fondle the child Rol.

Sweyn stood near them both, intent upon White Fell also; but how differently! She seemed unconscious of the gaze of both—neither aware of the chill dread in the eyes of Christian, nor of Sweyn's warm admiration.

These two brothers, who were twins, contrasted greatly, despite their striking likeness. They were alike in regular profile, fair brown hair, and deep blue eyes; but Sweyn's features were perfect as a young god's, while Christian's showed faulty details. Thus, the line of his mouth was set too straight, the eyes shelved too deeply back, and the contour of the face flowed in less generous curves than Sweyn's. Their height was the same, but Christian was too slender for perfect proportion, while Sweyn's well-knit frame, broad shoulders, and muscular arms, made him pre-eminent for manly beauty as well as for strength. As a hunter Sweyn was without rival; as a fisher without rival. All the countryside acknowledged him to be the best wrestler, rider, dancer, singer. Only in speed could he be surpassed, and in that only by his younger brother. All others Sweyn could distance fairly; but Christian could outrun him easily. Ay, he could keep pace with Sweyn's most breathless burst, and laugh and talk the while. Christian took little pride in his fleetness of foot, counting a man's legs to be the least worthy of his members. He had no envy of his brother's athletic superiority, though to several feats he had made a moderate second. He loved as only a twin can love—proud of all that Sweyn did, content with all that Sweyn was; humbly content also that his own great love should not be so exceedingly returned, since he knew himself to be so far less love-worthy.

Christian dared not, in the midst of women and children, launch the horror that he knew into words. He waited to consult his brother; but Sweyn did not, or would not, notice the signal he made, and kept his face always turned towards White Fell. Christian drew away from the hearth, unable to remain passive with that dread upon him.

'Where is Tyr?' he said suddenly. Then, catching sight of the dog in a distant corner, 'Why is he chained there?'

'He flew at the stranger,' one answered.

Christian's eyes glowed. 'Yes?' he said, interrogatively.

'He was within an ace of having his brain knocked out.'

'Tyr?'

'Yes; she was nimbly up with that little axe she has at her waist. It was well for old Tyr that his master throttled him off.'

Christian went without a word to the corner where Tyr was chained. The dog rose up to meet him, as piteous and indignant as a dumb beast can be. He stroked the black head. 'Good Tyr! brave dog!'

They knew, they only; and the man and the dumb dog had comfort of each other.

Christian's eyes turned again towards White Fell: Tyr's also, and he strained against the length of the chain. Christian's hand lay on the dog's neck, and he felt it ridge and bristle with the quivering of impotent fury. Then he began to quiver in like manner with a fury born of reason, not instinct; as impotent morally as was Tyr physically. Oh! the woman's form that he dare not touch! Anything but that, and he with Tyr would be free to kill or be killed.

Then he returned to ask fresh questions.

'How long has the stranger been here?'

'She came about half-an-hour before you.'

'Who opened the door to her?'

'Sweyn: no one else dared.'

The tone of the answer was mysterious.

'Why?' queried Christian. 'Has anything strange happened? Tell me.'

For answer he was told in a low undertone of the summons at the door thrice repeated without human agency; and of Tyr's ominous howls; and of Sweyn's fruitless watch outside.

Christian turned towards his brother in a torment of impatience for a word apart. The board was spread, and Sweyn was leading White Fell to the guest's place. This was more awful: she would break bread with them under the roof-tree!

He started forward, and touching Sweyn's arm, whispered an urgent entreaty. Sweyn stared, and shook his head in angry impatience.

Thereupon Christian would take no morsel of food.

His opportunity came at last. White Fell questioned of the landmarks of the country, and of one Cairn Hill, which was an appointed meeting-place at which she was due that night. The house-mistress and Sweyn both exclaimed.

'It is three long miles away,' said Sweyn; 'with no place for shelter but a wretched hut. Stay with us this night, and I will show you the way tomorrow.'

White Fell seemed to hesitate. 'Three miles,' she said; 'then I should be able to see or hear a signal.'

'I will look out,' said Sweyn; 'then, if there be no signal, you must not leave us.'

He went to the door. Christian rose silently, and followed him out.

'Sweyn, do you know what she is?'

Sweyn, surprised at the vehement grasp, and low hoarse voice, made answer: 'She? Who? White Fell?'

'Yes.'

'She is the most beautiful girl I have ever seen.'

208

'She is a werewolf.'

Sweyn burst out laughing. 'Are you mad?' he asked.

'No; here, see for yourself.'

Christian drew him out of the porch, pointing to the snow where the footmarks had been. Had been, for now they were not. Snow was falling fast, and every dint was blotted out.

'Well?' asked Sweyn.

'Had you come when I signed to you, you would have seen for yourself.'

'Seen what?'

'The footprints of a wolf leading up to the door; none leading away.'

It was impossible not to be startled by the tone alone, though it was hardly above a whisper. Sweyn eyed his brother anxiously, but in the darkness could make nothing of his face. Then he laid his hands kindly and re-assuringly on Christian's shoulders and felt how he was quivering with excitement and horror.

'One sees strange things,' he said, 'when the cold has got into the brain behind the eyes; you came in cold and worn out.'

'No,' interrupted Christian. 'I saw the track first on the brow of the slope, and followed it down right here to the door. This is no delusion.'

Sweyn in his heart felt positive that it was. Christian was given to day-dreams and strange fancies, though never had he been possessed with so mad a notion before.

'Don't you believe me?' said Christian desperately. 'You must. I swear it is sane truth. Are you blind? Why, even Tyr knows.'

'You will be clearer headed tomorrow after a night's rest. Then come too, if you will, with White Fell, to the Hill Cairn; and if you have doubts still, watch and follow, and see what footprints she leaves.'

Galled by Sweyn's evident contempt Christian turned abruptly to the door. Sweyn caught him back.

'What now, Christian? What are you going to do?'

'You do not believe me; my mother shall.'

Sweyn's grasp tightened. 'You shall not tell her,' he said authoritatively.

Customarily Christian was so docile to his brother's mastery that it was now a surprising thing when he wrenched himself free vigorously, and said as determinedly as Sweyn, 'She shall know!' but Sweyn was nearer the door and would not let him pass.

'There has been scare enough for one night already. If this notion of yours will keep, broach it tomorrow.' Christian would not yield.

'Women are so easily scared,' pursued Sweyn, 'and are ready to believe any folly without shadow of proof. Be a man, Christian, and fight this notion of a werewolf by yourself.'

'If you would believe me' began Christian.

'I believe you to be a fool,' said Sweyn, losing patience. 'Another, who was not your brother, might believe you to be a knave, and guess that you had transformed White Fell into a werewolf because she smiled more readily on me than on you.'

The jest was not without foundation, for the grace of White Fell's bright looks had been bestowed on him, on Christian never a whit. Sweyn's coxcombery was always frank, and most forgiveable, and not without fair colour.

'If you want an ally,' continued Sweyn, 'confide in old Trella. Out of her stores of wisdom, if her memory holds good, she can instruct you in the orthodox manner of tackling a werewolf. If I remember aright, you should watch the suspected person till midnight, when the beast's form must be resumed, and retained ever after if a human eye sees the change; or, better still, sprinkle hands and feet with holy water, which is certain death. Oh! never fear, but old Trella will be equal to the occasion.'

Sweyn's contempt was no longer good-humoured; some touch of irritation or resentment rose at this monstrous doubt of White Fell. But Christian was too deeply distressed to take offence.

'You speak of them as old wives' tales; but if you had seen the proof I have seen, you would be ready at least to wish them true, if not also to put them to the test.'

'Well,' said Sweyn, with a laugh that had a little sneer in it, 'put them to the test! I will not object to that, if you will only keep your notions to yourself. Now, Christian, give me your word for silence, and we will freeze here no longer.'

Christian remained silent.

Sweyn put his hands on his shoulders again and vainly tried to see his face in the darkness.

'We have never quarrelled yet, Christian?'

'I have never quarrelled,' returned the other, aware for the first time that his dictatorial brother had sometimes offered occasion for quarrel, had he been ready to take it.

'Well,' said Sweyn emphatically, 'if you speak against White Fell to any other, as tonight you have spoken to me—we shall.'

He delivered the words like an ultimatum, turned sharp round, and re-entered the house. Christian, more fearful and wretched than before, followed.

'Snow is falling fast: not a single light is to be seen.'

White Fell's eyes passed over Christian without apparent notice, and turned bright and shining upon Sweyn.

'Nor any signal to be heard?' she queried. 'Did you not hear the sound of a seahorn?'

'I saw nothing, and heard nothing; and signal or no signal, the heavy snow would keep you here perforce.'

She smiled her thanks beautifully. And Christian's heart sank like lead with a deadly foreboding, as he noted what a light was kindled in Sweyn's eyes by her smile.

That night, when all others slept, Christian, the weariest of all, watched outside the guest-chamber till midnight was past. No sound, not the faintest, could be heard. Could the old tale be true of the midnight change? What was on the other side of the door, a woman or a beast? he would have given his right hand to know. Instinctively he laid his hand on the latch, and drew it softly, though believing that bolts fastened the inner side. The door yielded to his hand; he stood on the threshold; a keen gust of air cut athim; the window stood open; the room was empty.

So Christian could sleep with a somewhat lightened heart.

In the morning there was surprise and conjecture when White Fell's absence was discovered. Christian held his peace. Not even to his brother did he say how he knew that she had fled before midnight; and Sweyn, though evidently greatly chagrined, seemed to disdain reference to the subject of Christian's fears.

The elder brother alone joined the bear hunt; Christian found pretext to stay behind. Sweyn, being out of humour, manifested his contempt by uttering not a single expostulation.

All that day, and for many a day after, Christian would never go out of sight of his home. Sweyn alone noticed how he manoeuvred for this, and was clearly annoyed by it. White Fell's name was never mentioned between them, though not seldom was it heard in general talk. Hardly a day passed but little Rol asked when White Fell would come again: pretty White Fell, who kissed like a snowflake. And if Sweyn answered, Christian would be quite sure that the light in his eyes, kindled by White Fell's smile, had not yet died out.

Little Rol! Naughty, merry, fair-haired little Rol. A day came when his feet raced over the threshold never to return; when his chatter and laugh were heard no more; when tears of anguish were wept by eyes that never would see his bright head again: never again, living or dead.

He was seen at dusk for the last time, escaping from the house with his puppy, in freakish rebellion against old Trella. Later, when his absence had begun to cause anxiety, his puppy crept back to the farm, cowed, whimpering and yelping, a pitiful, dumb lump of terror, without intelligence or courage to guide the frightened search.

Rol was never found, nor any trace of him. Where he had perished was never known; how he had perished was known only by an awful guess—a wild beast had devoured him.

Christian heard the conjecture 'a wolf'; and a horrible certainty flashed upon him that he knew what wolf it was. He tried to declare what he knew, but Sweyn saw him start at the words with white face and struggling lips; and, guessing his purpose, pulled him back, and kept him silent, hardly, by his imperious grip and wrathful eyes, and one low whisper.

That Christian should retain his most irrational suspicion against beautiful White Fell was, to Sweyn, evidence of a weak obstinacy of mind that would but thrive upon expostulation and argument. But this evident intention to direct the passions of grief and anguish to a hatred and fear of the fair stranger, such as his own, was intolerable, and Sweyn set his will against it. Again Christian yielded to his brother's stronger words and will, and against his own judgement consented to silence.

Repentance came before the new moon, the first of the year, was old. White Fell came again, smiling as she entered, as though assured of a glad and kindly welcome; and, in truth, there was only one who saw again her fair face and strange white garb without pleasure. Sweyn's face glowed with delight, while Christian's grew pale and rigid as death. He had given his word to keep silence; but he had not thought that she would dare to come again. Silence was impossible, face to face with that Thing, impossible. Irrepressibly he cried out:

'Where is Rol?'

Not a quiver disturbed White Fell's face. She heard, yet remained bright and tranquil. Sweyn's eyes flashed round at his brother dangerously. Among the women some tears fell at the poor child's name; but none caught alarm from its sudden utterance, for the thought of Rol rose naturally. Where was little Rol, who had nestled in the stranger's arms, kissing her; and watched for her since; and prattled of her daily?

Christian went out silently. One only thing there was that he could do, and he must not delay. His horror overmastered any curiosity to hear White Fell's smooth excuses and smiling apologies for her strange and uncourteous departure; or her easy tale of the circumstances of her return; or to watch her bearing as she heard the sad tale of little Rol.

The swiftest runner in the country-side had started on his hardest race: little less than three leagues and back, which he reckoned to accomplish in two hours, though the night was moonless and the way rugged. He rushed against the still cold air till it felt like a wind upon his face. The dim homestead sank below the ridges at his back, and fresh ridges of snowlands rose out of the obscure horizon-level to drive past him as the stirless air drove, and sink away behind into obscure level again. He took no conscious heed of landmarks, not even when all sign of a path was gone under depths of snow. His will was set to reach his goal with unexampled speed; and thither by instinct his physical forces bore him, without one definite thought to guide.

And the idle brain lay passive, inert, receiving into its vacancy restless siftings of past sights and sounds; Rol, weeping, laughing, playing, coiled in the arms of that dreadful Thing: Tyr—O Tyr!—white fangs in the black jowl: the women who wept on the foolish puppy, precious for the child's last touch: footprints from pine wood to door: the smiling face among furs, of such womanly beauty—smiling—

smiling: and Sweyn's face.

'Sweyn, Sweyn, O Sweyn, my brother!'

Sweyn's angry laugh possessed his ear within the sound of the wind of his speed; Sweyn's scorn assailed more quick and keen than the biting cold at his throat. And yet he was unimpressed by any thought of how Sweyn's anger and scorn would rise, if this errand were known.

Sweyn was sceptic. His utter disbelief in Christian's testimony regarding the footprints were based upon positive scepticism. His reason refused to bend in accepting the possibility of the supernatural materialised. That a living beast could ever be other than palpably bestial—pawed, toothed, shagged, and eared as such, was to him incredible; far more that a human presence could be transformed from its god-like aspect, upright, freehanded, with brows, and speech, and laughter. The wild and fearful legends that he had known from childhood and then believed, he regarded now as built upon facts distorted, overlaid by imagination, and quickened by superstition. Even the strange summons at the threshold, that he himself had vainly answered, was, after the first shock of surprise, rationally explained by him as malicious foolery on the part of some clever trickster, who witheld the key to the enigma.

To the younger brother all life was a spiritual mystery, veiled from his clear knowledge by the density of flesh. Since he knew his own body to be linked to the complex and antagonistic forces that constitute one soul, it seemed to him not impossibly strange that one spiritual force should possess divers forms for widely various manifestation. Nor, to him, was it great effort to believe that as pure water washes away all natural foulness, so water, holy by consecration, must needs cleanse God's world from that supernatural evil Thing. Therefore, faster than ever man's foot had covered those leagues, he sped under the dark, still night, over the waste, trackless snow-ridges to the far-away church, where salvation lay in the holy-water stoup at the door. His faith was as firm as any that wrought miracles in days past, simple as a child's wish, strong as a man's will.

He was hardly missed during these hours, every second of which was by him fulfilled to its utmost extent by extremest effort that sinews and nerves could attain. Within the homestead the while, the easy moments went bright with words and looks of unwonted animation, for the kindly, hospitable instincts of the inmates were roused into cordial expression of welcome and interest by the grace and beauty of the returned stranger.

But Sweyn was eager and earnest, with more than a host's courteous warmth. The impression that at her first coming had charmed him, that had lived since through memory, deepened now in her actual presence. Sweyn, the matchless among men, acknowledged in this fair White Fell a spirit high and bold as his own, and a frame so firm and capable that only bulk was lacking for equal strength. Yet the white skin was moulded most smoothly, without such muscular swelling as made his might evident. Such love as his frank self-love could concede was called forth by an ardent admiration for this supreme stranger. More admiration than love was in his passion, and therefore he was free from a lover's hesitancy and delicate reserve and doubts. Frankly and boldly he courted her favour by looks and tones, and an address that came of natural ease, needless of skill by practice.

Nor was she a woman to be wooed otherwise. Tender whispers and sighs would never gain her ear; but her eyes would brighten and shine if she heard of a brave feat, and her prompt hand in sympathy fall swiftly on the axe-haft and clasp it hard. That movement ever fired Sweyn's admiration anew; he watched for it, strove to elicit it, and glowed when it came. Wonderful and beautiful was that wrist, slender and steel-strong; also the smooth shapely hand, that curved so fast and firm, ready to deal instant death.

Desiring to feel the pressure of these hands, this bold lover schemed with palpable directness, proposing that she should hear how their hunting songs were sung, with a chorus that signalled hands to be clasped. So his splendid voice gave the verses, and, as the chorus was taken up, he claimed her hands, and, even through the easy grip, felt, as he desired, the strength that was latent, and the vigour that quickened the very fingertips, as the song fired her, and her voice was caught out of her by the rhythmic swell, and rang clear on the top of the closing surge.

Afterwards she sang alone. For contrast, or in the pride of swaying moods by her voice, she chose a mournful song that drifted along in a minor chant, sad as a wind that dirges:

'Oh, let me go!
Around spin wreaths of snow;
The dark earth sleeps below.
Far up the plain
Moans on a voice of pain:
"Where shall my babe be lain?"
In my white breast
Lay the sweet life to rest!
Lay, where it can lie best!
"Hush! hush its cries!
Dense night is on the skies:
Two stars are in thine eyes."
Come, babe, away!
But lie thou till dawn be grey,
Who must be dead by day.
This cannot last;
But, ere the sickening blast,
All sorrow shall be past;

And kings shall be
Low bending at thy knee,
Worshipping life from thee.
For men long sore
To hope of what's before,—
To leave the things of yore.
Mine, and not thine,
How deep their jewels shine!
Peace laps thy head, not mine.'

Old Trella came tottering from her corner, shaken to additional palsy by an aroused memory. She strained her dim eyes towards the singer, and then bent her head, that the one ear yet sensible to sound might avail of every note. At the close, groping forward, she murmured with the high-pitched quaver of old age:

'So she sang, my Thora; my last and brightest. What is she like, she whose voice is like my dead Thora's? Are her eyes blue?'

'Blue as the sky.'

'So were my Thora's! Is her hair fair, and in plaits to the waist?'

'Even so,' answered White Fell herself, and met the advancing hands with her own, and guided them to corroborate her words by touch.

'Like my dead Thora's,' repeated the old woman; and then her trembling hands rested on the fur-clad shoulders, and she bent forward and kissed the smooth fair face that White Fell upturned, nothing loth, to receive and return the caress.

So Christian saw them as he entered.

He stood a moment. After the starless darkness and the icy night air, and the fierce silent two hours' race, his senses reeled on sudden entrance into warmth, and light, and the cheery hum of voices. A sudden unforeseen anguish assailed him, as now first he entertained the possibility of being overmatched by her wiles and her daring, if at the approach of pure death she should start up at bay transformed to a terrible beast, and achieve a savage glut at the last. He looked with horror and pity on the harmless, helpless folk, so unwitting of outrage to their comfort and security. The dreadful Thing in their midst, that was veiled from their knowledge by womanly beauty, was a centre of pleasant interest. There, before him, signally impressive, was poor old Trella, weakest and feeblest of all, in fond nearness. And a moment might bring about the revelation of a monstrous horror—a ghastly, deadly danger, set loose and at bay, in a circle of girls and women and careless defenceless men; so hideous and terrible a thing as might crack the brain, or curdle the heart stone dead.

And he alone of the throng prepared!

For one breathing space he faltered, no longer than that, while over him swept the agony of compunction that yet could not make him surrender his purpose.

He alone? Nay, but Tyr also; and he crossed to the dumb sole sharer of his knowledge.

So timeless is thought that a few seconds only lay between his lifting of the latch and his loosening of Tyr's collar; but in those few seconds succeeding his first glance, as lightning-swift had been the impulses of others, their motion as quick and sure. Sweyn's vigilant eye had darted upon him, and instantly his every fibre was alert with hostile instinct; and, half divining, half incredulous, of Christian's object in stooping to Tyr, he came hastily, wary, wrathful, resolute to oppose the malice of his wild-eyed brother.

But beyond Sweyn rose White Fell, blanching white as her furs, and with eyes grown fierce and wild. She leapt down the room to the door, whirling her long robe closely to her. 'Hark!' she panted. 'The signal horn! Hark, I must go!' as she snatched at the latch to be out and away.

For one precious moment Christian had hesitated on the half-loosened collar; for, except the womanly form were exchanged for the bestial, Tyr's jaws would gnash to rags his honour of manhood. Then he heard her voice, and turned—too late.

As she tugged at the door, he sprange across grasping his flask, but Sweyn dashed between, and caught him back irresistibly, so that a most frantic effort only availed to wrench one arm free. With that, on the impulse of sheer despair, he cast at her with all his force. The door swung behind her, and the flask flew into fragments against it. Then, as Sweyn's grasp slackened, and he met the questioning astonishment of surrounding faces, with a hoarse inarticulate cry: 'God help us all!' he said. 'She is a werewolf.'

Sweyn turned upon him, 'Liar, coward!' and his hands gripped his brother's throat with deadly force, as though the spoken word could be killed so; and as Christian struggled, lifted him clear off his feet and flung him crashing backward. So furious was he, that, as his brother lay motionless, he stirred him roughly with his foot, till their mother came between, crying shame; and yet then he stood by, his teeth set, his brows knit, his hands clenched, ready to enforce silence again violently, as Christian rose staggeringand bewildered.

But utter silence and submission were more than he expected, and turned his anger into contempt for one so easily cowed and held in subjection by mere force. 'He is mad!' he said, turning on his heel as he spoke, so that he lost his mother's look of pained reproach at this sudden free utterance of what was a lurking dread within her.

Christian was too spent for the effort of speech. His hard-drawn breath laboured in great sobs; his limbs were powerless and untrusting in utter relax after hard service. Failure in his endeavour induced a stupor of misery and despair. In addition was the wretched humilation of open violence and strife with his brother, and the distress of hearing misjudging contempt expressed without reserve; for he was aware that Sweyn had turned to allay the scared excitement half by imperious mastery, half by explanation and argument, that showed painful disregard of brotherly consideration. All this unkindness of his twin he charged upon the fell Thing who had wrought this their first dissension, and, ah! most terrible thought, interposed between them so effectually, that Sweyn was wilfully blind and deaf on her account, resentful of interference, arbitrary beyond reason.

Dread and perplexity unfathomable darkened upon him; unshared, the burden was overwhelming: a foreboding of unspeakable calamity, based upon his ghastly discovery, bore down upon him, crushing out hope of power to withstand impending fate.

Sweyn the while was observant of his brother, despite the continual check of finding, turn and glance when he would, Christian's eyes always upon him, with a strange look of helpless distress, discomposing enough to the angry aggressor. 'Like a beaten dog!' he said to himself, rallying contempt to withstand compunction. Observation set him wondering on Christian's exhausted condition. The heavy labouring breath and the slack inert fall of the limbs told surely of unusual and prolonged exertion. And then why had close upon two hours' absence been followed by open hostility against White Fell?

Suddenly, the fragments of the flask giving a clue, he guessed all, and faced about to stare at his brother in amaze. He forgot that the motive scheme was against White Fell, demanding derision and resentment from him; that was swept out of remembrance by astonishment and admiration for the feat of speed and endurance. In eagerness to question he inclined to attempt a generous part and frankly offer to heal the breach; but Christian's depression and sad following gaze provoked him to self-justification by recalling the offence of that outrageous utterance against White Fell; and the impulse passed. Then other considerations counselled silence; and afterwards a humour possessed him to wait and see how Christian would find opportunity to proclaim his performance and establish the fact, without exciting ridicule on account of the absurdity of the errand.

This expectation remained unfulfilled. Christian never attempted the proud avowal that would have placed his feat on record to be told to the next generation.

That night Sweyn and his mother talked long and late together, shaping into certainty the suspicion that Christian's mind had lost its balance, and discussing the evident cause. For Sweyn, declaring his own love for White Fell, suggested that his unfortunate brother, with a like passion, they being twins in loves as in birth, had through jealousy and despair turned from love to hate, until reason failed at the strain, and a craze developed, which the malice and treachery of madness made a serious and dangerous force.

So Sweyn theorised, convincing himself as he spoke; convincing afterwards others who advanced doubts against White Fell; fettering his judgement by his advocacy, and by his staunch defence of her hurried flight silencing his own inner consciousness of the unaccountability of her action.

But a little time and Sweyn lost his vantage in the shock of a fresh horror at the homestead. Trella was no more, and her end a mystery. The poor old woman crawled out in a bright gleam to visit a bed-ridden gossip living beyond the fir-grove. Under the trees she was last seen, halting for her companion, sent back for a forgotten present. Quick alarm sprang, calling every man to the search. Her stick was found among the brushwood only a few paces from the path, but no track or stain, for a gusty wind was sifting the snow from the branches, and hid all sign of how she came by her death.

So panic-stricken were the farm folk that none dared go singly on the search. Known danger could be braced, but not this stealthy Death that walked by day invisible, that cut off alike the child in his play and the aged woman so near to her quiet grave.

'Rol she kissed; Trella she kissed!' So rang Christian's frantic cry again and again, till Sweyn dragged him away and strove to keep him apart, albeit in his agony of grief and remorse he accused himself wildly as answerable for the tragedy, and gave clear proof that the charge of madness was well founded, if strange looks and desperate, incoherent words were evidence enough.

But thenceforward all Sweyn's reasoning and mastery could not uphold White Fell above suspicion. He was not called upon to defend her from accusation when Christian had been brought to silence again; but he well knew the significance of this fact, that her name, formerly uttered freely and often, he never heard now: it was huddled away into whispers that he could not catch.

The passing of time did not sweep away the superstitious fears that Sweyn despised. He was angry and anxious; eager that White Fell should return, and, merely by her bright gracious presence, reinstate herself in favour; but doubtful if all his authority and example could keep from her notice an altered aspect of welcome; and he foresaw clearly that Christian would prove unmanageable, and might be capable of some dangerous outbreak.

For a time the twins' variance was marked, on Sweyn's part by an air of rigid indifference, on Christian's by heavy downcast silence, and a nervous apprehensive observation of his brother. Superadded to his remorse and foreboding, Sweyn's displeasure weighed upon him intolerably, and the remembrance of their violent rupture was a ceaseless misery. The elder brother, self-sufficient and insensitive, could little know how deeply his unkindness stabbed. A depth and force of affection such as Christian's was unknown to him. The loyal subservience that he could not appreciate had encouraged him to domineer; this strenuous opposition to his reason and will was accounted as furious malice, if not sheer insanity.

Christian's surveillance galled him incessantly, and embarrassment and danger he foresaw as the outcome. Therefore, that suspicion might be lulled, he judged it wise to make overtures for peace. Most easily done. A little kindliness, a few evidences of consideration, a slight return of the old brotherly imperiousness, and Christian replied by a gratefulness and relief that might have touched him had he understood all, but instead, increased his secret contempt.

So successful was this finesse, that when, late on a day, a message summoning Christian to a distance was transmitted by Sweyn, no doubt of its genuineness occurred. When, his errand proved useless, he set out to return, mistake or mis-apprehension was all that he surmised. Not till he sighted the homestead, lying low between the night-grey snow-ridges, did vivid recollection of the time when he had tracked that horror to the door rouse an intense dread, and with it a hardly-defined suspicion.

His grasp tightened on the bear-spear that he carried as a staff; every sense was alert, every muscle strung; excitement urged him on, caution checked him, and the two governed his long stride, swiftly, noiselessly, to the climax he felt was at hand.

As he drew near to the outer gates, a light shadow stirred and went, as though the grey of the snow had taken detached motion. A darker shadow stayed and faced Christian, striking his life-blood chill with utmost despair.

Sweyn stood before him, and surely, the shadow that went was White Fell.

They had been together—close. Had she not been in his arms, near enough for lips to meet?

There was no moon, but the stars gave light enough to show that Sweyn's face was flushed and elate. The flush remained, though the expression changed quickly at sight of his brother. How, if Christian had seen all, should one of his frenzied outbursts be met and managed: by resolution? by indifference? He halted be-tween the two, and as a result, he swaggered.

'White Fell?' questioned Christian, hoarse and breathless.

'Yes?'

Sweyn's answer was a query, with an intonation that implied he was clearing the ground for action.

From Christian came: 'Have you kissed her?' like a bolt direct, staggering Sweyn by its sheer prompt temerity.

He flushed yet darker, and yet half-smiled over this earnest of success he had won. Had there been really between himself and Christian the rivalry that he imag-ined, his face had enough of the insolence of triumph to exasperate jealous rage.

'You dare ask this!'

'Sweyn, O Sweyn, I must know! You have!'

The ring of despair and anguish in his tone angered Sweyn, misconstruing it. Jealousy urging to such presumption was intolerable.

'Mad fool!' he said, constraining himself no longer. 'Win for yourself a woman to kiss. Leave mine without question. Such an one as I should desire to kiss is such an one as shall never allow a kiss to you.'

Then Christian fully understood his supposition.

'I—I!' he cried. 'White Fell—that deadly Thing! Sweyn, are you blind, mad? I would save you from her: a werewolf!'

Sweyn maddened again at the accusation—a dastardly way of revenge, as he conceived; and instantly, for the second time, the brothers were at strife violently.

But Christian was now too desperate to be scrupulous; for a dim glimpse had shot a possibility into his mind, and to be free to follow it the striking of his brother was a necessity. Thank God! he was armed, and so Sweyn's equal.

Facing his assailant with the bear-spear, he struck up his arms, and with the butt end hit hard so that he fell. The matchless runner leapt away on the instant, to follow a forlorn hope.

Sweyn, on regaining his feet, was as amazed as angry at this unaccountable flight. He knew in his heart that his brother was no coward, and that it was unlike him to shrink from an encounter because defeat was certain, and cruel humiliation from a vindictive victor probable. Of the uselessness of pursuit he was well aware: he must abide his chagrin, content to know that his time for advantage would come. Since White Fell had parted to the right, Christian to the left, the event of a sequent encounter did not occur to him.

And now Christian, acting on the dim glimpse he had had, just as Sweyn turned upon him, of something that moved against the sky along the ridge behind the homestead, was staking his only hope on a chance, and his own superlative speed. If what he saw was really White Fell, he guessed she was bending her steps towards the open wastes; and there was just a possibility that, by a straight dash, and a desperate perilous leap over a sheer bluff, he might yet meet her or head her. And then: he had no further thought.

It was past, the quick, fierce race, and the chance of death at the leap; and he halted in a hollow to fetch his breath and to look: did she come? had she gone?

She came.

She came with a smooth, gliding, noiseless speed, that was neither walking nor running; her arms were folded in her furs that were drawn tight about her body; the white lappets from her head were wrapped and knotted closely beneath her face; her eyes were set on a far distance. So she went till the even sway of her going was startled to a pause by Christian.

'Fell!'

She drew a quick, sharp breath at the sound of her name thus mutilated, and faced Sweyn's brother. Her eyes glittered; her upper lip was lifted, and shewed the teeth. The half of her name, impressed with an ominous sense as uttered by him, warned her of the aspect of a deadly foe. Yet she cast loose her robes till they trailed ample, and spoke as a mild woman.

'What would you?'

Then Christian answered with his solemn dreadful accusation:

'You kissed Rol—and Rol is dead! You kissed Trella: she is dead! You have kissed

Sweyn, my brother; but he shall not die!'

He added: 'You may live till midnight.'

The edge of the teeth and the glitter of the eyes stayed a moment, and her right hand also slid down to the axe haft. Then, without a word, she swerved from him, and sprang out and away swiftly over the snow.

And Christian sprang out and away, and followed her swiftly over the snow, keeping behind, but half-a- stride's length from her side.

So they went running together, silent, towards the vast wastes of snow, where no living thing but they two moved under the stars of night.

Never before had Christian so rejoiced in his powers. The gift of speed, and the training of use and endurance were priceless to him now. Though midnight was hours away, he was confident that, go where that Fell Thing would, hasten as she would, she could not outstrip him nor escape from him. Then, when came the time for transformation, when the woman's form made no longer a shield against a man's hand, he could slay or be slain to save Sweyn. He had struck his dear brother in dire extremity, but he could not, though reason urged, strike a woman.

For one mile, for two miles they ran: White Fell ever foremost, Christian ever at equal distance from her side, so near that, now and again, her out-flying furs touched him. She spoke no word; nor he. She never turned her head to look at him, nor swerved to evade him; but, with set face looking forward, sped straight on, over rough, over smooth, aware of his nearness by the regular beat of his feet, and the sound of his breath behind.

In a while she quicked her pace. From the first, Christian had judged of her speed as admirable, yet with exulting security in his own excelling and enduring whatever her efforts. But, when the pace increased, he found himself put to the test as never had he been before in any race. Her feet, indeed, flew faster than his; it was only by his length of stride that he kept his place at her side. But his heart was high and resolute, and he did not fear failure yet.

So the desperate race flew on. Their feet struck up the powdery snow, their breath smoked into the sharp clear air, and they were gone before the air was cleared of snow and vapour. Now and then Christian glanced up to judge, by the rising of the stars, of the coming of midnight. So long—so long!

White Fell held on without slack. She, it was evident, with confidence in her speed proving matchless, as resolute to outrun her pursuer as he to endure till midnight and fulfil his purpose. And Christian held on, still self-assured. He could not fail; he would not fail. To avenge Rol and Trella was motive enough for him to do what man could do; but for Sweyn more. She had kissed Sweyn, but he should not die too: with Sweyn to save he could not fail.

Never before was such a race as this; no, not when in old Greece man and maid raced together with two fates at stake; for the hard running was sustained unabated, while star after star rose and went wheeling up towards midnight, for one hour, for two hours.

Then Christian saw and heard what shot him through with fear. Where a fringe of trees hung round a slope he saw something dark moving, and heard a yelp, followed by a full horrid cry, and the dark spread out upon the snow, a pack of wolves in pursuit.

Of the beasts alone he had little cause for fear; at the pace he held he could distance them, four-footed though they were. But of White Fell's wiles he had infinite apprehension, for how might she not avail herself of the savage jaws of these wolves, akin as they were to half her nature. She vouchsafed to them nor look nor sign; but Christian, on an impulse to assure himself that she should not escape him, caught and held the back-flung edge of her furs, running still.

She turned like a flash with a beastly snarl, teeth and eyes gleaming again. Her axe shone, on the upstroke, on the downstroke, as she hacked at his hand. She had lopped it off at the wrist, but that he parried with the bear-spear. Even then, she shore through the shaft and shattered the bones of the hand at the same blow, so that he loosed perforce.

Then again they raced on as before, Christian not losing a pace, though his left hand swung useless, bleeding and broken.

The snarl, indubitable, though modified from a woman's organs, the vicious fury revealed in teeth and eyes, the sharp arrogant pain of her maiming blow, caught away Christian's heed of the beasts behind, by striking into him close vivid realisation of the infinitely greater danger that ran before him in that deadly Thing.

When he bethought him to look behind, lo! the pack had but reached their tracks, and instantly slunk aside, cowed; the yell of pursuit changing to yelps and whines. So abhorrent was that fell creature to beast as to man.

She had drawn her furs more closely to her, disposing them so that, instead of flying loose to her heels, no drapery hung lower than her knees, and this without a check to her wonderful speed, nor embarrassment by the cumbering of the folds. She held her head as before; her lips were firmly set, only the tense nostrils gave her breath; not a sign of distress witnessed to the long sustaining of that terrible speed.

But on Christian by now the strain was telling palpably. His head weighed heavy, and his breath came labouring in great sobs; the bear spear would have been a burden now. His heart was beating like a hammer, but such a dulness oppressed his brain, that it was only by degrees he could realise his helpless state; wounded and weaponless, chasing that terrible Thing, that was a fierce, desperate, axe-armed woman, except she should assume the beast with fangs yet more formidable.

And still the far slow stars went lingering nearly an hour from midnight.

So far was his brain astray that an impression took him that she was fleeing from the midnight stars, whose gain was by such slow degrees that a time equalling days and days had gone in the race round the northern circle of the world, and days and days as long might last before the end—except she slackened, or except he failed.

But he would not fail yet.

How long had he been praying so? He had started with a self-confidence and reliance that had felt no need for that aid; and now it seemed the only means by which to restrain his heart from swelling beyond the compass of his body, by which to cherish his brain from dwindling and shrivelling quite away. Some sharp-toothed creature kept tearing and dragging on his maimed left hand; he never could see it, he could not shake it off; but he prayed it off at times.

The clear stars before him took to shuddering, and he knew why: they shuddered at sight of what was behind him. He had never divined before that strange things hid themselves from men under pretence of being snow-clad mounds or swaying trees; but now they came slipping out from their harmless covers to follow him, and mock at his impotence to make a kindred Thing resolve to truer form. He knew the air behind him was thronged; he heard the hum of innumerable murmurings together; but his eyes could never catch them, they were too swift and nimble. Yet he knew they were there, because, on a backward glance, he saw the snow mounds surge as they grovelled flatlings out of sight; he saw the trees reel as they screwed themselves rigid past recognition among the boughs.

And after such glance the stars for awhile returned to steadfastness, and an infinite stretch of silence froze upon the chill grey world, only deranged by the swift even beat of the flying feet, and his own—slower from the longer stride, and the sound of his breath. And for some clear moments he knew that his only concern was, to sustain his speed regardless of pain and distress, to deny with every nerve he had her power to outstrip him or to widen the space between them, till the stars crept up to midnight.

Then out again would come that crowd invisible, humming and hustling behind, dense and dark enough, he knew, to blot out the stars at his back, yet ever skipping and jerking from his sight.

A hideous check came to the race. White Fell swirled about and leapt to the right, and Christian, unprepared for so prompt a lurch, found close at his feet a deep pit yawning, and his own impetus past control. But he snatched at her as he bore past, clasping her right arm with his one whole hand, and the two swung together upon the brink.

And her straining away in self preservation was vigorous enough to counterbalance his headlong impulse, and brought them reeling together to safety.

Then, before he was verily sure that they were not to perish so, crashing down, he saw her gnashing in wild pale fury as she wrenched to be free; and since her right hand was in his grasp, used her axe left- handed, striking back at him.

The blow was effectual enough even so; his right arm dropped powerless, gashed, and with the lesser bone broken, that jarred with horrid pain when he let it swing as he leaped out again, and ran to recover the few feet she had gained from his pause at the shock.

The near escape and this new quick pain made again every faculty alive and intense. He knew that what he followed was most surely Death animate: wounded and helpless, he was utterly at her mercy if so she should realise and take action. Hopeless to avenge, hopeless to save, his very despair for Sweyn swept him on to follow, and follow, and precede the kiss-doomed to death. Could he yet fail to hunt that Thing past midnight, out of the womanly form alluring and treacherous, into lasting restraint of the bestial, which was the last shred of hope left from the confident purpose of the outset?

'Sweyn, Sweyn, O Sweyn!' He thought he was praying, though his heart wrung out nothing but this: 'Sweyn, Sweyn, O Sweyn!'

The last hour from midnight had lost half its quarters, and the stars went lifting up the great minutes; and again his greatening heart, and his shrinking brain, and the sickening agony that swung at either side, conspired to appal the will that had only seeming empire over his feet.

Now White Fell's body was so closely enveloped that not a lap nor an edge flew free. She stretched forward strangely aslant, leaning from the upright poise of a runner. She cleared the ground at times by long bounds, gaining an increase of speed that Christian agonised to equal.

Because the stars pointed that the end was nearing, the black brood came behind again, and followed, noising. Ah! if they could but be kept quiet and still, nor slip their usual harmless masks to encourage with their interest the last speed of their most deadly congener. What shape had they? Should he ever know? If it were not that he was bound to compel the fell Thing that ran before him into her truer form, he might face about and follow them. No—no—not so; if he might do anything but what he did—race, race, and racing bear this agony, he would just stand still and die, to be quit of the pain of breathing.

He grew bewildered, uncertain of his own identity, doubting of his own true form. He could not be really a man, no more than that running Thing was really a woman; his real form was only hidden under embodiment of a man, but what it was he did not know. And Sweyn's real form he did not know. Sweyn lay fallen at his feet, where he had struck him down—his own brother—he: he stumbled over him, and had to overleap him and race harder because she who had kissed Sweyn leapt so fast. 'Sweyn, Sweyn, O Sweyn!'

Why did the stars stop to shudder? Midnight else had surely come!

The leaning, leaping Thing looked back at him with a wild, fierce look, and laughed in savage scorn and triumph. He saw in a flash why, for within a time measurable by seconds she would have escaped him utterly. As the land lay, a slope of ice sunk on the one hand; on the other hand a steep rose, shouldering forwards; between the two was space for a foot to be planted, but none for a body to stand; yet a juniper bough, thrusting out, gave a handhold secure enough for one with a resolute grasp to swing past the perilous place, and pass on safe.

Though the first seconds of the last moment were going, she dared to flash back a wicked look, and laugh at the pursuer who was impotent to grasp.

The crisis struck convulsive life into his last supreme effort; his will surged up indomitable, his speed proved matchless yet. He leapt with a rush, passed her before her laugh had time to go out, and turned short, barring the way, and braced to withstand her.

She came hurling desperate, with a feint to the right hand, and then launched herself upon him with a spring like a wild beast when it leaps to kill. And he, with one strong arm and a hand that could not hold, with one strong hand and an arm that could not guide and sustain, he caught and held her even so. And they fell together. And because he felt his whole arm slipping, and his whole hand loosing, to slack the dreadful agony of the wrenched bone above, he caught and held with his teeth the tunic at her knee, as she struggled up and wrung off his hands to overleap him victorious.

Like lightning she snatched her axe, and struck him on the neck, deep—once, twice—his life-blood gushed out, staining her feet.

The stars touched midnight.

The death scream he heard was not his, for his teeth had hardly yet relaxed when it rang out; and the dreadful cry began with a woman's shriek, and changed and ended as the yell of a beast. And before the final blank overtook his dying eyes, he saw that She gave place to It; he saw more, that Life gave place to Death—causelessly, incomprehensibly.

For he did not presume that no holy water could be more holy, more potent to destroy an evil thing than the life-blood of a pure heart poured out for another in free willing devotion.

His own true hidden reality that he had desired to know grew palpable, recognisable. It seemed to him just this: a great glad abounding hope that he had saved his brother; too expansive to be contained by the limited form of a sole man, it yearned for a new embodiment infinite as the stars.

What did it matter to that true reality that the man's brain shrank, shrank, till it was nothing; that the man's body could not retain the huge pain of his heart, and heaved it out through the red exit riven at the neck; that the black noise came again hurtling from behind, reinforced by that dissolved shape, and blotted out for ever the man's sight, hearing, sense.

In the early grey of day Sweyn chanced upon the footprints of a man—of a runner, as he saw by the shifted snow; and the direction they had taken aroused curiosity, since a little farther their line must be crossed by the edge of a sheer height. He turned to trace them. And so doing, the length of the stride struck his attention—a stride long as his own if he ran. He knew he was following Christian.

In his anger he had hardened himself to be indifferent to the night-long absence of his brother; but now, seeing where the footsteps went, he was seized with compunction and dread. He had failed to give thought and care to his poor frantic twin, who might—was it possible?—have rushed to a frantic death.

His heart stood still when he came to the place where the leap had been taken. A piled edge of snow had fallen too, and nothing but snow lay below when he peered. Along the upper edge he ran for a furlong, till he came to a dip where he could slip and climb down, and then back again on the lower level to the pile of fallen snow. There he saw that the vigorous running had started afresh.

He stood pondering; vexed that any man should have taken that leap where he had not ventured to follow; vexed that he had been beguiled to such painful emotions; guessing vainly at Christian's object in this mad freak. He began sauntering along, half unconsciously following his brother's track; and so in a while he came to the place where the footprints were doubled.

Small prints were these others, small as a woman's, though the pace from one to another was longer than that which the skirts of women allow.

Did not White Fell tread so?

A dreadful guess appalled him, so dreadful that he recoiled from belief. Yet his face grew ashy white, and he gasped to fetch back motion to his checked heart. Unbelievable? Closer attention showed how the smaller footfall had altered for greater speed, striking into the snow with a deeper onset and a lighter pressure on the heels. Unbelievable? Could any woman but White Fell run so? Could any man but Christian run so? The guess became a certainty. He was following where alone in the dark night White Fell had fled from Christian pursuing.

Such villainy set heart and brain on fire with rage and indignation: such villainy in his own brother, till lately love-worthy, praiseworthy, though a fool for meekness. He would kill Christian; had he lives many as the footprints he had trodden, vengeance should demand them all. In a tempest of murderous hate he followed on in haste, for the track was plain enough, starting with such a burst of speed as could not be maintained, but brought him back soon to a plod for the spent, sobbing breath to be regulated. He cursed Christian aloud and called White Fell's name on high in a frenzied expense of passion. His grief itself was a rage, being such an intolerable anguish of pity and shame at the thought of his love, White Fell, who had parted from his kiss free and radiant, to be hounded straightway by his brother mad with jealousy, fleeing for more than life while her lover was housed at his ease. If he had but known, he raved, in impotent rebellion at the cruelty of events, if he had but known that his strength and love might have availed in her defence; now the only service to her that he could render was to kill Christian.

As a woman he knew she was matchless in speed, matchless in strength; but

Christian was matchless in speed among men, nor easily to be matched in strength. Brave and swift and strong though she were, what chance had she against a man of his strength and inches, frantic, too, and intent on horrid revenge against his brother, his successful rival?

Mile after mile he followed with a bursting heart; more piteous, more tragic, seemed the case at this evidence of White Fell's splendid supremacy, holding her own so long against Christian's famous speed. So long, so long that his love and admiration grew more and more boundless, and his grief and indignation therewith also. Whenever the track lay clear he ran, with such reckless prodigality of strength, that it soon was spent, and he dragged on heavily, till, sometimes on the ice of a mere, sometimes on a wind-swept place, all signs were lost; but, so undeviating had been their line that a course straight on, and then short questing to either hand, recovered them again.

Hour after hour had gone by through more than half that winter day, before ever he came to the place where the trampled snow showed that a scurry of feet had come—and gone! Wolves' feet—and gone most amazingly! Only a little beyond he came to the lopped point of Christian's bear-spear; farther on he would see where the remnant of the useless shaft had been dropped. The snow here was dashed with blood, and the footsteps of the two had fallen closer together. Some hoarse sound of exultation came from him that might have been a laugh had breath sufficed. 'O White Fell, my poor, brave love! Well struck!' he groaned, torn by his pity and great admiration, as he guessed surely how she had turned and dealt a blow.

The sight of the blood inflamed him as it might a beast that ravens. He grew mad with a desire to have Christian by the throat once again, not to loose this time till he had crushed out his life, or beat out his life, or stabbed out his life; or all these, and torn him piecemeal likewise: and ah! then, not till then, bleed his heart with weeping, like a child, like a girl, over the piteous fate of his poor lost love.

On—on—on—through the aching time, toiling and straining in the track of those two superb runners, aware of the marvel of their endurance, but unaware of the marvel of their speed, that, in the three hours before midnight had overpassed all that vast distance that he could only traverse from twilight to twilight. For clear daylight was passing when he came to the edge of an old marlpit, and saw how the two who had gone before had stamped and trampled together in desperate peril on the verge. And here fresh blood stains spoke to him of a valiant defence against his infamous brother; and he followed where the blood had dripped till the cold had staunched its flow, taking a savage gratification from this evidence that Christian had been gashed deeply, maddening afresh with desire to do likewise more excellently, and so slake his murderous hate. And he began to know that through all his despair he had entertained a germ of hope, that grew apace, rained upon by his brother's blood.

He strove on as best he might, wrung now by an access of hope, now of despair, in agony to reach the end, however terrible, sick with the aching of the toiled miles that deferred it.

And the light went lingering out of the sky, giving place to uncertain stars.

He came to the finish.

Two bodies lay in a narrow place. Christian's was one, but the other beyond not White Fell's. There where the footsteps ended lay a great white wolf.

At the sight Sweyn's strength was blasted; body and soul he was struck down grovelling.

The stars had grown sure and intense before he stirred from where he had dropped prone. Very feebly he crawled to his dead brother, and laid his hands upon him, and crouched so, afraid to look or stir farther.

Cold, stiff, hours dead. Yet the dead body was his only shelter and stay in that most dreadful hour. His soul, stripped bare of all sceptic comfort, cowered, shivering, naked, abject; and the living clung to the dead out of piteous need for grace from the soul that had passed away.

He rose to his knees, lifting the body. Christian had fallen face forward in the snow, with his arms flung up and wide, and so had the frost made him rigid: strange, ghastly, unyielding to Sweyn's lifting, so that he laid him down again and crouched above, with his arms fast round him, and a low heart-wrung groan.

When at last he found force to raise his brother's body and gather it in his arms, tight clasped to his breast, he tried to face the Thing that lay beyond. The sight set his limbs in a palsy with horror and dread. His senses had failed and fainted in utter cowardice, but for the strength that came from holding dead Christian in his arms, enabling him to compel his eyes to endure the sight, and take into the brain the complete aspect of the Thing. No wound, only blood stains on the feet. The great grim jaws had a savage grin, though dead-stiff. And his kiss: he could bear it no longer, and turned away, nor ever looked again.

And the dead man in his arms, knowing the full horror, had followed and faced it for his sake; had suffered agony and death for his sake; in the neck was the deep death gash, one arm and both hands were dark with frozen blood, for his sake! Dead he knew him, as in life he had not known him, to give the right meed of love and worship. Because the outward man lacked perfection and strength equal to his, he had taken the love and worship of that great pure heart as his due; he, so unworthy in the inner reality, so mean, so despicable, callous, and contemptuous towards the brother who had laid down his life to save him. He longed for utter annihilation, that so he might lose the agony of knowing himself so unworthy such perfect love. The frozen calm of death on the face appalled him. He dared not touch it with lips that had cursed so lately, with lips fouled by kiss of the horror that had been death.

He struggled to his feet, still clasping Christian. The dead man stood upright within his arm, frozen rigid. The eyes were not quite closed; the head had stiffened, bowed slightly to one side; the arms stayed straight and wide. It was the figure of one crucified, the blood-stained hands also conforming.

So living and dead went back along the track that one had passed in the deepest passion of love, and one in the deepest passion of hate. All that night Sweyn toiled through the snow, bearing the weight of dead Christian, treading back along the steps he before had trodden, when he was wronging with vilest thought, and cursing with murderous hatred, the brother who all the while lay dead for his sake.

Cold, silence, darkness encompassed the strong man bowed with the dolorous burden; and yet he knew surely that that night he entered hell, and trod hellfire along the homeward road, and endured through it only because Christian was with him. And he knew surely that to him Christian had been as Christ, and had suffered and died to save him from his sins.

How these papers have been placed in sequence will be made manifest in the reading of them. All needless matters have been eliminated, so that a history almost at variance with the possibilities of later-day belief may stand forth as simple fact. There is throughout no statement of past things wherein memory may err, for all the records chosen are exactly contemporary, given from the standpoints and within the range of knowledge of those who made them.

Thus Ends The Tale